Advanced Praise for *The Practical Guide to Colorado Real Estate In*

Your book is a concise, practical guide for all current and potential real estate investors. their investment plans, manage the properties and monitor returns. It's a perfect reference. It was immediately beneficial to me and I will with my clients!

Terry McCullough, Broker Associate, Kentwood Cherry Creek
Terry works with owner occupant as well as investor clients.

I would recommend this book to our clients. This book is straightforward and pragmatic. It doesn't sell or pitch. It gives the direction and guidance that all new real estate investors need to get started. I would recommend this book to anyone getting started with real estate investing. This book serves as both a compass and a map.

Mark Struznik, owner HomeVestors, Metro Properties Inc.
Mark and his team have bought and sold hundreds of investment properties.

It's imperative in today's uncertain economic environment to cover all your bases when looking at an investment property. This book provides the investor with a comprehensive template that should increase the probability of them achieving success. The book provides a good road map.

Bobby Hutchinson, Senior Advisor, Pinnacle Real Estate Advisors
Pinnacle helps investors buy and sell mid-size apartments.

This book is just what I need to help educate my clients. It will help me save a lot of time and it'll help my clients make better decisions.

William Roberts, Past-President, Denver Board of Realtors
Will is a developer and also helps investors buy and sell property.

The Practical Guide to Colorado Real Estate Investments is a clear reflection of the knowledge and expertise exhibited by Your Castle Real Estate. Even in a severe housing market and economic downturn Your Castle Real Estate's methods benefit their customers. As a professional statistician I am impressed with Your Castle's creative use of data to put them leagues ahead of their competitors.

Kieron Dey BSc, MBA, FSS
Consulting Statistician

The Practical Guide to Colorado Real Estate Investing is a great field guide for both the experienced real estate investor as well as the novice. This book clearly describes all aspects of real estate development with thoughtful detail and real life experience. A "must read" for anyone contemplating this type of venture.

Jeff Cline, Cline Design Group

Great for the new or average investor, I also think that it provides an insight for the Contractor in working with a new investor/partner with the issues or concerns that they might be dealing with.

John Henry, John Henry Development, Quality Real Estate Partners, LLC

This is among the best guides to real estate investing that I have read. It is practical and informative. Your Castle is truly a great leader in our industry and I continue to learn from their experience and wisdom.

Paul Barrow, Professional Real Estate Investor, Co-Owner, HomeVestors Franchise
Paul has bought and sold hundreds of investment properties.

There are no guarantees in real estate, but this book is the next best thing. If my clients would simply follow the guidelines and suggestions offered in your book, they would be a lot happier and wealthier.

Archie Warthen, Unique Properties, LLC

One of the most honest and realistic books for investors I have seen. None of the usual false information in real estate books. It has everything an investor needs to make a realistic decision - not how to be a millionaire overnight sort of book.

Verne Harris, owner Public Real Estate Brokerage

Verne has been listing foreclosure properties and working with investors for over 25 years.

The counsel, information, and ready-to-use forms in this book provide a jump-start to anyone ready to invest in real estate. The research-based, field-tested methods are sure to increase returns on investments and save investors from costly mistakes.

Mark Hafley, Small Business Owner and Future Landlord

I bought my house through Your Castle Real Estate. I am a student in their real estate investment seminars. I see the same quality of work in this book that I have experienced in my experience with them. The advice is practical, succinct, and actionable. It is clearly written and has all the component parts needed to guide my investment decisions.

Robert Andrews, VP of Global Services, Flash Global Logistics and Real Estate Investor

This book is a must read for any new investor or property manager. A true step-by-step detail on every aspect of a Real Estate transaction.

Sean Moudry, President, Ascent Wealth Strategies

The Practical Guide to Colorado Real Estate Investing

Your Castle Real Estate
Lon Welsh
Charles Roberts
Greg Parham
Joe Massey

Also by the Authors

<u>Current Editions Available Now</u>

Game Changers, 2014 edition
Steve Murray, Lorne Wallace, Lon Welsh

How to Thrive with Social Media and Blogging, 2011 edition
Kris Andrea, Steve Depperschmidt, LaTonia Gore, Greg Parham, Lon Welsh

Unlocked: Revealing the Eight Secrets of Highly Efficient Sales Professionals
Darice Johnston, Lon Welsh, Bruce Gardner, Drew Shope

Thrive: How Realtors Can Succeed in a Down Market, 2009 edition
Lon Welsh, Bruce Gardner, Mike Welk, Drew Shope

The Real Estate IRA Retirement Planning Guide
Jeff Sibel, with Lon Welsh and Charles Roberts

<u>Older Editions</u>

The Practical Guide to Colorado Real Estate Investing (2016)
Lon Welsh, Charles Roberts, Greg Parham, Joe Massey

The 2013 Guide to Colorado Real Estate Investing
Lon Welsh, Charles Roberts, Jon Roberts, Tony Girard, John Dovenbarger, Greg Parham

The 2011 Guide to Colorado Real Estate Investing
Lon Welsh, Charles Roberts, Ben Dorland, Jon Sommer, Tony Girard

The 2009 Guide to Denver Real Estate Investing
Lon Welsh, Charles Roberts, Michael Canon, Mike Welk

Editing and layout design by Charles Roberts, Lon Welsh
Cover design by Brandi Howard, Your Castle Real Estate

For information to reproduce selections from this book, write to:

Permissions
Your Castle Real Estate, Inc.
9085 E. Mineral Circle, Suite #360
Centennial, Colorado 80112

Fifth Edition

ISBN 978-0-9914070-2-6

About the Authors

Lon Welsh is the founder and Chairman of Your Castle Real Estate (YCRE). YCRE has over 750 Realtors. He personally has 80 rental units and has built 19 homes in the Denver area. His team will complete 12 Fix and Flips this year. Mr. Welsh is a frequent speaker at real estate investing clubs and on radio shows. He frequently contributes articles on real estate trends to the *Denver Post*, the *Denver Business Journal* and the four Denver Realtor boards.

Prior to founding YCRE, Mr. Welsh spent eight years working as a consultant, first with Deloitte & Touche and later with Arthur Andersen (Accenture). At Deloitte, he managed merger and acquisition engagements. At Accenture, Mr. Welsh was a senior manager providing strategy consulting services to high tech clients. Mr. Welsh also held several finance and accounting positions with a Fortune 100 consumer products company. He has a BBA in Finance from the University of Iowa and an MBA in Finance from Vanderbilt.

Charles Roberts is President of both Your Castle Real Estate and Shorewood Real Estate. He is a registered appraiser, licensed Realtor, and a former loan officer. He has invested in Denver real estate for the past 20 years, completing dozens of fix up projects along the way, and currently manages his own portfolio of properties in metro Denver. His specialty is helping investors buy cash flow properties.

He is a frequent lecturer on the Denver real estate market and is quoted regularly by the Denver Post, 5280 Magazine, Money Magazine, CASA Magazine, Inman News, and the Denver Business Journal. He co-hosted a local real estate radio show and appears regularly on NBC's 9 News, ABC's News7, ABCs Nightline, Colorado Public Radio, Inman Real Estate Conferences, American Real Estate Media Radio, 560 KLZ AM, and 760 AM KKZN to help make sense of the state of Denver real estate. He serves as an attorney's expert witness on real estate related cases. He was a Board Director at the 5,000-person Denver Metro Association of Realtors from 2009-2014 and was also the Chair of their Professional Development & Education Committee.

He is currently President of the Colorado Broker's Association. He is also a Board Director and the Education Chair of the Colorado/Wyoming chapter commercial CCIM organization.

Greg Parham earned his Law Degree from University of Denver's College of Law in 1994. He is a current member of the Colorado and Denver Bar Associations, and is admitted to practice before the Colorado trial and appellate courts, as well as the United States District Court for the 10th Circuit. His legal career began with a boutique law firm in Colorado that specialized in handling transactional and litigation matters for clients in the health industry. Greg later served as General Counsel for a a large multi-state mortgage banking firm. Eventually he opened his own law firm, The Parham Law Firm, P.C., which provides representation to real estate investors and small business owners.

Greg is co-founder and general manager of First Alliance Title, LLC, a full service title and escrow company that specializes in complex investment transactions. Greg is a frequent lecturer on real estate topics including foreclosure laws, real estate contracting, seller finance, short sale transactions, landlord tenant matters, and the structuring of complex transactions.

Joe Massey is a graduate of the Colorado School of Mines with a degree in Economics and Business. Joe has been a lender since 2002; has been recognized as a "Million Dollar Loan Officer" since 2007 and recognized by 5280 Magazine as a Five Star Mortgage Professional from 2012 - 2018. Joe was recently recognized by National Mortgage News as the #230 loan originator for 2015, #202 loan originator for 2016 and National Mortgage News ranked him in the top 1% of all originators nationwide for 2015, 2016 and 2017. Prior to working with residential mortgages, Joe was a commercial lender, underwriter and financial analyst which prepared him for his mortgage career and taught him the specifics of how to get loans approved and how to find the best terms for the customer.

Joe now works as a Senior Loan Officer for Castle & Cooke Mortgage, a Billion Dollar mortgage lender based in Salt Lake City, Utah. In addition to his Loan Officer responsibilities, Joe co-manages the DTC office for Castle & Cooke Mortgage, which is their top office nationwide for the last 5 years and remains their top office for 2018 YTD. In partnership with Your Castle Real Estate, First Alliance Title, Pine Financial and other real estate companies in Denver, Joe has closed hundreds of loans for both experienced and first-time homebuyers as well as all levels of property investors. Joe continues to contribute to the real estate and mortgage community with his monthly presentations on financing options and continuing education.

Table of Contents

Introduction 11
Chapter 1: What Type of Investment is Best for You? 14
Determining Where You are Now 15
Which Investing Category is Best for Your Unique Situation? 26
Chapter 2: How Successful Investors Build Their Team 30
The Inside Story on How Investors are Perceived 31
Finding a Lender 32
What You Need to Know about Inspectors 39
Finding a Property Manager 43
Finding a CPA 44
Finding an Attorney 44
Finding a Closing Agent 44
Chapter 3: Where the Pros Get the Money 45
How to Improve Your Credit Score 48
Top Ten Things to Do Between Loan Application and Closing 49
Basic Mortgage Topics 52
The Truth About Owner Carry 54
All About "Grant" Programs 54
Chapter 4: How the Pros Manage the Buying Process 55
The Ideal Purchasing Process 56
Lowball Offers 58
Negotiation 59
Things to Monitor During the Closing Process 61
Special Purchasing Circumstances 61
Chapter 5: Rental Property Fundamentals 63
Categories of Rentals 64
What Types of Investor Should Consider Rentals? 64
Pros and Cons of Different Rental Types 79
Analyzing Your Investment – One Year Projection 84
Chapter 6: Buy a Great Rental Home, Condo or 2-4 Unit 95
What Types of Investor Should Buy a Small Rental? 95
How Much Can You Pay and Break Even? 97
Impact of Property Condition on Rents and Cash flow 100
Looking at Potential Properties 101
How to Analyze Your Potential Investment's Return in Year One 103
Chapter 7: Short Sales 106
Chapter 8: House Hacking 114
Chapter 9: Property Management 120
Tenant Management – Getting New Tenants 121
Step-by-Step Guide to the Lease 124
Maintenance Management 132
General Management 132
Who is Going to Do all of this Work? 133
Chapter 10: How the Pros Sell Their Properties 135
Understanding and Negotiating Commissions 138
Tips for a Smooth Close 141
Appendix A – Sample Lender Letter 142
Appendix B – Hiring a Mortgage Broker 143
Appendix C – Hiring a Real Estate Agent – Investor Buyers Agent 145
Appendix D – Hiring an Agent – Residential Listing Agent 147

Appendix E – Sample LOI (Letter of Intent) 149

Appendix F – Sample Lender Letter 150

Introduction

"The best investment on earth is earth."
        -- Louis J. Glickman, real estate owner

Why We Wrote This Book

There's no shortage of real estate investing books on the market. Most of them do a good job on the "academic" perspective of how to invest, but they don't get their hands dirty and tell you the specifics of how to do it, and how to do it successfully. They miss the common traps many investors fall into. They also tell you what you WANT to hear, instead of what you NEED to know.

Investing in real estate is serious business, not a game. The authors of this book actually own and manage rental properties, from small condos to forty-unit apartment buildings. We've been doing it for over 15 years, through good economic times and bad. We have managed dozens of fix and flip projects for our own accounts, and our team of real estate agents has helped thousands of real estate investor clients do the same. We've watched them over time to determine what works and what doesn't. This combined experience is packed into the following chapters in five ways that you won't find in other books on real estate investing. We hope you find it helpful!

Who Should Read This Book

There are several audiences:

-   **Consumers** considering investing in real estate, but are not sure how to get started. You will discover if investing is right for you, and if so, what type of investment will be the best fit for your unique situation.
-   **Newer Investors** that have properties and need guidance on how to improve performance.
-   **Experienced Investors** that want to improve performance or perhaps take their game to the next level.
-   **Realtors that want to work with investors.** Many talented Realtors that have focused on "traditional" real estate (that is, helping people purchase homes they will live in) want to learn about investing. They might want to expand their practice to help their clients in a new way, or they might want to learn to invest themselves.
-   **Experienced investor Realtors** that want to increase the knowledge and expertise they can share with their clients.
-   **Managing Brokers** that want to be better prepared to answer questions from Realtors on their teams about investing.

Five Features of This Book You Will Not Find Elsewhere

1. **Road Map.** Many investors early in the process are eager to get started, but don't know where to begin. We start with an **assessment of where you are currently** – your finances, time, and skills – and **where you want to go**. We then match your unique situation to the best type(s) of real estate investments that will be compatible with your situation… and not keep you up at three o'clock in the morning. Look for the map icons.

2. **Case Studies.** Rather than just giving you the academic perspective, we give you lots of real world case studies of what worked well, and what sounded like a great idea at the time that proved to not work as well as we hoped. You can learn from our mistakes. Look for the house icon.

3. **Best Practices.** We distill the experience of hundreds of clients and transactions into short lists of best practices. Many of these will seem like common sense, but every day we see that common sense is not common practice. If you review a list of twelve ideas and you pick up one that is new to you, you will be more successful as a result. Look for the sparkle icons.

4. **Checklists and Guides.** Many of our prospective clients asked us for sample checklists and interview guides to shorten their learning curve from newbie to experienced investor. We will share the "insider questions" that we give to our close friends and family members. You can learn from our experience and avoid some of our mistakes. Look for the checklist icons.

5. **Analytical Templates.** How can you examine your investments before you buy them? Not everyone likes math, but a little time and effort invested up front will do a lot to improve your chances of success. The key difference between our book and others is that we provide some ideas of what the assumptions should be and where the models have sometimes differed from reality for us and our clients. The models are a tool, and an important one no investor can be without, but they are not perfect. We'll reveal those imperfections. Look for the magnifying icons.

6. **Glossary.** A concise description of some of the common industry jargon. A complete glossary can be found in the back of the book.

Seminars and Tours

This book on its own will offer a lot of practical advice. But to propel your knowledge even further, please join us for our **free seminars and real-world tours**. No bull. No selling. Just great real estate related information you can use to build your business. Go to www.yourcastle.com and click on "Training" to see our training and tour schedule.

Disclaimers from the Attorneys

The intention of this book is to provide a set of tools and checklists for real estate investors, new and experienced. The reader acknowledges that the publisher and authors are not providing accounting, tax, or legal services.

Real estate investing is an outstanding opportunity for the individual investor to generate profits. As with any investment, it is also possible to lose money. Events beyond the authors' control could cause financial losses. Such events include, but are not limited to, changes in the macro economic climate, the local real estate environment, or the performance of individual investments selected by the investor.

The reader assumes all responsibility for the successes or failures in their investing decisions. The reader should consult experts, including but not limited to certified public accountants, attorneys, real estate agents, property inspectors and mortgage brokers in their quest to identify and purchase any investment property.

The authors shall have no liability or responsibility to any person and/or entity for any loss or damage stemming from reliance on the information provided in this book

Chapter 1: What Type of Investment is Best for You?

What's in this Chapter?

This is a summary of each investment category covered in this book; there is a lot more detail in the individual chapters that follow. To get a sense of which categories are best for your skills and personality, the second half of this chapter will have some questions to help you decide. Many of the categories will not be a good fit for some investors, so this can help you save a lot of time.

Executive Summary of Real Estate Investment Categories

- A brief summary of the categories of real estate investing. Each category is explored in much more depth in its individual chapter.
- Next, we review the skills, time and monetary resources that you can devote to your real estate investments – this is "what you give."
- Finally, we make some recommendations of which types of investments you might wish to consider, given your unique situation.

Assignments

If you don't have much equity (e.g., cash to use as a down payment), and/or if your credit power is limited, assignments can be a way to get started in real estate investing. You will need to have a strong "sales" personality to succeed at it, though.

GLOSSARY

Assign or *Assignment* – usually "*Assign a Contract.*" An investor who is interested in assignments gets a property under contract for an attractive price, and then assigns the contract to another buyer, usually another investor. The first investor will be paid a fee for the work. The purchaser of the contract gets all the rights and accepts all the responsibilities of the contract.

Rental Condo or Rental Home

This is the purchase of a residential property to be rented out to tenants, usually on a 6-12 month lease term. This is how most new landlords get started. You may hire out all of the property management functions, but in many cases you will do many of them on your own. There are smaller down payment requirements for homes and condos than for larger rental buildings. The purchase process and financing process is very similar to what you experienced buying the home you live in now. It's a great way for beginners to get started.

Small Apartment Building (2-4 units)

This is the purchase of a duplex, triplex or quad to be rented to tenants, usually for 12-month terms. This is often what the rental condo or home landlords graduate to. In most markets they cost a little more than a rental home, but are much more likely to generate positive cash flow. This results in less cash flow risk; if one unit is empty you have other tenants that still help you with the mortgage payment so it doesn't all come out of your pocket. Many owners will start to delegate some of the property management tasks to an on-site assistant (typically the most responsible tenant), such as yard maintenance and showing empty units. The financing process is only slightly more involved than a residential loan. The purchase process is also very similar to purchasing a home. It is also a good way for beginners to get started.

Large Apartment Building (5 and more units)

With five units and up you are still targeting tenants for 12 months at a time (buildings with more than five units are considered "commercial" property). The loans are somewhat more difficult to qualify for, and usually a larger down payment percentage is needed. Large apartment buildings are a less frequent choice for the new investor; this is usually what landlords with several years of experience "trade up" to. That said, we have had newbie landlords purchase 12 unit buildings and do very well. Cash flows on larger buildings are more stable than for smaller buildings, and the economies of scale make it practical (and desirable) to hire a property manager to take over most of the day-to-day work for you. This reduces the hassle factor of the landlord process dramatically. If you are a busy professional that doesn't need another hobby, this might be a good fit.

Fix and Flips

Fix and Flips involve purchasing a property that needs work. The scope can range from the basic "paint and carpet" to extensive overhauls, to scraping a decrepit property and completely starting over. It usually does not involve tenants, and the objective is to get in and out of the property as quickly as possible. Great for beginners with the right skill sets or the willingness to learn.

Conversion of Apartments into Condos

Condo conversions are a synthesis of the fix and flip and rental operations – purchasing an apartment building in a neighborhood dominated by owner occupants, then converting the building from apartment building to condominium. Often requires renovation of the units to meet the expectations of owner-occupant buyers in that area. Though complex and time consuming, condo conversions have wonderful tax advantages compared to fix and flips and often have superior returns to all other asset classes. Ideally suited for the sophisticated investor with extensive experience.

Scrapes, Pops and New Construction

These projects often involve purchasing a small home in an expensive neighborhood that may or may not need work. The home is bulldozed and a new home or duplex is put on the lot, or the existing home is renovated and more square footage is added on. A pop-top is adding a second story to an existing home to add more square footage (commonly, a master bedroom suite). The investor that succeeds in this segment usually has quite a bit of real estate experience.

Determining Where You are Now

Let's evaluate where you are now, and what you like to do, with eight criteria. Let's begin by reviewing what the typical requirements are for successful investing in a given investment category. You can compare those requirements to the self assessment that you complete here to get an idea of how appropriate the investment class is for your current situation. **This takes time and effort. Trust us, it's worth it. We've seen hundreds of clients learn critical aspects of themselves and their investing potential by evaluating these criteria.**

Equity Needed is how much liquid assets you and/or your investment team will need to have. Purchasing a large apartment building, for example, usually requires at least 20% down on a purchase price that might start at $500,000. 25-30% is not uncommon. You would need $100,000 in cash just to get into the game.

Credit Score will be important for some types of investments. Large apartment loans require nearly impeccable credit for the best terms. A small rental or fix and flip might require solid, though not perfect, credit. If you can put down 20%, you can often purchase a small rental even if your credit is far less than perfect. In general, if your credit score is under 620, you have poor credit. From 620 to 680 might be average, and above 680 would be good. 740 and above is great! We'll discuss the breakpoints for excellent, average, and poor credit in the "Where the Pros Get the Money" chapter and provide suggestions of how to improve your score.

GLOSSARY

Credit Score – An independent, third party assessment of how well you have managed your credit in the past. Three national companies track your credit scores; a lender will usually request all three and take the middle value (the *mid score*) for determining the terms of your loan. As slang, you will often hear the *Loan Officer* say that they need to "pull your credit," which is to get the three credit reports to discover your mid score.

Experience with Contractors will make some types of projects more pleasant. Fix and flips, as a category, benefit the most from this type of experience. We did not have much experience when we undertook our first projects and we still managed to muddle through (but we learned a lot on our first projects and made lots of mistakes). We have worked with many investors with the same experience. On the other hand, if you purchase a larger apartment building that already has a competent property manager in place, you won't need any experience with contractors.

Experience with Property Managers makes purchasing a rental property easier. It certainly is not essential and you can learn by doing. We'll outline the advantages and disadvantages in the rental chapters.

Time Required Each Week varies on the project specifics, but we'll make some broad generalizations so you have a sense of the level of commitment you'll have to make to improve your chances of success.

The Number of Monthly Interactions (e.g., how many times you visit the property or get phone calls about it) is also important to some people. They are happy spending one or two long sessions on the property, but would be highly annoyed to have twenty very short interactions. Others, due to personal commitments, might have the opposite preference. We'll help set your expectations.

Property Manager - A third party that takes on some of your responsibilities in the ongoing operations of your rental property. Some of the tasks include cleaning and maintenance, collecting rents, showing units to prospective tenants, answering questions, and managing tenants as they move out of the building. Some Property Managers will also run the operating account for you and pay the building's bills.

Perception of Hassle varies as much by individual as it does by project, but again, we can offer some broad guidelines.

Risk Tolerance is the level of comfort that you and the key people that influence your decisions have with risk and ambiguity. If you are going to be awake at 3AM every morning worrying about this decision it may not be the right asset category for you.

Reality Check. As you read through the criteria and how they vary among the different types of real estate investments, you'll detect a pattern of tradeoffs. For example, you can bring a lot of equity and a very strong credit score, and then purchase a large apartment building with a property manager – little effort is required on your part. Or… if you have no money and no credit, you will have to have a lot of time available and a high degree of willingness to accept hassles. There are, of course, a few options in the middle that require a degree of both. Finally, if you have great credit, lots

Equity – The difference between net market value after closing costs and the mortgage amount or the amount of money the Seller clears after the closing. Also used to refer to the amount of cash you have available to invest in a project.

of money, lots of skill, and lots of time to focus on the project, you are a developer – and you can focus on the very high return projects such as converting apartments to condos or scraping old buildings and putting up new ones in the most expensive neighborhoods.

Unlike late night TV infomercials, **there are no reliable and ethical methods to make money with no risk, no credit, no cash, and no effort**. They don't exist in the real world. Period. Anybody who tells you different is selling something. You'll have to bring something to the table to get a reward. Before people begin their career in real estate investing they often think they need to have a lot of cash on hand to get started. The truth is, there are certain types of investments that will not require large sums of equity up-front.

As in anything in life, however, more cash does make things easier. Hopefully, as you progress in your investing career and build up your funds, additional investment opportunities will become available to you. The following chart will give you a summary of the equity requirements for different types of real estate investments. You can explore each type of investment in more detail in each of the following chapters. Loans are discussed in more detail in the chapter "Where the Pros Get the Money."

Equity Needed

There are many potential sources for the funds. You could use your checking and savings accounts, take a loan out against your 401(k), get a HELOC (home equity line of credit) if your residence has any equity, or borrow from friends and family members. We have seen clients take cash advances from their credit cards to get their funds. That is more aggressive than many investors might want to get, but it is an option. This is where evaluating your risk tolerance becomes critical.

Investment Type	Equity requirements
Assignments	**$0 is typical.** One of the appealing attributes of Assignments is you don't need any money or credit to play. Alas, this tends to be the most competitive sector of real estate investing since the entry barriers are so low.
Rental Condo Rental Home Small (2-4 unit) Apartment	**$25,000 and up.** 15-20% of the purchase price is generally required to be put down on the loan. Lenders will also require six months of operating expenses in reserves. For example, you might put 20% down on a $150k property and deposit $5k into your operating account. Three and four unit properties usually require 25%-30% down. Ex: Cos 1Br CND: $150K and 15% down + closing costs. Denver & Northern Co DSF: $300k and 20% down = $60k + closing costs
Large (5+ unit) Apartment	**$120,000-$225,000 and up.** Buildings over four units require a commercial loan. Sometimes a lender will loan up to 80% of the purchase price, requiring 20% down. Frequently 25% will be needed. You'll need to have a few months of reserves in your operating account as well. Most new investors start with smaller rental buildings to build experience and build equity. Prices for buildings will vary by market and neighborhood. Ex: Pueblo might have a 6 unit bldg. @ $100k/door or $600k total. 20% down = $120k. Denver & Northern Co more likely @$150k/door or $900k total. 25% down = $225k.
Lease Options (Owner Carry)	**$0 is typical.** Like Assignments, one of the appealing attributes of owner carry L/O's is that your credit score is not impacted by the transaction and neither is your checking account. However, also like Assignments, this tends to be a very competitive sector of real estate investing since the entry barriers are so low.
Lease Options (Investor Carry)	**$20,000 and up. $55,000 might be typical.** 20% of the purchase price down is typical. Since you are bringing some money to the deal, you'll have a lot more flexibility than the L/O investors that don't bring money. Can be a wonderful tool for the right investor in the right phase of the market. The typical estimate is for the investor that puts down 20% on a $250,000 property and deposits $5,000 to the operating account.
Fix and Flips	**$70,000 and up.** 20% of the purchase price down is typical. Usually the investor pays for the renovation work out of pocket. A "typical" estimate is based on a 20% down payment for a $250,000 property, a $5,000 reserve for purchase costs and holding costs, and $20,000 for renovation work. If you don't have this much money, you may find *hard money* loans for projects with compelling economics.
Converting Apartments to Condos	**$385,000 and up.** Realistically you will need at least 25% of the purchase price. Some renovation work is required; the investor sometimes pays for the renovation work out of pocket. A "typical" estimate is based on a 25% down payment for a $1,000,000 property (6 units for example), $25,000 reserve for purchase costs and holding costs, $10,000 to legally divide the property, and $20,000 for renovation work per door. Quickly requires more equity for larger projects. Local banks that portfolio (don't sell) their loans are the best sources.
Scrapes & New Construction	**$190,000 and up.** On land, plan to put down, in Denver, 50%. On land at $300k., that's $150k you may need to front. Engineering, survey, design and architecture at $40,000 or more. You can probably get a construction loan for the rest. Northern Co won't be much less.

Credit Score

A common misperception that new investors have is that they need to have perfect credit in order to invest in real estate. That is not true for all asset types – some require no credit at all. On the other hand, once new investors see an infomercial on TV or go to their first investing seminar they get a perspective that they can do anything with terrible credit. That's not true either – the truth, as usual, is in the middle.

The following chart gives you an initial idea of the relative importance of your credit score with different types of investments. The following chapters will explore this in more detail. See the Chapter on the "Where the Pros Get the Money" to see how to improve your scores.

Investment Type	Minimum Credit Score Requirement
Assignments	**Terrible.** You won't use your credit score for this type of investment, which makes it open to anyone!
Rental Condo Rental Home	**Average.** You'll be purchasing the property, usually as a non-owner occupant (since you probably already have a primary residence). The mortgage companies will look at your credit score a little more closely than they will for your primary residence. As a rule of thumb, if you can qualify (even with a high interest rate) to buy a home to live in, you will be able to qualify to buy a home to rent out. However, the interest rates will be a little higher.
Small (2-4 unit) Apartment	**Average +.** The discussion for rental home and condo applies, but the standards, are a little tighter when you get a slightly bigger building.
Large (5+ unit) Apartment	**Average+/ Near Perfect.** You can get a commercial loan with a credit score that is a little better than the average, but you'll pay a higher interest rate. On larger buildings, the economics are very sensitive to your financing, so if you have just above average credit, not as many buildings will make sense for you. Conversely, if you have perfect or near perfect credit, you'll be able to get the most favorable commercial rates which will increase the number of buildings that are economical to invest in. Most investors believe only the building matters and their credit is not considered. That is very rarely true.
Lease Options (Owner Carry)	**Terrible.** You won't use your credit score for this type of investment, which makes it open to anyone.
Lease Options (Investor Carry)	**Average.** Same commentary as for "Rental Home" above.
Fix and Flips	**Terrible.** If you have terrible credit, you will turn to a hard money lender. They typically focus on the economics of the deal and not your credit. As a result, the number of potential investments available to you will be somewhat (but not significantly) smaller than the pool of properties available to the investor with better credit.
Converting Apartments to Condos	**Perfect.** The bank considers these to be high risk projects.
Scrapes and New Construction	**Perfect.** Very similar to "Converting Apartments to Condos."

As you can see, having terrible credit will not prevent you from getting involved in real estate investing, but it will reduce some of your choices and will make the choices you make less profitable than if you had better credit. Get started with a project and start learning, and in the meantime, take any steps you can to improve your credit scores. Make improving your credit score a permanent pursuit.

Experience with Contractors

If you enjoy improvement projects on the home that you live in now (or, at least, can tolerate them), you will probably enjoy working with contractors on your real estate projects. For many of our investors, this is a highly rewarding part of their work (at least when things are going right). Other investors find it very frustrating. To learn how to find a good contractor, refer to the Chapter on "How Successful Investors Build Their Team."

Investment Type	Importance of Experience with Contractors (or Willingness to Learn)
Assignments	**None.**
Rental Condo	**None / Very Limited.** Things will break in the rental units a little more often than they do at your home. But, if you overpay to get a deluxe contractor that holds your hand through every step of the process (e.g., go to Home Depot and hire their people), you are not going to significantly change the economics of your investment.
Rental Home	
Small (2-4 unit) Apartment	
Large (5+ unit) Apartment	**1-2 Projects.** As you buy a building with more units, you are going to have to fix more things more frequently. Getting good at managing contractors will make your building more profitable. If you don't, you'll leave money on the table.
Lease Options (Owner Carry)	**None / Very Limited.** See discussion for "Rental Condo."
Lease Options (Investor Carry)	
Fix and Flips	**Very Important.** Experience with contractors is what will make or break your project's profitability (and to a large extent, your enjoyment of the project, too). Even if you have at least some experience in hiring, managing and firing contractors this could be a great choice for you. If not, you should be willing to be actively involved to learn these skills.
Converting Apartments to Condos	**Crucial.** Don't consider this type of real estate investing until you have mastered the management of contractors. Do some small fix and flip projects first.
Scrapes and New Construction	**Crucial.** Don't consider this type of real estate investing until you have mastered the management of contractors. Do a few small fix and flip projects first.

Experience with Property Managers

This table outlines the relative importance of prior experience working with Property Managers for different types of real estate investments. As you review the chart below, you will see that extensive experience with property managers is not a requirement for any of these real estate investment types. To learn how to find a good property management company, please see the chapter on "How Successful Investors Build Their Team."

Investment Type	Importance of Experience with Property Managers (or Willingness to Learn)
Assignments	**None.**
Rental Condo Rental Home	**None / Limited.** We always advise our clients to manage their own property for at least the first year. It's invaluable experience. If you decide to hire a property manager, you'll need to get some experience in managing them, but know that most investors for this size of a rental manage the properties on their own. For most investors, it makes more economic sense to do it on their own and they learn many lessons first hand that enable them to better select and manage property managers in the future on their larger investments.
Small (2-4 unit) Apartment	**Limited.** For many investors, this is their follow-up rental investment. They often start to experiment with delegation of at least some of the property management functions in this size property.
Large (5+ unit) Apartment	**Limited – Somewhat Important.** As your rental buildings get bigger, you'll be increasingly likely to outsource at least some of the elements of the management job.
Lease Options (Owner Carry) Lease Options (Investor Carry)	**None / Limited.** See discussion under "Rental Condo" above.
Fix and Flips	**None.** Hopefully, you sell the property immediately after completing the renovation work.
Converting Apartments to Condos	**Limited – Somewhat Important.** Depending on the size of the building you are working, see the discussion above. The property management elements are a bit more complex in this environment, as you may have some owners in the building alongside your tenants, with contractors improving units to the frustration of everyone. It can get a little exciting.
Scrapes and New Construction	**None.** Hopefully, you sell the property immediately after completing the renovation work.

Time Required

Some real estate investments are relatively hands-off once they are set up and running properly. Others are very hands on. Depending on what other commitments you are trying to juggle in your life, you may not have time for a hands-on investment. This is a common source of failure for newer investors. Don't purchase an investment if you don't have the time necessary to commit to it! We segment the discussion into the number of hours to get started, then the number of recurring hours of effort each week to keep the investment working well.

Here is a rough guideline to what you can expect to get your project started. The table after that will outline your time commitments after the project is started (e.g., after you close):

Investment Type	What's required to *GET STARTED* (time you invest just once, up through and including the purchase of the property)
Assignments	**Can be extensive (60+ hours).** Usually you will start by finding a motivated seller, then negotiating the terms. Depending on the conditions in your market this can take some time. Once you have located the property you need to find an investor to match to the property. Again, depending on the market, this can also take time. Once you have located all of the parties there is some paperwork to fill out on a one-time basis.
Rental Condo Rental Home Small (2-4 unit) Apartment	**40+ hours.** You will want to spend time with your real estate agent discussing your needs, then hunt for properties, then manage the closing process. Once you close, there will be some one-time setup activities (set up checking account for building, notify tenants of new landlord and payment procedure, etc).
Large (5+ unit) Apartment	**20+ hours.** Similar to the smaller rental buildings but the allocation of the time is different since you have probably purchased a rental building before. It will take less time to assess your needs, and you will probably be more efficient at finding a building. However, the change-over process once you close takes longer since there are more tenants to be managed. You'll probably have a property management firm helping with at least some of the tasks, and they will need setup time (involving your input) to get up and running.
Lease Options (Owner Carry)	**Can be extensive (60+ hours).** Usually you will start by finding a motivated seller, then negotiating the lease terms. Depending on the conditions in your market, this can take some time. Once you have located the property you need to find a tenant to match to the property. Again, depending on the market, this can also take time. Once you have located all of the parties there is some paperwork to fill out on a one-time basis (the leases, the option, etc.).
Lease Options (Investor Carry)	**Can be extensive (40+ hours), though significantly easier than L/O Owner Carry.** Often you will start with finding the tenant (it depends on what is currently going on in your market). Once you find the tenant, matching them to an appropriate home usually doesn't take as long as the L/O Owner Carry method. Once you have located all of the parties there is some paperwork to fill out on a one-time basis (the leases, the option).
Fix and Flips	**Almost always extensive (80+ hours).** There are many steps to finding a good project, and the more time you invest up front the higher your chances for success.
Converting Apartments to Condos	**Extremely extensive (160+ hours).** Like the F&F project (and basically, this is a F&F project on steroids) there are many steps to finding a good project, and the more time you invest up front the higher your chances for success.
Scrapes and New Construction	**Almost always extensive (160+ hours).** There are many steps to finding a good project. The more time you invest up front, the better your chances for success.

Investment Type	What's required to *KEEP GOING* (time you invest every week, after you close on the purchase)
Assignments	**None.**
Rental Condo Rental Home Small (2-4 unit) Apartment	**0 – 3 hours / week.** For the months when the property is full you'll just have to mow the grass, shovel snow, or deal with the occasional tenant question. If you get someone on site to do the yard work, you'll have many weeks where you do nothing at all. When you have a vacancy you'll have to run an advertisement, answer some phone calls and do some showings (again, you might hire someone to do much of this for you), but it shouldn't take too much time once you are in the rhythm of doing it.
Large (5+ unit) Apartment	**0 – 20 hours / week.** If you hire a property management company, this should be closer to zero hours. If you elect to do it on your own, it still might not be much if you have a person on-site to do yard work and show vacant units for you. If you do it all yourself it will depend on the size of the building, but will generally be among the least time intensive of the real estate investments.
Lease Options (Owner Carry) Lease Options (Investor Carry)	**0 – 3 hours / week.** Very similar to the "rental condo" above, and if done properly it can even be less work than working with a traditional tenant, since the lease-option tenant often does their own minor repairs.
Fix and Flips	**Likely 10+ hours / week.** If you have extensive contractor management experience, you can get by with a lot less. If this is your first project with contractors, you'll want to be around frequently, and ideally getting your hands dirty, to build your skills and improve your chances of success.
Converting Apartments to Condos	**Likely 10+ hours / week.** Similar to the F&F discussion above, there will be a lot of work to do.
Scrapes and New Construction	**Likely 10+ hours / week.** If you have extensive contractor management experience, you can get by with a lot less. If this is your first project with contractors, you'll want to be around frequently, and ideally getting your hands dirty, to build your skills and improve your chances of success.

Number of Monthly Interactions

By interactions, we mean how often you will have to visit the property or take phone calls to answer questions. In addition to understanding the number of hours required to be successful, different investors have different preferences for the number of interactions they will need to have. Due to the balancing act of work and family, some prefer to have a smaller number of longer interactions, while others prefer many interactions of shorter duration. Which do you prefer?

Investment Type	Typical number of monthly interactions (e.g., phone calls, meetings, on-site visits)
Assignments	**None.**
Rental Condo Rental Home	**Average 1 – 5.** Should not require much on-going effort for the months when the unit is occupied; more effort when you are filling a vacancy, less if you have management assistance. Most of the interactions will be very brief (e.g., following up on why rent is late, answering questions about a vacant unit)
Small (2-4 unit) Apartment	**Average 1 – 10.** Similar to "Rental Condo" above; but you will have vacancies more frequently.
Large (5+ unit) Apartment	**Average 1 – 20+.** Similar to "Small Apartment." If you hire out all of the property management it can be relatively easy. You'll have some longer discussions with your property manager on a monthly "status call."
Lease Options (Owner Carry) Lease Options (Investor Carry)	**Average 1 – 5.** Similar to "Rental Condo"; likely to have even fewer interactions (longer durations for the tenants than typical rental, they handle many small maintenance issues for you).
Fix and Flips	**Average 10 – 20+.** If you are not experienced, you will want to check in at least several times a week with each major contractor on the team. Many of these interactions will be longer discussions (10+ minutes) as contractors explain problems that have appeared and you discuss alternative options to resolve the issue and select the best approach. You'll probably want to be on site frequently. You might also lower your project costs by buying materials for the contractors and delivering them to the job site, which can be time consuming.
Converting Apartments to Condos	**Average 20+.** This is a combination of running an apartment building with a F&F at the same time; anticipate lots of phone calls. There will be plenty of longer phone calls and meetings to resolve problems, and you will work with attorneys on the HOA documents, etc. Not for the faint of heart.
Scrapes and New Construction	**Average 5 - 10.** If you hire a general contractor to oversee the project, he or she will be responsible for handling most of the phone calls and resolving most of the problems. If you want to be the General Contractor, then you have a new part time job.

Perception of "Hassle"

This is the toughest area to assess – what annoys one investor might be a challenging and fun puzzle to solve for the next. Look within yourself. We'll discuss how to manage some of the most common hassles later on in the book. Specifically, how to select and manage contractors is covered in the chapter "How Successful Investors Build Their Team" and working with tenants is covered in the chapter "Property Management." However, there are some broad observations we can share:

Investment Type	How Much Hassle is Required
Assignments	**High – Very High.** If you don't bring a credit score or cash, you are going to have to bring your time and willingness to deal with a lot of nonsense to find a good deal. The seminars and infomercials make it sound easy, but most people find it's more hassle than it's worth. Consider yourself warned.
Rental Condo Rental Home Small (2-4 unit) Apartment	**Very Low – Moderate.** People are people and tenants are tenants. Most are fine but some will drive you crazy. You will have the occasional person that never pays on time, irritates other tenants, or is the one complaining about every possible issue. Hopefully it is the exception and not the rule. Unless you are in a dreadfully bad renter's market, keeping your building occupied usually will not be too much of a problem if you work hard and pay attention. This is not, however, a turnkey business. See the chapter on "Property Management" to learn more.
Large (5+ unit) Apartment	**Very Low – Moderate.** Most investors don't buy a larger building until they have some experience with a smaller building for a very good reason. They've already learned many lessons on tenant selection, and hopefully how to get a property manager to help them. A good property manager will make this score "very low." If you do a lot of the work yourself, you'll make more money but you'll have more headaches, too.
Lease Options (Owner Carry) Lease Options (Investor Carry)	**Before "closing": High – Very High.** If you don't have a high credit score or cash you are going to have to bring your time and willingness to deal with a lot of nonsense to find a good deal. The seminars and infomercials make it sound easy. It isn't. **After "closing": Very Low – Moderate.** Looks like "Rental Condo" but sometimes even more favorable.
Fix and Flips	**Before closing on purchase: Medium – High.** You will want to do a lot of *due diligence* (e.g., verifying all of the facts that the listing agent gave you that you relied on to make a decision) to avoid making a mistake. This takes time. **After closing to completion of renovation: Medium** (if you have experience) **– Very High** (if you do not have experience). This can be a great way to build equity in a hurry, but it would be misleading for us to tell you that it's a walk in the park. It can be a lot of fun for the projects where everything goes well (and this does happen), but most projects will involve at least some headaches.
Converting Apartments to Condos	**Very High.** Similar to the "Fix and Flip" discussion above.
Scrapes and New Construction	**Before closing on purchase: Medium – High.** You will want to do a lot of due diligence to avoid making a mistake… this takes time and the discipline to walk away from projects that don't make sense. **After closing to completion of renovation:** • **Medium** (if you hire a general contractor) • **Very High** (if you are the GC). This can be a great way to build equity in a hurry, but it would be misleading for us to tell you that it's a walk in the park. It can be a lot of fun for the projects where everything goes well (and this does happen), but most projects will involve at least some headaches.

Risk Tolerance

"It was a high counsel that I once heard given to a young person,—'Always do what you are afraid to do.'"
     -- Ralph Waldo Emerson (1803–1882), U.S. essayist, poet, philosopher

"Courage is resistance to fear, mastery of fear - not absence of fear."
     -- Mark Twain

Some investors (and their spouses and/or co-investors and/or bankers) are more comfortable with risk and ambiguity than others. This chart will give you an initial orientation to the degree of risk you are accepting with different types of real estate investments.

Investment Type	Relative Degree of Risk and/or Uncertainty
Assignments	**None.**
Rental Condo	**Very Low.** This investment is relatively easy to assess, purchase, and sell if you don't like it. A small condo is probably the easiest category of rental to manage. Like all rentals, the returns are fairly predictable and are not too volatile.
Rental Home	**Low.** Similar to rental condo, only you'll have to make arrangements for outside maintenance on your own. On the other hand, you won't have HOA fees, noisy neighbors, etc.
Small (2-4 unit) Apartment	**Low.** Less risky than rental condos and homes since you have more than one unit, so it's unlikely you would ever have to make a mortgage payment completely on your own. A little more risky than a condo or rental home since it (typically) costs more to purchase, and might take a little longer to sell.
Large (5+ unit) Apartment	**Low – Medium.** Less risky than other rentals insofar as the cash flow should be the most stable of any rental group. More risky than other rentals since they cost more, require more equity, and take longer to sell. In the hands of a landlord seasoned with experience from smaller buildings there's a relatively low degree of risk. Returns are certainly more predictable and controllable than the stock market.
Lease Options (Owner Carry)	**Low.** The owner (not you!) is still responsible to the bank for the mortgage payments.
Lease Options (Investor Carry)	**Low - Medium.** You are responsible for the mortgage payments, which is similar to the Rental Home category above. However, the number of tenants you have to work with is quite a bit smaller since you have more particular requirements in seeking a lease-option tenant than a traditional landlord.
Fix and Flips	**Medium – High.** High risk, high effort, and high potential return. Requires more due diligence up front than rental investments. Your success is largely dependent on the performance of your contractors who you do not directly control. Be careful. Work with pros. Consider the risks.
Converting Apartments to Condos	**High/High+.** All of the factors for an apartment building and a Fix and Flip.
Scrapes and New Construction	**High.** High risk, high effort, and high potential return. Just like Fix and Flips, and then some.

Which Investing Category is Best for Your Unique Situation?

Follow the flow chart to determine which real estate investing categories are best suited for your unique situation. Begin in the upper left at the start box. Take your time and see what results.

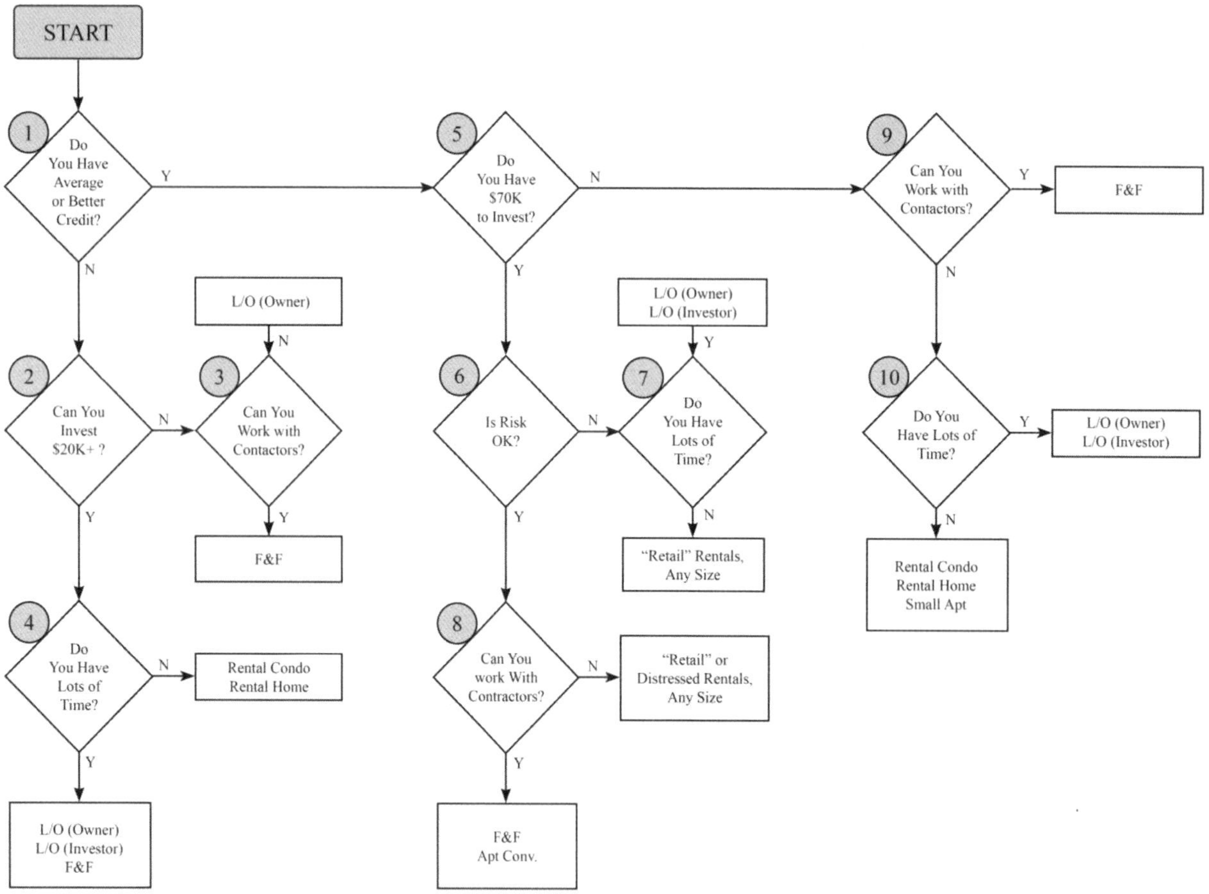

Question 1: Do you have average or better credit? We will explore credit scores in exhaustive detail in the chapter "Where the Pros Get the Money." For now, if your credit score is above 620 assume you have average credit. If your score is above 720, assume you have excellent credit. If the answer is yes, proceed to question 5. If not, go on to question 2.

Question 2: Can you make an investment of at least $10-20K? If the answer is no, go to question 3. If yes, go to question 4.

Question 3: In this case, you currently do not have a strong credit score and you are limited on the funds that you can invest. Do you enjoy (or at least be willing to try) working with contractors?

If you **are not willing** to work with contractors, you should consider a lease option strategy where you leverage owner financing. Focus on developing your credit score as you do this and/or looking for partners with cash to increase your options. Alternatively, you can also consider Assignments.

If you **are willing** to work with contractors, you can consider the L/O strategy above or you could also consider a fix and flip project. If you choose a F&F, you will likely need to get a Hard Money loan that finances both the acquisition costs and fix up costs. Since the project funding will be tight, you will probably have to do a lot of the work yourself. However, this could be a good method for you to build your equity reserves in a hurry if your marketplace currently has a good market for F&F.

Question 3

Question 4: Do you have a lot of time on an on-going basis to allocate to your real estate investing interests?

If you **do not** have a lot of on-going time, then you should consider getting a small rental property. With your current cash resources and credit score, you will most likely want to choose a rental condo or a smaller rental home. As you build equity in a few years, you can refinance your property and you will have more capital to deploy. Also focus on building your credit score and this will serve to increase the options that are available to you.

If you **do** have a lot of on-going time to invest, you have more choices. You can choose to pick a smaller rental as outlined above or you could choose to pursue a lease option strategy. Since you are short of cash, you will need to leverage an owner carry rather than purchasing the property on your own. Alternatively, if you like working with contractors (or have the desire to learn), you could work on a small fix and flip. If you choose a F&F, you will likely need to get a Hard Money loan that finances the acquisition costs and the fix up costs. Since the project funding will be tight you will probably have to do a lot of the work yourself. However, this could be a good method for you to build your equity reserves in a hurry if your marketplace currently has a good market for F&F.

Question 5: We have established that you have at least an average credit score. Do you have at least $70,000 to invest? If not, please jump to question 9. If you do have at least $70,000 you would like to invest, continue with question 6.

Question 6: Are you willing to take on at least a moderate level of risk to get higher returns? If yes, and you want to focus on the higher risk opportunities to earn higher returns, please skip to question 8. If you want to start with less risky investments and are accepting of lower returns, continue on to question 7.

Question 5

Question 7: We have established you have a good credit score, at least $40,000 to invest, but you want to limit your risk. Do you have a lot of time to invest with your real estate investments on an on-going basis?

If you **do not have time**, then a rental strategy is probably best for you. If this is your first time as a landlord, you'll want to start small. You can afford to go with a condo, home, or small apartment building. Condos and homes require less money, but they have more cash flow volatility (e.g., if the tenant moves out you make all of the mortgage payment). Slightly larger buildings will require a little more money but the cash flow is more dependable (if one of the four tenants moves out, the other three tenants will pay most or all of mortgage for you). If you have some experience as a landlord you should consider a larger (more than five unit) building. With your experience, this will also be a low risk investment and with a competent property manager it won't take too much of your time either. In any case, you will probably want to purchase a building without a lot of risks (e.g., not many vacancies, in a nice part of town, and/or not much deferred maintenance) to reduce your exposure.

If you **do have time** you could either pursue the rental options above or you could also pursue a lease option strategy. Since you have capital and a good credit score, you don't have to depend exclusively on the owner-carry strategy, which will greatly increase your options.

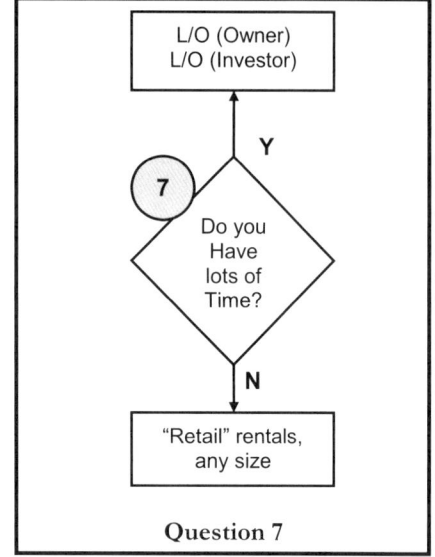

Question 7

Question 8: We have established you have a good credit score, at least $70,000 to invest, and you are willing to accept more risk to get more return. Are you experienced working with contractors?

If you **are not experienced** but are willing to learn, a fix and flip project would work. You will not have the constraints that a Hard Money lender will often apply to applicants with less credit power, and you will have the financial freedom to hire contractors to do the work. If it is your first F&F project, start with something simple even if you are willing to take on more risk. Don't be a hero! Once you have had a successful project, feel free to move on to more complex projects. Walk before you run and you won't be a statistic!

If you **are experienced** with contractors, you should consider whether an apartment conversion or a scrape and new construction is right for you. This is probably the highest risk category, but it also can have the highest returns and affords considerable tax planning flexibility that the other investment choices do not offer.

If you have strong credit, ample cash, and willingness to take on risk but you don't want to deal with contractors, your best choice may be to buy a rental building. (We will explore the difficulties of working with contractors later in the book). If you don't have much property management experience (either first-hand or managing the managers), buy a less ambitious project (e.g., a "retail" building), learn about how to manage a building, and then consider a more difficult project (e.g., a "distressed" building). If you do have property management experience, you could consider buying a distressed building that is being sold below market. Many rental investors do not have deep property management skills so you won't be competing with as many people for the investment, thus you can often get a better price. Examples of factors that cause distress are high vacancy rates, significant deferred maintenance, and/or weak property management (often manifested as below-market rents). Since buildings usually sell as a multiple of cash flow, you can buy the under-performing building at an attractive price, fix the issues causing distress, then re-sell the building at a higher price. This is a great strategy if you have the time and inclination to do it!

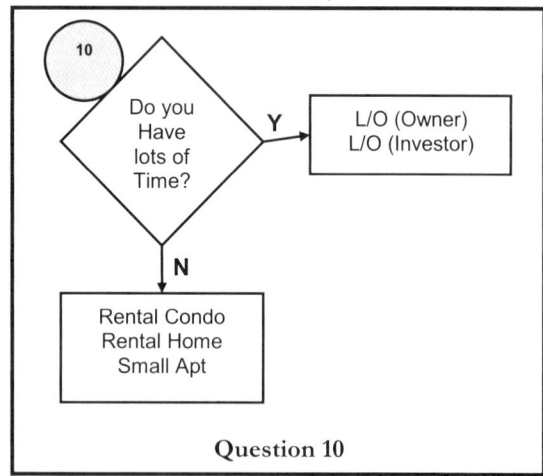

Question 10

Question 9: You have at least an average credit score but you have less than $70,000 available. Do you enjoy working with contractors? Or are you willing to try? If not, proceed to question 10. If you are willing to work with contractors you should consider a fix and flip project. You will not have the constraints that a Hard Money lender will often apply to applicants with less credit power, and you will have the financial freedom to hire contractors to do the work. If it is your first F&F project start with something simple even if you are willing to take on more risk. Once you have had a successful project, feel free to move on to more complex projects. Slow and steady wins the race so be the tortoise, not the hare.

Question 10: You have at least an average credit score, you have less than $70,000 to work with and you don't want to duke it out with your contractor every Friday afternoon. Do you have a lot of time, on an on-going basis, to allocate to your real estate investments?

If you **do not** have a lot of on-going time, then you should consider getting a small rental property. With your current cash resources you will mostly likely want to choose a rental condo, a smaller rental home or a small (2 – 4 unit) building. As you build equity in a few years, you can refinance your property, and you will have more capital to deploy.

If you **do** have a lot of on-going time to invest, you have more choices. You can choose to pick a rental as outlined above, or you could choose to pursue a lease option strategy. Since you are not short of cash, you are not limited to owner carry – you could also purchase the property on your own.

Summary

This chapter requires a great deal of self-analysis, a discipline which does not come naturally to many of us. We suggest you return to the beginning of the chapter and walk through the flowchart again… slowly and deliberately… with someone you trust. It's critical you spend the time to get this right. Otherwise, you risk pursuing the wrong type of real estate investment and severely reducing your chance of success.

Chapter 2: How Successful Investors Build Their Team

"Where no counsel is, the people fall; but in the multitude of counselors there is safety."
    -- Proverbs, 11:14

"The important thing to recognize is that it takes a team, and the team ought to get credit for the wins and the losses. Successes have many fathers, failures have none."
    -- Philip Caldwell

What's in this Chapter: Having worked with hundreds of investors over the years, we have observed that the most successful investors always have a great team helping them. This chapter reviews the key people you need to have on your team, their roles, and considerations in how to hire them. The appendices have detailed interview guides to help you select team members. We'll also spend a lot of time on how to interpret and use the information that your team members provide you. Finally, we'll examine how you can present yourself to your team members to get the best from them.

There are a lot of new terms in this chapter. You can find them in the Glossary with a detailed definition. Some of the new terms are called out in the Glossary boxes in the text.

Executive Summary – Best Practices

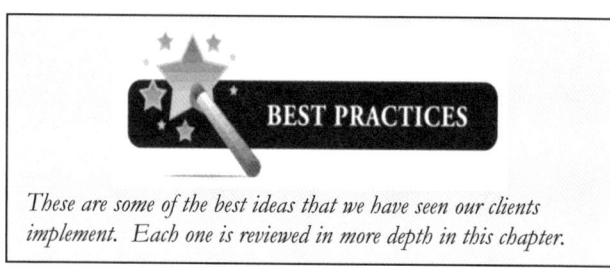

These are some of the best ideas that we have seen our clients implement. Each one is reviewed in more depth in this chapter.

- **Solicit referrals** from members of your real estate investor groups and from other successful investors for all of your team members. However, don't hire a team member based solely on referral – go through the interview screening steps. This takes time and you are probably too busy to do it, but it will pay rewards in the long haul. Don't take shortcuts!

- **Realistic expectations** – get as educated as you can before you start your interviews. Most likely, the real estate professionals on your team will have had a lot of experience with investors and many of those experiences will have been bad. If you come across as serious, knowledgeable and realistic, they will take you seriously and you will get much better results. If you act like a clown expect to work with clowns.

- **Find specialists.** Outstanding **residential** mortgage brokers and real estate agents rarely achieve even modest success with **investors**. Insist on full-time professionals that don't dabble in other things. You're looking for a track record of success.

- **Understand loan tradeoffs.** Take the time to get mortgage quotes from several lenders, specifically mortgage brokers that specialize in working with investors. Study hard and learn the differences and tradeoffs among different loan types. This may be painful, but it **will** save you a lot of money and frustration down the road. One of the authors preaches that lending is where the new investor spends the least amount of time but where they should spend the most amount of time. He's probably right.

- **Understand your strengths and weaknesses.** Before searching for your real estate agent, develop an honest self-assessment of your strengths and weaknesses. If possible, recruit a seasoned agent with strengths in the areas where you need help. As a team, you will make better decisions.

- **Interview** several real estate agents and briefly work with a handful before making a final decision to sign a buyer's agency contract. Make sure you have a clause to cancel if you are not satisfied. Commit to working with only one agent after your due diligence period so they will bring you the best deals. Non-committal buyers see only left-over deals after preferred clients have picked over them.

- **Inspections.** When you get a property under contract, spend some time thinking about what sort of inspection report you need and your negotiation strategy with the seller. Pick an inspector accordingly.

- **Manage contractors.** To get the best results, be willing to make the investment of time and effort to manage the contractors doing the repair work on your fix-up project. Depending on your availability and prior experiences, there are several proven ways to accomplish this.

Get as educated as you can before doing your interviews so you have realistic expectations. All of the prospective real estate professionals on your team will have had a lot of experience with investors, and many of those experiences have been bad. If you come across as serious, knowledgeable and realistic, they will take you seriously and you will get much better results!

Building a Team to Get the Best Results

One of the first things you will want to do is to assemble a team of professionals. You'll need to find a *Mortgage Broker*, *Real Estate Agent*, *Inspector*, *Appraiser*, *Insurance Broker* and *CPA*. You may also need the support of an *Attorney* and a *Property Manager*.

The Inside Story on How Investors are Perceived

You should know that there has been an incredible surge in the number of people interested in investing in real estate in the past 20 years. Many of these investors watch late night TV infomercials and Reality TV or go to seminars that set them up with unrealistic expectations about how they can make money with little or no effort or risk. Many investment "gurus" charge thousands of dollars for courses on how you can buy properties with nothing down and no risk. Hogwash! These people are in the business of selling get-rich-quick books, tapes, and more seminars. Caveat emptor.

Real Estate Agent – A person who has passed your state's regulatory board requirements and has some minimal level of training to offer real estate services to the general public. A real estate agent that has joined the National Association of REALTORS® is allowed to use the trade name of REALTOR®. About half of the people with a license are also REALTOR®.

When you approach a mortgage broker or a real estate agent to get help as an investor, don't expect a universally warm welcome. Most full time agents have had many unpleasant experiences with investors that have wasted their time – and for full time professionals that means less money for their families. Many agents do not work with investors at all because of the get-rich-quick attitude prevalent among beginners.

For the agents that do work with investors, the successful and busy agents have dozens of investors who want to be clients, so they will quickly sort through the prospective clients to determine what small percentage are likely to ever result in a closed deal. The best agents won't work with investors with unrealistic expectations, so those investors get bounced down to less-experienced agents. In tracking the statistics in our office, we find any given real estate agent is more than twice as likely to close a deal with a residential buyer than with an investor. If you were making a living as an agent, who would

Mortgage Broker – Independent loan broker that works with multiple lenders to find the best loan for your specific needs. In most states they are licensed and regulated.

you be more excited to work with? To balance this though, our best investor clients buy multiple properties per year and make decisions quickly. One of the authors has closed over 2 dozen deals with the same client.

For you to be taken seriously, it is very important for you to have realistic expectations about what can and cannot be accomplished with different investing approaches. This chapter will arm you with much of the information that you need. The more educated you are about how things actually work in your market, the more successful you will be in recruiting the most skilled and competent professionals.

Finding a Lender

Hopefully, the previous chapter helped you determine what type of investment to pursue. Once you know what you want to buy, your next step is to locate a source of funds. Then when you know what you can qualify for, you can begin looking for properties that match your criteria. The major choices for funding are to use your own cash (a goal for most of us), *Hard Money*, or a *Mortgage* – either from your current bank or a mortgage broker. If you are pursuing a lease option strategy leveraging owner carry, then you will not need to line up financing.

GLOSSARY

Hard Money Lenders – Individuals or groups that lend you money based on the value of the property you are purchasing. If the property is worth $200,000 and you are able to purchase it for $150,000, a Hard Money Lender may give you a loan even if you have bad credit. However, the fees and the interest rate will be much less desirable than more conventional forms of financing. Hard Money lenders can usually close very quickly.

When Should You Pay Cash? If you can pay cash, you probably also have a strong enough credit score that you won't have to use it. But, your terms will usually be attractive enough that it may be better to use someone else's money. The exception is when you are buying a property that does not conform to most lenders' guidelines and you can't get a loan (at least, not on terms you find acceptable). An example would be an apartment building with more than four units that has a poor occupancy level. You might need to purchase the building with your own cash, fix the management problem, lease up the building, and then take out a loan or sell the building to capture your gains. Similarly, if you are buying a trashed house that you plan to fix and flip, most appraisers will document the problems and you will not qualify for a traditional mortgage.

When Should You Use "Hard Money?" Banks evaluate your credit scores and your capacity to repay a loan when determining how much money they will loan you. Hard Money lenders are more concerned with the value of the property you are purchasing than your qualifications. Basically, they figure if you stop making payments to them they'll just take over the property. If you are getting the property for significantly less than market value, then they often will give you a loan even if your credit is marginal. However, the fees, interest rates, and restrictions are much more onerous than any other source of funds (think 4 points and 14% interest for a 6-month loan). Hard Money lenders are often the lenders of last resort when the property has equity but cannot be purchased via another channel.

GLOSSARY

Cash – When purchasing a property, most state-regulated real estate contracts allow you to put provisions into the contract that state that if you cannot get the loan you want on the terms you want, you can back out of the deal. A purchase of a property using cash does not have the "loan conditions" contractual right to get out of the contract.

Other times to use Hard Money are when…

- Time is of the essence (e.g., you need to close in 48 hours). They can usually make a decision very rapidly, whereas a more traditional loan might take three weeks or more to close.
- You are buying a multi-unit building with low occupancy (lower than 80%).
- You are buying a fix and flip property that is uninhabitable in its current condition (e.g., no kitchen or furnace).

If you are interested in a Hard Money loan, attend a local real estate investing club meeting to ask for referrals. Most large cities will have many Hard Money lenders in operation. It pays to shop your deal around to get the best rates and terms.

How Do Mortgages Work? Most investors are somewhere in the middle – not wealthy enough to pay cash, but not in a situation where they have to use Hard Money. Let's review how the mortgage process works, reveal the meaning of some of the jargon that you will hear in the process, and examine the different ways you can find mortgage products.

GLOSSARY

Loan Officer (LO) – the person who gathers your financial information in a standardized format (the *1003*), gathers rate and term quotes from lenders, helps you select the best loan for your situation, then helps coordinate the closing of the loan.

Picking the Lender and the Loan Program

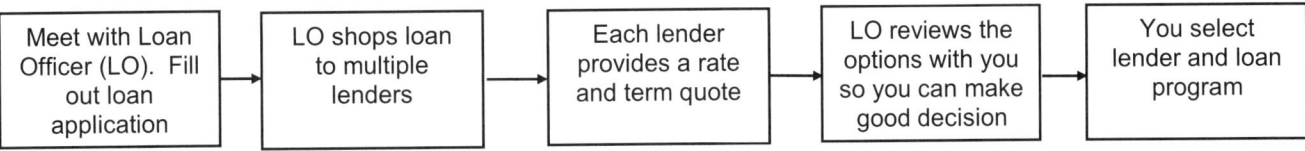

Your first step is to meet with a *Loan Officer* (LO). You might start with an application page on the Internet, a mortgage loan officer at the bank you are currently using, or an independent mortgage broker. You'll fill out a standardized loan application called a *1003*. The full form is four pages long. It'll review your sources of income (e.g., salary, alimony, rapidly growing real estate investment income…), your debt payments (e.g., the mortgage on your primary residence, credit card debt, your car payment), your *Assets* (money in checking/savings accounts, stocks, bonds, etc.), and your *Liabilities* (what you owe; e.g., your mortgage balance, your car loan balance).

If you are working with your local bank, the LO will give the 1003 to the bank's underwriters. They will evaluate your financial position and will develop a rate quote for their most suitable loan product. If you are working with a mortgage broker, they will choose among multiple lenders to find the one with the best match for your needs. Each will develop a rate quote for you.

> **GLOSSARY**
>
> *1003* – The standardized loan application form for *Residential* (i.e., non-commercial) mortgages. It consists of a list of your sources of income, your *Balance Sheet*, your *Credit Score* and other information needed by the Lender to determine which loan products for which you qualify.

After the quotes are in, the LO should sit with you to review your options as well as the advantages and disadvantages of each loan program so you can make the best decision for your unique situation.

You now have your loan program picked out and it is time to start looking at properties. The LO will print out a *Lender Letter* which outlines the general terms of your loan program. Your real estate agent will provide this to the *Listing Agent* to prove that you have the financial capacity to purchase the property. See Appendix for a sample lender letter.

Closing on the Transaction

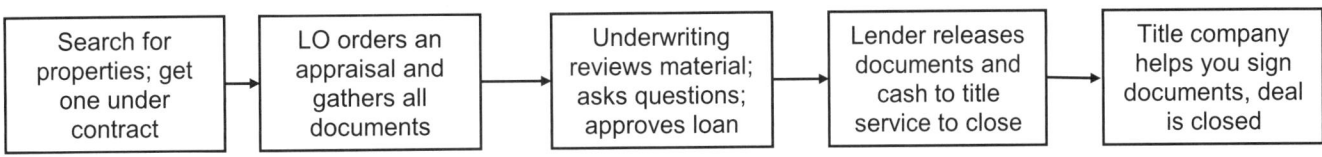

Once you have identified your property, your real estate agent will help you put it under contract. The agent sends a copy of the contract to the Loan Officer. For residential purchases, the buyer usually will conduct an inspection of the property with an *Inspector*, and then the Buyer and Seller negotiate over what repairs and/or allowances, if any, the Seller will provide. Once that has been agreed upon, the Buyer gives the Loan Officer permission to order the appraisal.

The appraisal is usually ordered after the inspection so the cost of the appraisal won't be borne if the parties cannot come to terms over the repair work. If you are confident that you will not be

> **GLOSSARY**
>
> *Inspector* – Independent party that you may hire to inspect a property you are considering purchasing. In many states, inspectors are not regulated, so anyone can call themselves an inspector without any minimum level of training or certification.

requesting much repair work, or if the property is in good condition, you could decide to order the appraisal at the same time as the inspection. You would take on a little risk in that you might waste the cost of the appraisal, but you would shorten the closing process by at least a week.

While the appraisal is being completed, the underwriters at the bank should be reviewing your file to ensure the file is complete. They may ask you, via the Loan Officer, for more documents. In the ideal situation, they will give final approval to your loan, subject to a successful appraisal, within a few days. When the appraisal comes in, they release the funds so you can close on your transaction.

The closing agent at the Title Company will help you sign and notarize the loan documents at the closing table. Voila! The Title Company records the appropriate documents with the County and sends the rest back to the lender; the mortgage origination process is complete.

When Should You Go Directly to Your Bank? The bank where you keep your checking and savings accounts will often provide mortgages, too. You should definitely call them to explore their rates and terms. Often times, your current bank will not have many options for a non-owner occupied investment loan and you can do better by going to a mortgage broker to shop many banks to get the best terms. Call and find out.

GLOSSARY

Closing Agent or *Closer* – the person at the Title Company that conducts the closing and manages the blizzard of paperwork and checks.

The exception is for a second mortgage. A HELOC (home equity line of credit) is usually less expensive from your local banker than from almost any other source. Not all banks will do a HELOC for an investment property, but if you simply need to tap the equity in your house to get some money for a down payment, this is frequently the most efficient way.

When Should You Go to a Mortgage Broker? Unlike the loan officer at your bank, which can usually only sell that one bank's loan products, the mortgage broker sets up relationships with many lenders. Each lender may have a different focus area and product line. Representing a large number of lenders means that almost every unique situation will have a product tailored to its specific needs. Any one bank would find it cost-prohibitive to offer this much variety, so they usually offer a few owner-occupied loan products, and that is it. This is the value of a good mortgage broker. If you find a good one, treat him or her very well.

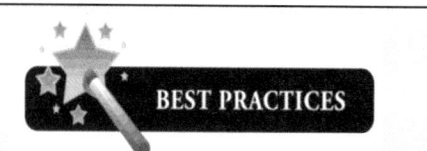

BEST PRACTICES

Talk to your friends and fellow investors to get referrals, but be sure to follow the interview guide "How to Hire a Mortgage Broker" in the appendix. Interview at least three. Getting this right is critical!

For most non-owner occupied properties, you should always find a mortgage broker that specializes in working with investors to get some quotes from multiple banks. It should not cost you anything to do this and if the mortgage broker pulls your credit within a few days of the time that your local bank does, it does not have an adverse impact on your credit score. The credit rating agencies expect that you will shop for a loan when you make a major purchase (e.g., a car, your primary residence, or an investment property).

GLOSSARY

Underwriters – The underwriter is the person who works for the Lender that examines all of the Borrower's documents to be sure they are credit worthy and examine the appraisal to ensure the property is worth what the Buyer is paying for the property. They check all facets of the loan to make sure they are within the lending guidelines of the program. When they are satisfied that all conditions are met, they approve the release of funds from the Lender so you can complete your purchase.

How to Find a Great Mortgage Broker. The best source is likely your real estate investor club meetings. Ask the investors, particularly the people that are doing things similar to what you plan to do, and you will hear stories – good, bad, and downright scary. You'll also be certain to meet a lot of mortgage brokers there, too. Be sure to screen them like you screen anyone else you bring on to your team. If this is your first time hiring an investor-oriented mortgage broker, you should consider interviewing at least three.

Don't rely too heavily on the recommendations of friends and family members that have purchased residential property that they live in – the requirements to set up a loan for an owner occupant are significantly different than the requirements for an investor loan. Excellent residential mortgage brokers (and there are many out there) usually are not very good with investors since they don't get much practice working with them.

Differences between Residential and Investment Mortgage Brokers. In most states there is at least a nominal amount of supervision provided by regulators to the mortgage brokers. In many cases, however, there isn't any distinction on what types of services the mortgage broker may offer to clients. Most mortgage brokers will spend the majority of their time working on owner occupied loans for primary residences. This type of loan makes up the majority of the market. So while you (or your real estate agent) likely already know someone who can find a mortgage, they usually won't be the best pick for your needs as an investor. Mortgage brokers that specialize in working with investors will have a multitude of lenders with products tailored to your needs. This results in more selection, better pricing, and better terms.

Commercial property –Commercial properties, for the purpose of this book, are apartment buildings with more than four units. Financing for these buildings is more difficult to arrange than for residential properties.

Avoid Part Time Mortgage Brokers. The majority of people who call themselves mortgage brokers also have other methods to sustain themselves. There is an amazing array of lenders competing for loan business, and a nearly limitless set of permutations on how a loan can be structured. It is difficult enough for someone who thinks about it all day, every day, to get good at the business. It is virtually impossible for someone who does it part-time. Be sure to hire a full time mortgage broker. Similarly, your real estate agent might tell you they can "set up the loan for you." If you have great credit and are purchasing a home that you will live in, they may certainly be able to do a competent job for you. However, if you are not going to be living in the house, think twice. They should be able to refer you to a mortgage broker that specializes in working with investors.

Difference between Lenders with Wholesale Lines versus Resellers. Most mortgage brokers resell loan products from other investors. They are an intermediary that gathers your information in a standardized way, identifies loan alternatives, then explains the advantages and disadvantages of each of your options so you can make an informed choice. They also do a lot of other value added tasks so your loan can close efficiently. They don't control the whole process, though -- underwriting decisions are usually made at a place called "headquarters" in a galaxy far, far away. If you have ever had a real estate closing that experienced a delay, it might have been because the underwriter didn't look at your loan file until the very last minute, had a question, and it could not be resolved before your closing.

These problems – which are much more common for non-owner occupied property – can be reduced by using a wholesale lender. This specialized set of mortgage brokers actually can do the underwriting in their own office. As a result, there is much more local control over the whole process. Sometimes these lenders will cost a little more, but the mitigation of hassle and worry is worth it to some investors.

Talk to your friends and fellow investors to get referrals. Use the interview guides in the appendix. There is one for an Investor Broker and one for a Residential Listing Agent since your needs will be different. Interview at least three if you can.

When to Fire Your Mortgage Broker. Alas, not everything in life works out well. If your mortgage broker cannot seem to communicate with your real estate agent, if you are experiencing long delays in getting calls back, or if your questions simply are not being answered… it might be time to find a new mortgage broker. If you are mid-way through a deal, it might be a bad time to change brokers and you might have to tough it out. Start interviewing to find a new person for the next deal.

Finding a Real Estate Agent

Your real estate agent is a critical member of your team. In our opinion they should be investors themselves so they have firsthand knowledge of what you are looking for and can (from experience) point out traps and good opportunities. Experience and hands-on knowledge makes all the difference. Accept no substitutes.

Difference between a "real estate agent" and a REALTOR®. Many investors are confused about the difference between a licensee and a REALTOR®. A licensee is anyone who has passed the state's regulatory exam and has a legal license to practice real estate. This is what we are referring to as a "real estate agent." A REALTOR® is a real estate agent who has joined the National Association of Realtors trade group. Joining the group gives them the privilege of using the REALTOR® designation. REALTORS® take additional classes in ethics that other real estate agents can, but do not have to, take. About half of the 2,000,000 licensed real estate agents in the U.S. are also REALTORS®.

Many, though certainly not all, Realtors are full time and take a significant number of on-going training courses to increase their skills. Be sure to ask about the training classes your real estate agent has taken.

Avoid Part Time Agents. The majority of real estate agents complete only one or two deals a year! Many have other jobs that they rely on to sustain themselves, and the intermittent commissions they earn from friends and family generate some welcome extra income. You need an experienced full time agent to help you navigate this business. For example, in the Denver market, about 24,000 people have a real estate license. Around 4,000 of them are full time and they do about 82% of the business. The majority of these productive, experienced agents are REALTORS®, not licensees.

Develop an honest self-assessment of your strengths and weaknesses. If possible, recruit a seasoned Broker with strengths in the areas where you need help. As a team, you will make better decisions.

How to Find a Great Real Estate Agent. As usual, a good source is likely your local real estate investor club meetings. Ask the investors, particularly the people that are doing things similar to what you plan to do and you will hear stories – good, bad, and frightening. You'll also be certain to meet a lot of real estate agents there, too. Keep in mind that many of the agents you contact at these meetings will be newer agents with little experience themselves. Be sure to screen them like you screen anyone else you bring on to your team. If this is your first time hiring an investor-oriented agent, you should consider interviewing at least three.

Just like with mortgage brokers, don't rely too heavily on the recommendations of friends and family members that have purchased residential property that they live in – the requirements to find a nice house for an owner occupant are significantly different than the requirements for an investor.

Most licensees don't make a good living from Real Estate (and this is why the vast majority of people who enter the field leave within two years). For the minority of agents that are full time, they take whatever work they can find in any part of the city, since their survival depends on it. You don't want that person representing you, since there is a conflict of interest – they want you to get a good investment, so you are happy, but they also really want you to buy *something*, so they can get a commission. These agents tend to be pushier about trying to get you to close on something. Ideally, you want to work with an agent that is busy enough that they are not concerned about where their next mortgage payment is coming from, so they can really be patient in helping you to find the right deal. An agent that is always available to wait on you probably isn't busy enough to have the market knowledge and transaction experience you will need to be successful.

Finally, and perhaps most importantly, try to develop an honest self-assessment of what you, as an investor, are good at and not so good at. Try to find an agent that rounds out your skills set. For example, if you really don't like doing the math to determine if an investment is solid choice or not, try to find a real estate agent that is really good at math that can help you with this part of the investment process.

Recognize that you are not delegating responsibility, but are simply looking for help. It's irresponsible for an investor to try to get the real estate agent to make a decision for them. As the investor, you always have the final say and must take full responsibility for your decisions.

Differences between Residential and Investment Agents. Similar to the discussion about mortgage brokers, you want a real estate agent that mainly works with investors, and primarily investors in your particular area of interest. The search process and thought process for investments should be highly numbers-driven: How much money can the investor make? How much risk do they have to accept? In contrast, the residentially-focused agent's clients are mainly focused on the emotional appeal of the home and how well it fits their lifestyle.

What are Designations? Real Estate Agents have many continuing education opportunities available to them that result in "designations." There are at least a dozen such designations; generally these agents have more of a commitment to continuing education than the average agent. Most of the designations are relatively easy to obtain – for example, ABR (Accredited Buyers Representative) requires a twelve hour course and five closed residential transactions of any size. The designations that investors will find interesting are the CCIM and SIOR. The other accreditations are interesting but not particularly relevant to investors.

What is a CCIM and Does it Matter? The CCIM (Certified Commercial Investment Member) is a recognized professional in commercial real estate brokerage, leasing, asset management, valuation, and investment analysis. As an experienced expert, a CCIM is an invaluable resource to the commercial real estate owner, investor, and user. The Commercial Investment Real Estate Institute (CIREI), through its education program, has been conferring the CCIM designation since 1969. The 240 hours of graduate-level curriculum leading to the designation represents a rigorous level of education. It includes several graduate-level courses in real estate finance and a minimum of either 20 completed commercial deals, $40 million of commercial volume, or ten commercial deals of at least $10 million each. If you are considering purchasing a larger apartment building then an agent with a CCIM designation is worth seeking out. If you are doing smaller investment project under $1 million then most CCIMs probably would not be willing to work with you, as they focus on larger commercial deals.

The SIOR (Society of Industrial and Office REALTORS®) designation is available to agents with five years of industrial and office real estate experience who fulfill all educational requirements, pass a comprehensive membership exam, or hold the CCIM designation. Further, they must meet an annual minimum in closed transactions by number, volume or square footage as set by local chapters. If you are branching out from the investment types reviewed in this book to explore larger commercial investments, an agent with a SIOR designation would be a valuable addition to your team.

Keep in mind there are many highly qualified commercial Brokers that do not carry these designations – they are just too busy working with clients to have the time to get the designation.

BEST PRACTICES

The clients the Broker perceives as the most loyal and willing to close quickly will see the best deals first. The best deals don't get shown to clients perceived as un-loyal. Balance this, though, with an early exit clause in your Buyer Agency contract if things don't work out.

What the Real Estate Agent Does and Doesn't Do for You. Your agent is a powerful ally in your journey to becoming a successful real estate investor. After reading the first few chapters of this book, you should have a better **theoretical idea** of what you want to invest in. But you won't know for sure until you get out of your armchair and see some properties! Once you are face to face with a fix up home, you will start to get a gut feeling and a **true understanding** if it is the right choice for you or not. Your agent is your passport to discover which investment group(s) is/are the best fit for you. They can provide you with war stories and coaching, but you will need to decide which is the best type of investment for your situation.

Once you have settled on a type of investment, you'll need to narrow it down to a few neighborhoods that make sense. Again, your agent can provide you with a lot of information and show you properties, but the final decision on the best value/potential for appreciation will be yours.

Finally, and most importantly, estimating the future value of a property is one of the most difficult things that investors and their teams work on. It's also an area where we most commonly see investors take a back seat role, and ask their agent "what will this be worth when I finish fixing it up?" The agent can provide the data to you, and show you comparables (comps) and competitor homes, but the ultimate determination on the project valuation rests with you. Your money. Your risk. Your responsibility. **Don't outsource your thinking or your responsibility!**

Should You Sign a Buyer's Agency Contract? Yes, but not immediately. Good agents with lots of clients will ask you to sign a Buyer's Agency agreement. It states that you are hiring that agent to work for you and that you commit to work with only that agent. Obviously this is a great thing for the agent but it limits your options as an investor. Consider interviewing a number of agents and ask a few of them (perhaps two or three) to spend an hour or two showing you some properties that meet your needs. Ask the interview questions in the appendix. You will get a strong gut feeling when you find the right agent. If you sign a Buyer's Agency with them, they will be a lot more willing to invest time in research, showings, and mentoring for you than if you do not sign a Buyer's Agency. Life is a two-way street. Investing in real estate is no different.

Consider also asking the agent to put in an Additional Provision that you can cancel the agreement at any time. One of the authors puts that in ALL his Buyer Agency and Listing agreements. This is a good compromise between protecting your needs (getting out of the agreement if it turns out the agent isn't getting what you need) and assuring the agent that if they put in the extra effort to get a great deal for you they will be paid for it. If they won't agree to this clause then put in a shorter time period for the Buyer Agency – perhaps a month versus the six months they will often ask for. As you will see in the next section, in most states it will be very easy for you to cancel this contract should the need arise.

What you don't want to do is appear to be a flaky investor that tries to work with multiple agents simultaneously. Get a bad reputation in this business and no one who is competent will want to work with you. The real estate market is highly competitive and the number of truly exceptional deals is very limited. If an agent comes across a great deal and is currently working with twenty clients (and this is the type of agent you need to work with), who will they call first? They'll start with the investors with whom they have closed deals in the past. Then they will call the buyers with whom they have a Buyer's Agency contract and a lender letter, so the agent has a high degree of certainty the deal will close and they will be paid. The last people they will call are the investors that are "playing the field" with a number of agents and/or the investors that will not sign a Buyer's Agency agreement. Good deals do not make it to the bottom of the call list. Ever.

When to Fire Your Agent and How to Do it. If your agent cannot seem to communicate well with you, if you are experiencing long delays in getting calls back, or if your questions simply are not being answered well… it might be time to change agents. Start by trying to have a conversation with the agent about what you need that you are not getting. In many cases that will help. If you are mid-way through a deal, it might be a bad time to change agents and you might have to tough it out. Start interviewing to find a new person for the next deal.

If you signed a Buyer Agency agreement, tell the agent you are no longer comfortable working with him or her and you want to cancel it. Usually they will do it. Get it in writing – a brief paragraph that both parties sign is sufficient; it does not need to be fancy. If the agent is stubborn and won't do it, escalate the issue to their real estate office Managing Broker. Outline what you need that you are not getting, and review the discussion that you had with the agent to try to get them to improve. Usually the Managing Broker will solve the problem by either canceling the Buyer Agency or asking if you would consider working with a different agent in the office. If you get the rare Managing Broker that doesn't seem to comprehend what you are telling them, politely suggest that you could take it to the State Real Estate Commission and file a complaint. In most states, the Commission is required to investigate every complaint. Usually, this will get you the flexibility you need.

What You Need to Know about Inspectors

After you find a home and put it under contract, the usual next step is to find an Inspector to look over the home in detail. The Inspector is hired by the Buyer and reports to the Buyer. Often times the buyer relies on the recommendation of the real estate agent in making this selection. That is a great place to start, but by being a little more educated about Inspectors you can make a better decision.

Are They Licensed in Your State? The first thing you might want to investigate is if Inspectors in your state are licensed. In many states they are not, and anyone can call themselves a home inspector with no training or certification from the state. Begin by learning what regulations, if any, your state has.

Regardless of your state's level of regulation, there are some other criteria you can use to assess your Inspector. You might ask if they are a member of ASHI, the American Society of Home Inspectors. This group has some minimum levels of education that are required for membership, so you can be confident that your Inspector has a baseline level of training. You can learn more at http://www.ashi.org/

Do They Need to be an Engineer? No. For newer properties in areas where structural issues are uncommon, an engineer might be more expensive than you need. However, if you are purchasing an older property and/or your neighborhood does have some history of structural issues, you might want to spend more money to get a more thorough assessment.

We recommend you get a sewer scope for virtually any property you are buying. For $100 - $200, a sewer inspector will insert a camera down the sewer line and look for root blockages, offset sewer pipes, and even complete breaks. It's well worth the investment since a crushed sewer can set you back as much as $10,000. You'll get a VHS or DVD tape of the camera going through your sewer line along with an analysis from the sewer tech. Some companies even give you a bag of microwave popcorn so you can watch the movie at home with the kids!

The Inside Scoop on Appraisals

"I think we ought always to entertain our opinions with some measure of doubt."

-- Bertrand Russell

You will not need an appraisal if you are planning to use cash to purchase the property. In some cases, Hard Money Lenders will not require an appraisal either. Lenders, however, almost always will require a completed appraisal to give you final approval for the mortgage request.

Overview. The main objective of the appraisal is to get an independent assessment of the property's value. If you default on your mortgage, the bank can be reasonably sure that they can resell the property if they foreclose on it and recover the money they paid out in the loan.

Who does the appraiser work for? While you will be paying for the appraisal in your closing costs, the hiring relationship is technically between the bank (or mortgage broker) and the appraiser. The appraiser is accountable to the bank, not you, for answering questions. Technically, the appraiser is not a member of your team; they are part of the lender's team. Appraisal Management Company's (AMCs) came into being after the housing meltdown and most appraisers are now selected from a pool working for an AMC that has a relationship with a lender. This mechanism was established to break the alleged collusion between loan officers and appraisers. The jury is still out on whether it's done more harm than good.

GLOSSARY

Comps – Slang for "sales comparables." If you are purchasing a three bedroom, two bathroom home with a two car garage and 2,000 square feet, the homes that generally meet those same parameters and sold in the last six to twelve months in a half mile to mile radius would be the "comps" for your property. There will be a bit of a range in price, as some homes will have been sold in better condition than others, or will have had more upgrades than others. An investor will often ask their real estate agent to "pull comps" for them for a property they like.

BEST PRACTICES

Be willing to make the investment of time and effort to manage the contractors doing the repair work on your fix-up project to get the best results. Depending on your availability and prior experiences, there are several proven ways to accomplish this.

How long will it take and what will it cost? Here are some rough estimates, which will vary by market:

- Most residential, owner-occupied appraisals can be completed in a week for $400 - $500.
- **Small rental buildings** (less than five units) might take two weeks and run $500 - $700. They cost more and take longer since the appraiser needs to gather rental information as well as the building valuation.
- **Larger rental buildings** (more than four units) will usually run from $1,000 - $3,500 and might take two to four weeks. You might also need an environmental review as well. A basic assessment should only take a few weeks and should be around $1,000 - $3,000. This can be completed concurrently with the appraisal. This appraisal will include a sales comp assessment, a rent assessment and usually a cost valuation as well.
- **Construction loans** for condo conversions are the most complicated. They will include all of the elements of a larger rental appraisal and they'll also evaluate the value of the building after it has been converted. There will usually be some commentary about project construction budget and timing as well. The shortest amount of time that we've seen a construction loan appraisal completed in took three weeks. Expect to pay at least $3,000. You might also need an environmental assessment, as outlined in "larger rental buildings" above.

Since the work of the appraiser has an important impact on your transaction, we'll review their activities here to round out your understanding of the overall purchase process.

How a Residential Appraisal Works. Usually the appraiser will visit your property, take some photos, and measure the building to confirm the square footage reported in the county records. Then they will research the MLS for recently sold properties (ideally in the last six months, though sometimes they will have to go back further in time) to find properties that are similar. Typically they will try to find between three and five. These properties are called *Sales Comps*.

The appraiser will examine the comps and make some adjustments based on their judgment. For example, if your home does not have a fireplace and if one of the three comps did have a fireplace, they would adjust the value of that comp down by some value (say, $1,000), since the fireplace adds some value to the sales comp. If one of the comps was in significantly better condition than the others, the appraiser will make a value adjustment for

CASE STUDIES

Fact is, every contractor we've spoken to has been screwed by an investor at one time or another, and many would rather not work with investors – they tend to run out of money, they are too tight on the budget, etc. They are evaluating you to see if you are going to stiff them too. As a result, if you are a good, decent person, acknowledge that this is a problem in the real estate investor industry and be cognizant of how you present yourself. If you win their confidence early on, you'll get a better bid (or, at least, get a bid… many contractors never come back to provide one).

that, too. After the adjustments have been made for the features and conditions of the homes, the appraiser adjusts the prices of the sales comps to compensate for the fact they are larger or smaller than the property you are trying to purchase. They can then average the values to determine a target price for your home.

Working with Contractors

Finding a Contractor. If you have done some renovation work in the past, you might already have a network of contractors that you like and trust. If not, ask friends and family members for referrals. Meet several (three at a minimum and ideally five). You should also consider attending a few meetings of local real estate investor groups. You will learn a lot by networking with your peers, and you can ask them for recommendations of who to use – and not to use – since this group of investors will likely interact with many different trades people. Ask your real estate agent, too.

As a last resort, you can pick up the yellow pages, go to your local REALTOR® association, go to Craigslist or do an Internet search and call around. We usually find that many of the best contractors are very busy, even in a slower economy, due to strong word-of-mouth referrals. The contractors that run ads are not as busy and are running advertisements in the yellow pages to get business. Sometimes they are fine craftspeople that are new to an area and do not have a book of business. Other times, they are not as good, don't get many referrals, and have to rely on advertising to get work. At the other end of the spectrum, you will find large operations (especially for electrical and plumbing work) that do outstanding work, and will charge very high prices. They usually drive very expensive trucks. Sometimes that is what you want, but make sure that you get a number of bids so you are not taken advantage of.

In our experience, if we call ten contractors only a few will ever answer the phone or return the call. Of those we talk to, many don't keep their appointment and fail to show up to give a bid. Amazingly, few ever submit a bid. You'll be able to weed down the list considerably just based on this.

Communicating What You Want with Your Contractor.
Before you even talk to them, figure out what you want. It sounds obvious, but many contractors tell us that most investors have no idea of what needs to be done, and they outsource all of their thinking to the contractor. This is not a best practice! Then, a detailed "meeting of the minds" is absolutely essential for a contractor/investor relationship to be successful. Don't skimp on this. Write everything down. Work out every last detail. **Over document**; you'll be glad you did.

Have Realistic Expectations About the Bid.
The bid should outline the scope of work and the quality of materials to be used in a reasonable level of detail. You'll certainly discuss the project until you have a shared verbal understanding of what needs to be done, but memorializing it on paper will help both of you as the

BEST PRACTICES

Consider spending some time at your community college or at Home Depot ® attending some do-it-yourself classes before you interview contractors to ask for bids. If you have gone to the trouble to learn about tile floors at a ninety minute class, you will have a much better idea of what you want, what is reasonably possible with your project (and budget), and how best to communicate it. There are many books and video tapes you could review to get a basic knowledge if the class schedules don't work for you. This is a very inexpensive way to educate yourself.

weeks go by and memories fade. Keep in mind that many good craftspeople are likely to enjoy paperwork even less than you do – there may not be much correlation between the quality of the bid paperwork and the work they do. High priced contractors will usually have a much better looking presentation and bid, but the work quality is often very similar. Remember to put it in writing! The more detail, the better.

How to Pay the Contractor.
Most projects have a degree of risk in estimating their cost. If you are doing new construction, the risk is relatively small since there are fewer unknowns. If you are renovating a hundred year old Victorian house there could be many issues that are discovered during a renovation that take more time and/or money to resolve. Try moving a wall in an old house sometime and you'll see what we mean.

BEST PRACTICES

As a quick, rough rule of thumb, the labor costs for installation are usually about the same as the material costs.

There are two main methods for compensation – a fixed bid or "time and materials." A fixed bid puts the project risk on the contractor. It specifies what will be done and a fixed price for the work. If the work goes exactly as planned, the contractor enjoys a high profit margin. If one problem after another pops up, the contractor loses money on the job and you still pay your fixed price, unless the contractor just gives up and leaves a mess on your hands. (You wouldn't believe how often this happens.)

BEST PRACTICES

After you have talked through the project with the contractor, explore whether paying in cash will yield a better price. Many times it will. Ask for proof of liability and workman's compensation insurance.

Fixed bids are nice because they give you a high degree of certainty of what the project will cost. However, as you shift the risk of a project problem from you to the contractor, they will have to charge you more to cover the inevitable problems that crop up that no one could have reasonably anticipated. The higher the possibility of unforeseen problems, the more risk that that contractor takes on -- and the higher "safety factor" that the contractor will have to add on to the quote.

Sometimes there will be caveats in the bid for unforeseen problems that come up during the course of the rehab. For example, you might decide to remove a wall between a dining room and a living room to create one large room. The contractor might give you a fixed bid to perform this work, with the assumption that there is nothing in the walls but some minor electrical cables that will need to be relocated. There could be a caveat that if something unexpected shows up in the walls (e.g., a plumbing vent), there would be an additional charge for the additional work to relocate the plumbing.

On the other hand, you could elect to pay for the project on a time and material basis. The contractor might give you a rough idea of what it will cost verbally, but you agree to pay $X per hour and actual cost for materials (or often, a 10% premium on the materials to cover the contractor's shopping and driving time). You take on the risk of unforeseen problems. If there are few problems, you save money. If there are lots of problems, you probably would have been better off with a fixed bid. Of course, the contractor might not work as fast as they can on a time and material bid, and if you don't have a sense of how long some activities should take (e.g., tiling a kitchen floor), you might pay more than you should.

Which method should you choose? If you are an experienced investor that has been actively involved with your contractors, you should have a well-developed idea of what common job site problems are, and you'll develop an instinct to look for potential problems when you are shopping for a property. You will also have a good idea of how long different sorts of projects should take and what they should cost. You'll have made mistakes in the past and learned when to choose a fixed bid versus a time and material approach.

If you are new, try to find an experienced person to mentor you. Be willing to pay a bit for it. The real estate investor club meeting you attended to find some contractors might also give you some contacts of experienced investors that would be willing to look over your shoulder and give you advice on this. Keep in mind the most successful investors will be too busy to do this, but there are often people who are willing to share their thoughts on your specific situation. Many times if they have a project in process they will be willing to give you a tour of what they have done and what different activities cost.

You might want to try to start with fixed bids (and get several quotes). As you gain experience, you will probably shift to time and materials as you learn. Take the time to ask around and get as much advice as you can – experience is the best teacher, but often at a high price. Also consider putting in a bonus for finishing ahead of schedule and a penalty for finishing after the commitment date.

Self Contracting. As you gain experience or if you come from a construction or contracting background you may consider "self contracting". This may include you actually doing all or part of the renovation work yourself.

The advantages include:
1. More control over the timing of the project
2. Ongoing monitoring of quality and finishes
3. Close control of the budget
4. Savings on contractor and permitting fees

This is not recommended for the novice! The first thing it takes is knowledge and experience with your sub-contractors: painters,

Property Manager -- A third party that takes on some of your responsibilities in the ongoing operations of your rental property. Some of the tasks include cleaning and maintenance, collecting rents, showing units to prospective tenants, answering questions, and managing tenants as they move out of the building. Some Property Managers will also run the operating account for you and pay the building's bills.

flooring people, roofers, HVAC professionals, etc. It takes some careful planning, particularly with regards to the timing of the various projects. It is important that the new paint go on the walls prior to the new carpeting being installed (as one example). The major drawback of this method is the time and potential aggravation of taking on the project. One of the authors has acted as a de-facto general contractor for more than 300 home rehabs over the course of his real estate career. In many cases he has found this method to actually be less aggravating than managing a general contractor.

Checking References. When you are setting up your appointment to meet the contractor at the job site, ask them to bring their photo album with them. Many (though certainly not all) contractors take before and after photos of their projects and are very proud of their work and happy to review it with you. Be sure to ask the contractor for several references of clients who had similar projects in the past. Take the time to call the clients to ask how they liked the work. For the major contractors on your team, consider asking the references if you can come to their home to see the work. If the project is recent and it turned out well, the client is often very enthusiastic about the results and proud to show it off to other people.

Call their insurance carrier to make sure their worker's compensation and liability insurance is paid and up to date. Call the government authority that manages licenses to make sure their contractor license, if needed, is still in good standing. Keep in mind many contractors that are capable of good quality work will not have insurance or licenses. If they get hurt on your property and they do not have medical insurance or workman's compensation, you could be liable for their injuries. Be aware of the risks you are taking hiring uninsured contractors. If their prices are significantly less than competitors with insurance, you could consider offering a little more money to pay for the insurance premiums. You might still come out ahead on the project budget and with less liability exposure.

Importance of Being Nice and Being Perceived as "Fun to Work With". Your mother told you this and we'll bring it up one more time – be really polite and courteous. A surprisingly large number of investors "look down" on contractors and are not very nice to them. It's very much to your advantage to be perceived as a client that will be polite and fun to work with. Bullying your contractors is a really bad idea.

Real estate agents have been known to quote a much higher commission rate to difficult or high maintenance clients (we're not saying WE'VE ever done that!). Many contractors have told us they do the same thing. Successful business people often have more clients than they can handle so they can pick and choose their clients. They make decisions on whom to work with based on project economics as well as how much fun the project is likely to be. Some contractors will never refuse to give a bid to an unpleasant customer, but they'll give a much higher bid price.

Managing Frustration with Contractors. Of all of the players on your team, contractors are the most likely to cause headaches. Unless you are extraordinarily lucky, you will experience a few delays that you didn't expect, things will cost more than you planned, and contractors will, for no obvious reason, sometimes disappear from the face of the earth for days at a time. Initially this can be very frustrating, but eventually you will consider it to be "normal." Full disclosure: the estimate for the first fix and flip project done by one of the authors was off by 600%! But he worked through it and more or less survived the project.

Finding a Property Manager

As always, ask for referrals at your real estate investor club. You will meet investors there with rental properties with great stories to share. Also consider investigating whether your city has an Apartment Owner's Association, like the Apartment Association of Metro Denver (AAMD). Most larger cities will have such a group, with subgroups for property managers and rental owners. Two of the authors met originally at our local Apartment Association meeting 15 years ago. Attend a few meetings and you will get a lot of insight on which property management firms are performing the best.

The key things to understand about Property Managers is how they are compensated. Many will have a relatively low monthly percentage, for e.g., 8-10% of gross rents. They will want 50% - 100% of the first month's rent "finder's fee" when they find a new tenant for a vacant unit. Additionally, there might be a fee for an onsite manager (at a minimum, free or discounted rent for their unit, depending on the size of the complex). Contractors that are dispatched to do work on your building might have a markup applied to their fees.

Be sure to ask a lot of questions and understand all of the various fees. You might be better off paying a higher base monthly percentage in lieu of the finder's fee. This aligns everyone's interests. As the owner, you would like to see the property manager go to a lot of trouble to screen out all but the best tenants and have them stay for a long time. If they get paid a bonus every time a unit turns over, you are not providing an incentive for the behavior you want.

Be sure to check their references, and if possible, visit some of the other buildings that they manage.

Some property managers have a la carte services. For example, their job might be only to find a suitable tenant and charge 2/3 of the first month's rent for this service.

Finding a CPA

"Only the little people pay taxes."
   -- Leona Helmsley, real estate magnate. Helmsley was convicted of tax evasion and served two years jail time.

You will want to have a strong CPA (Certified Public Accountant) on your team for at least three reasons:

<u>Advice on the right type of holding company</u>. You can choose from many options, including but not limited to, holding the property in your own name, in an LLC, or in a corporation (and there are several sub-types of corporations). Each has tax, risk and liability issues, and different options for what you can deduct. For your first project or two it might not matter much, but as your investments grow in number, size, and/or complexity, you will want to carefully consider your choices.

<u>Discussing trade-offs of different tax treatments</u>. In some cases, such as condo conversions, you will have some degree of latitude in how your profits are taxed – either as ordinary income or as long term capital gains. Small and relatively painless operational choices on your part can have a major impact on your tax liability.

<u>Preparing the end of year tax statements</u>. As you become a more advanced investor, the complexity of your tax returns will follow. Eventually it will become a better use of your time to delegate your tax preparation work.

Ideally you would like a CPA that owns real estate themselves, so they can relate to your issues most directly. If that isn't possible (and it probably won't be), try to find a CPA that does a lot of work with real estate investors.

Consider asking your real estate agent and attorney for referrals. Asking around at the real estate investors club is also a good source for referrals.

Finding an Attorney

The guidelines for hiring a CPA apply to hiring an attorney as well. For real-estate specific matters, take the time to try to find an attorney who mainly works within real estate. For serious questions, find a firm that specializes in real estate and usually each of the partners will focus on just one facet of the large real estate landscape. You can then get very deep advice and skill. This will usually cost more, but you should have to purchase fewer hours since less research time will be required. It would be desirable, but not essential, if the attorney was actually a real estate investor as well.

It might take some trial and error to find the right attorney. Like CPAs, some will naturally be very conservative – too conservative for most investors. If you get the feeling that your attorney doesn't know the subject area very well and is erring *too much* on the side the caution, find a new attorney. Ideally the attorney should identify your points of legal exposure with an idea, and outline mitigation steps or what the worst case would be if something went wrong. Then you as the investor can weigh the risks and the rewards with better information. Ultimately, as always, it is your responsibility to make the final decision.

The other time to find a deep specialist is for condo conversions, where you want to find an attorney that can guide you through the entire process and will have a good rolodex of professionals (e.g., surveyors, engineers) to refer. Often this type of work can be performed on a fixed-fee basis, which makes it easier to budget.

Finding a Closing Agent

Your real estate agent will have a sense of who is good at working with investors and can be trusted to go the extra mile to keep a deal together. Find a good closing agent (or perhaps, in your state, an attorney) and take very good care of them. Try to specify that you use their Title Company on the purchase side (see the "How the Pros Manage the Purchase Process" Chapter) *as well as* the sales side of the deals you do. For more information contact <u>Greg@FirstAllianceTitle.com</u> (303-523-5092)

Chapter 3: Where the Pros Get the Money

"I'd rather be a pimp with a purple hat ... than be associated with banks."
-- Real Estate Developer Pete Zamarello, in a bankruptcy court hearing

What's in this Chapter: In Chapter 1 we reviewed different types of real estate investments, and examined the process of determining which types of investments are best for you. In Chapter 2 we discussed building a winning real estate team. Now we'll tackle how to get the best loan.

- We'll start by discussing what is in your credit report and how it relates to your credit score.
- We share how to get your current credit score, and will demystify how it is calculated.
- If you have inaccurate information that is dragging it down, we'll outline what you can do about it.
- Then, we'll review some other considerations to the mortgage planning process – whether or not you plan to live in the property and how much money you should put down.

Executive Summary – Best Practices

These are some of the best ideas that we have seen our clients implement. Each one is reviewed in more depth in this chapter.

- Your credit score has a significant impact on the interest rate and terms for your real estate loans. Pull your credit report and correct errors several months before applying for a mortgage to improve your score and lower your interest costs.

- Assume you'll have to put 20-30% down on any investment property. (Note there are options for as little as 15% down but they cost a lot more in rates and points.)

- To get better terms, you could consider renting out your current personal residence and maintaining the existing owner-occupied financing, if the economics make sense. Then you could purchase a new personal residence and get a better interest rate. Ask your lender; most will require one year of owner occupation.

- For larger commercial deals, you'll usually get a variable rate loan. Choose the COFI index if you think rates are likely to go up over the next three to five years. Otherwise, the LIBOR index is probably the better choice.

- If you are highly confident you will be in your commercial property for a set time period, strongly consider a *Conduit* loan. Otherwise, a traditional Portfolio lender, while somewhat more expensive, will likely pose less risk. At the time of this writing, conduits loans were much less available than they were in the past, but it's worth inquiring.

Your credit score has a significant impact on the interest rate and terms for your real estate loans. Pull your credit reports and correct errors several months before applying for a mortgage to improve your score and lower your interest costs.

- Most of the "grant" programs that investors will be eligible for will not really be a free handout. In the majority of cases, the money is simply rolled into the mortgage for the property you are purchasing. The "grants" can reduce your equity requirements without increasing your interest rate. We can't think of a single investor who's used a grant program successfully in twenty years.

- Ask around for referrals for mortgage brokers, but still go through the interviewing process using the interview guide in the appendix.

- Ask for a written estimate of all of the fees on a Loan Estimate (LE). If you are in a state that requires *YSP* (Yield Spread Premium) disclosures, ask for your loan to be priced "*at par.*"

Your Credit Report and Credit Score

The Credit Report: There are three large credit reporting agencies in the United States. They track information about you and your spending habits. Whenever you apply for credit, it is noted in your file. Lenders make periodic reports about what credit products you have signed up for, your maximum credit line, how much of that credit you have used, and if you are making your payments on time. Closed accounts are tracked for seven to eleven years. If you fall behind, that will be tracked.

FICO stands for Fair Isaac Corporation, a company that created the most used credit scoring model in the United States. An individual's credit score is calculated through a statistical algorithm and is used as a factor in determining the likelihood of a borrower defaulting on a loan. FICO scores are generally used for obtaining mortgages, car loans or consumer credit. The scores are provided from the three major credit reporting agencies: Equifax, Experian and Transunion.

Employers and landlords, if you are still renting, also periodically report information about you. Finally, information from public records is also included. This includes items such as tax liens, late child support payments, judgments or bankruptcies.

Things not included on your *Credit Report* include where you bank (e.g., your checking or savings accounts, and their balances), where you save money in mutual funds or other investments and their balances, bankruptcy information that is more than ten years old, charged off debts that are more than seven years old, medical history, or criminal records.
Your Credit Report is available to a large number of audiences, including but not limited to potential lenders, landlords, insurance companies (people with higher credit scores have lower insurance payments in many states), employers, and some government agencies.

A *Credit Score* is developed from the information found in your credit report. The results of the score will be used by the lender to determine if they will extend credit to you or not, and if so, on what terms. Generally, the higher the score (indicating that you have managed your credit well in the past), the lower the interest rates and/or the better the terms you will be offered.

The credit reporting agencies each have a complex mathematical model that mysteriously transforms the information in your file into a single number which represents your credit score. Usually a loan officer will order all three credit reports and credit scores in what is known as a *Tri-Merge*. The middle score of the three credit scores (referred to as the *Mid Score*) is usually used for your loan application analysis. The purpose of the credit score is to estimate the risk that the lender is taking on by extending credit to you. Specifically, they want to estimate the chance that you won't pay them back in the next two to three years. The higher the credit score, the less risk that you will default on a loan. The details of the credit score calculation are not public, but there are some broad guidelines of what drives your score.

- **Payment History –** If you have had late payments

GLOSSARY

Credit Score – An independent, third party assessment of how well you have managed your credit in the past. Three national companies track your credit scores; a lender will usually request all three and take the middle value (the *Mid Score*) for determining the terms of your loan. As slang, you will often hear the *Loan Officer* say that they need to "pull your credit," which is to get the three credit reports to discover your mid score.

SAMPLE CHECKLIST

You can learn more about the credit agencies, the information they track about you, and how it is distilled into a credit score by contacting the three primary credit agencies.
www.equifax.com, **1-800-685-1111**
www.transunion.com, **1-800-916-8800**
www.experian.com, **1-888-EXPERIAN (397-3742)**

You might also find these sites to be helpful:
www.MyFico.com (more information about credit scores)
www.nolo.com (legal forms you may need to dispute incorrect information on your report)

in the past, it will reduce your credit score. Late payments in more recent history (e.g., 6 months ago) are weighted more heavily than late payments in the distant past (e.g., six years ago). Late payments do fall off your credit file entirely at the seven to ten year mark (except tax liens, which may stay for fifteen years). This is about 35% of your overall score.

- **Amount Owed** – The more money you have borrowed, the higher the risk that you won't be able to pay all of the loans back. Higher debt levels lower your credit score. As you get closer to the maximum lending limits of your credit cards and other loans, the higher the risk to the lender. To keep your score high, it has been recommended that you keep your balances less than 25% of the maximum credit limit. The amount owed comprises about 30% of the overall score. It's very important to be below the maximum credit amount on any given card or account.

- **Length of Credit History** – Generally, the longer you have been using credit products, the better you are likely to be able to handle them properly (e.g., pay on time). It also increases the confidence of the risk-predicting model, since they have more information with which to work. This is about 15% of the overall score.

- **Credit File Inquiries** – Whenever someone other than yourself requests your credit file, it is added to your account history. Your inquires have no impact on your credit score. A large number of recent inquiries can lower your score by two to fifty points per inquiry, up to a maximum of ten. The credit agencies claim that they can differentiate between unrelated inquires (e.g., loans for a car, furniture, and a mortgage) which suggest you are considering spending a lot of money versus related inquiries where you are simply shopping for the best rate (e.g., asking three mortgage brokers to compete for your business). We've been told that you can make up to twenty inquiries in one fourteen day period for auto or home loans and it will be treated as just one inquiry. This is about 10% of the overall score. Only inquires from the last year are evaluated.

- **Recently Opened New Accounts** – Opening multiple new accounts in a short period of time lowers your score as it increases your risk that you won't be able to keep up with all of the new accounts that you have opened. **Open Accounts** – Having too many (the number that constitutes "too many" is not disclosed) open accounts can lower your score, whether you are using the accounts or not. Collectively these are about 10% of your overall score. The more information you have on other parts of your credit report (e.g., more history to be examined), the less important this area is thought to be in influencing your overall score.

- **Public Records** – Bankruptcies, judgments (e.g., if you were to lose a lawsuit), pending lawsuits, and collections lower your score. Again, more recent problems have a bigger impact than issues from the distant past.

Importance of On-time Payment

An owner-occupied client put a condo under contract. When he qualified for his loan, his credit score was good enough to merit an attractive interest rate. Since he wrote the contract two months before the end of his lease, he had an extended closing period. Before closing, he missed a payment on a credit card and it went into collections (that's what he told us; we suspect he was behind before even applying for the loan). The underwriter had to pull his credit scores again a day before closing to authorize disbursement of loan funds. The client's credit score dropped precipitously from the collection and he could no longer qualify for the loan. The Loan Officer called him with this news as the buyer was finishing loading up the moving van! He had to move back into his apartment, resolve the collection issue, then reapply for a mortgage, which took several months.

Value of a Credit Dispute

A client had a mortgage and the bank holding the mortgage was acquired by another bank. When mortgage files for the two companies were merged, the mortgage payments received by the new bank were not properly applied for a few months. This client's credit report showed that the mortgage payments were received sixty days late, when in fact they were made on time. This had a severe negative impact on the client's credit score. The client disputed the information on-line. It took a few months of phone calls after the on-line dispute to resolve the issue, but eventually the incorrect late payments were removed from the file. This improved the client's score dramatically.

Credit reporting agencies developed their first credit risk scores about twenty years ago. Scores range from 350 to 850, but most people will have a score between 600 – 800. Your score is updated daily as new information is posted to your credit file.

How to Improve Your Credit Score

Before applying for any major loan, you should check on your credit score to see if it appears to be accurate. If you check a few months before you need the money, you will have time to make corrections. Your credit score is not carved in stone. It is recalculated every time something changes in your file, or as the file ages and old information is dropped. Most updates will be relatively minor, but occasionally the changes can be significant. There are many things you can do to improve your score.

Study Your File. The first step is to order your credit report from each agency. In some states you can do this once a year for free. You can also get a free report, in some situations, if you have been denied credit due to adverse information in your file. If not, you can always purchase it on the Internet directly from the credit agencies for around $10 to $13. The higher end of the range will include your credit report <u>and</u> your credit score. Go through all of the information and make sure that it is correct. To better understand what is impacting your score, each of the three credit bureaus will provide the four most important factors that made your score less than perfect. Start your efforts there.

Mid Score – The middle *Credit Score* from the three national companies that track your credit history. This value is the one most commonly used by your lender.

Get into the Habit of Paying on Time. This seems obvious, but it is the biggest driver of your score. If you are too busy to pay on time, consider setting up your bills for automatic payment from your checking account so you don't have to watch it as closely. This won't have an immediate impact on your score, but it will make improvements over time.

Dispute Incorrect Information. If you order your credit report on-line, there are automated tools to help you dispute incorrect information. If not, the credit report will have contact information for each lender so you can call them.

Manage Credit Cards. The ratio of the credit balances that you are carrying to the total credit lines that you have available is one of the calculations that impact your overall score. If you have credit cards that you do not use, keep them open – the larger the overall credit available, the lower your ratio. Try to keep the ratio under 25% (definitely under 75%). The formula also looks at the average age of your accounts, so keeping old credit cards helps to keep that average up – which increases your score.

Pay a Bit Earlier. If you are in the habit of paying off your credit cards each month, you will be disappointed to learn that many credit card companies still report your monthly spending as if you carried the balance to the next month. If you have relatively low credit line limits and your spending approaches the limit each month, it will have a negative impact on your score just as if you did not pay off the balance each month. To combat this, send in your payment before the monthly cycle deadline – the reported balance will then be zero and your score will improve.

Improve FICO with Early Payment
We had a client that traveled very extensively on business, and all of her expenses were reimbursed by their company. She was relatively young and had only been out of college for a few years. She did not have many credit lines, and the history she had was not extensive. The monthly tab for hotels, airlines, and entertaining usually approached the client's credit limit. The client always paid off the card balance each month, as her company's reimbursement policy was very quick. Nevertheless, from the credit score's point of view, the client was carrying about 80% of available credit each month! Shifting the timing of the payment to a few weeks earlier resulted in the agencies thinking the cards were at a zero balance, which caused a large improvement in her credit score.

Manage Inquiries. Don't let just anyone have access to your credit report – permit access only when absolutely necessary, as extra inquiries bring down your score. Don't sign up for department store or gas station credit cards if you already have enough credit cards to have a score. If you have so little trade line information that the credit agencies cannot compute your score (most common for young adults or people that pay cash for everything), opening three smaller credit accounts (called trade lines) will help you to get your first score after about twelve months of history.

When you order your credit score from one of the three agencies, they will have options for you to get advice on how to improve your score. Reading this material is often helpful. The overall idea to keep in mind is to only get credit when you need it.

About Credit Repair. Going to a credit repair clinic will not help you. There is nothing any credit repair clinic can legally do for you – including removing inaccurate credit information – which you can't do for yourself for free. Credit repair companies often charge significant fees, ranging from hundreds to thousands of dollars. The Credit Repair Organization Act is a federal law that prohibits credit repair clinics from taking a consumer's money until they have fully completed the services they promised. It also requires such firms to provide consumers with a written contract stating all the services to be provided and the terms and conditions of payment. Consumers also have three days to withdraw from the contract.

Top Ten Things to Do Between Loan Application and Closing

Sometimes a lender will need to pull your credit report a second time just before closing. If your credit score has dropped, you may no longer qualify for the loan! This can lead to interest rate changes, or worse, you may no longer qualify – and you might have to cancel the closing. The authors have developed the following list of ten things to do and not do between the date of your loan application and the closing. It will help reduce the odds of you being turned down:

1. **DON'T APPLY FOR NEW CREDIT OF ANY KIND.** Including those "You have been pre-approved" credit card invitations that you receive in the mail. Every time that you have your credit pulled by a potential creditor or lender, you lose points from your credit score immediately. Depending on the elements in your current credit report, you could lose anywhere from 2-50 points for one inquiry.

2. **DON'T PAY OFF COLLECTIONS OR CHARGE OFFS** during the loan process. Paying collections will decrease the credit score immediately due to the date of last activity becoming recent. If you want to pay off old accounts, do it through the closing process. Make sure that 1) you validate that the debt is yours (you'd be surprised how many mistakes there are in credit files), and 2) that the creditor agrees to give you a letter of deletion.

3. **DON'T CLOSE CREDIT CARD ACCOUNTS.** If you close a credit card account it will appear to the FICO that your debt ratio has gone up. Also, closing a card will affect other factors in the score such as length of credit history. If you have to close a credit card account, do it after closing, and make sure it is a more recent account. Ask your Mortgage Broker to review your credit history with you if you have any doubts about which cards would be most advantageous to close.

4. **DON'T MAX OUT OR OVER CHARGE ON YOUR CREDIT CARD ACCOUNTS.** Don't buy any new furniture or a car until after you close! This is the fastest way to bring your score down 50-100 points. Try to keep your credit card balances below 30% of their available limit at all times during the loan process. If you decide to pay down balances, do it across the board. In other words, make an extra payment on all of your cards at the same time.

5. **DON'T CONSOLIDATE YOUR DEBT ONTO 1 OR 2 CREDIT CARDS.** It seems like it would be the smart thing to do; however, when you consolidate all of

CASE STUDIES

Keep Your Job Until AFTER You Close
We have seen many prospective clients that want to quit their jobs and become full time investors. We advise them to pre-qualify for their loan and actually close on the loan before quitting their job. The interest rate you'll pay when you have been in the same line of work for several years is quite a bit lower than if you are freshly unemployed!

your debt onto one card, it appears that you are maxed out on that card, and the system will penalize you as mentioned above in 4. If you want to save money on credit card interest rates, wait until after closing.

6. **DON'T DO ANYTHING THAT WILL CAUSE A RED FLAG TO BE RAISED BY THE SCORING SYSTEM**. This would include adding new accounts, co-signing on a loan, changing your name or address with the bureaus. The less activity on your reports during the loan process, the better.

7. **DO JOIN A CREDIT WATCH PROGRAM**. If you join a credit watch program, you can check your reports weekly, or even daily depending on the program you select. (When you pull your own reports, your score does not get punished for a credit inquiry.) This way, if something does show up on your reports that has caused your score to go down, you'll know it immediately, and you may be able to take care of the problem before closing.

CASE STUDIES

Refinancing

One of our investors uses cash to purchase his rental investments. He likes to buy homes that need a lot of work. He'll do enough renovation to make them appealing to a renter, then he'll take out a mortgage after the renovation work is complete. Usually the increase in the value of the home is several times greater than the money he spends on the renovation work.

His goal is to get the property to appraise high enough that he can get an 80% LTV loan that pays back his initial purchase price plus his renovation costs. And, he wants the property to be (at least) slightly cash flow positive after the refinancing. If he can't meet both parameters, he reconsiders if he wants to buy the property. Most of the time he has been successful in doing this. As a result, he now owns a rental property where he effectively has zero cash invested and his mortgage is at a low interest rate.

Note, however, that increasing the value of a property substantially shortly after purchase can be a big red flag for an underwriter. The lender will likely require an appraisal review or second full appraisal to confirm the higher value is justified. Also, pulling cash out at the time of refinance shortly after purchasing an investment home is challenging. Most lenders now require the home to have been owned for at least six months, and more than likely, at least twelve months.

8. **DO STAY CURRENT ON EXISTING ACCOUNTS**. Your mortgage and car payments are particularly important. One 30-day late can cost you anywhere from 30-75 points on your overall credit score.

9. **DO CONTINUE TO USE YOUR CREDIT AS NORMAL.** Red Flags are raised easily with the scoring system. If it appears that you are changing your pattern, it will raise a red flag, and your score could go down.

10. **DO CALL YOUR MORTGAGE BROKER** if you receive something in the mail from a creditor or collection agency that you believe may affect your score during the loan process. Your broker may be able to supply you with the resources you need to stop any derogatory reporting to the bureaus.

GLOSSARY

Loan to Value – The amount of money that the Lender is willing to provide for the purchase of a given property. For example, if you are purchasing a home for $100,000 and you want to borrow $80,000, the LTV is 80%.

Mortgage Considerations

After learning about your credit score and taking steps to improve it, there are a few other factors to consider before getting your mortgage.

Owner Occupied versus non-Owner Occupied. If you are planning on living in the property you are purchasing, you are an owner occupant. The lender will perceive you to be a lower credit risk than an investor buying the exact same property who does not plan to live in it. Lenders have discovered that if times get tough, people will pay their mortgage payment to keep their homes before they will make the mortgage payments on their investments.

Low Down Payment Financing - In 2009, Federal Housing Authority (FHA) loans started requiring a 3.5% down payment for all owner-occupant financing; however, such funds can be a gift from friend or family member. Additionally, depending on where the home is purchased, many cities still offer down payment monies to assist borrowers with little or nothing down. There is even a program that permits someone to purchase a home for as little as $100 down. Keep in mind that when a borrower makes a very low down payment their interest rate will always be higher, since the loan will have greater perceived risk. For the most part, conventional loans require a 5% down payment.

At this time it is virtually impossible to buy an investment property with nothing down except with Hard Money. Current Fannie Mae/Freddie guidelines for conventional loans require 15% down. However, the guidelines change constantly so be sure to ask your mortgage broker.

How Much Money Should You Put Into a Down Payment: For most loans, 80% *Loan to Value (LTV)* is the most you can borrow on your first mortgage without having to pay mortgage insurance. Mortgage insurance protects lenders in case of default. Loans above 80% LTV are considered greater risk, thus, carry mortgage insurance. Borrowers can pay mortgage insurance separately per month or it can be built into the interest rate. Mortgage insurance premiums will vary based on the LTV. In the past, second mortgages were popular to avoid mortgage insurance. However, they are tougher to secure in this environment in light of the volume of second mortgage lenders that lost billions of dollars in defaulted loans. Since they were in second lien position, their priority in being repaid was subordinate to first lien holders. When homes were foreclosed upon, the second lien holders were typically paid back nothing.

The choice of how much money to put down depends mainly on what the next-best use of the money is. If you are purchasing a $100,000 property and you have $100,000 of cash, you could just pay cash. If you have no other potential investments that you can make, and if the money will just be sitting in a checking account drawing 0.5% interest, you might want to pay cash. You will save the interest costs of the mortgage, which, after tax, would be a lot more than you would earn in that checking account.

CASE STUDIES

Fixed versus Variable

Imagine you are purchasing a property for $200,000 and you plan to put 20% down and get 80% from a first mortgage. Your interest rate choices might be:

30 year fixed:	5%
5 year ARM:	4.5%
3 year ARM:	4%

Your initial payments on your $160,000 mortgage would be:

30 year fixed:	$859
5 year ARM:	$811
3 year ARM:	$764

If you ended up owning the property for just three years, the additional cost of the 30 year fixed mortgage over the three year ARM would be $859 - $764 = $95 per month. Over three years, you would save (before taxes) $3,420 with the three year ARM. That would increase your overall ROI by 8.5%! ($3,420 of extra pre-tax profit divided by your $40,000 investment.)

In most cases, though, you either won't have that much free cash, or if you do, you will have other things that you can invest in. For most investors, borrowing at least 80% LTV makes sense. In this example, you would borrow $80,000 on a first mortgage, and bring $20,000 of cash to the closing. You would be left with $80,000 in your checking account to make four more investments of a similar size.

If you have an opportunity to invest in a <u>fix and flip project</u>, for example, where you hope to make 50% on your money over the course of six months (or a 100% return on an annualized basis), it doesn't really matter much). The more you borrow and the more projects you complete, the better off you will be.

If you have the opportunity to invest in a <u>rental</u> property with <u>five or more units</u>, you'll be getting a commercial loan. In most cases you will need to put 20-25% down. Every once and a while, a commercial lender will allow a small second mortgage. Don't count on it though, unless you have a lot of assets and experience.

The main mitigating factor is that you should consider keeping some cash reserves on hand in case you have an emergency. Examples could include losing your job, having a sudden health issue, having a project develop a problem that requires more money than you initially expected, or having extra holding costs set aside in case a property takes longer to sell than you anticipated. To be conservative, you might want to estimate how much you might need in one of these scenarios and then double the value, and then keep at least this much in reserves. Many investors are able to sleep much better at night knowing they have some money set aside.

You can accomplish the same thing without a large up-front cash investment by selecting an initial mortgage to purchase the property that does not have a *Prepayment Penalty*. Be sure to discuss your plans and options with your Loan Officer before you purchase the property.

Stated Income Loans: There is no guaranty that an underwriter will approve a stated loan in today's mortgage market. Most lenders now require a 4506-T Tax Authorization Form to be fully processed prior to receiving final loan approval. The 4506-T will compare the income reported to the IRS to the income listed on the loan application. If the income on the application is higher, the loan may be rejected. A full documentation loan (Full Doc) is really the only income type of loan permissible for conventional loans currently. If you're self-employed, you will need to provide two years of full personal tax returns and two years of business returns if you own more than 25% of a company.

GLOSSARY

Stated Loan – As opposed to a *Full Doc* loan, you will not be required to fully document your income or your assets – you "state" what you have and the lender takes you at your word. Since there is more risk, the loan will usually have a higher interest rate and won't offer as high of a *LTV* as a Full Doc loan. This is the loan that many self-employed investors use. Like a 25-cent shoeshine, stated loans for investors no longer exist, or at least are extremely rare.

Basic Mortgage Topics

There are innumerable types of mortgages on the market and it is very easy to get overwhelmed by the large number of choices. This section will introduce the basic concepts and trade-offs, so you can make a good decision about what mortgage is best for your unique situation.

Full Documentation versus "Stated": If you have been working in the same line of work for more than two years, then it will probably be to your advantage to go with a *Full Documentation* (Full Doc) loan. You'll need to provide a paper trail to support all of the figures you provided on your loan application ("the *1003*"). Frequently, you will provide a few years of tax returns and W2's or 1099's, current pay stubs, several months of bank statements for your checking and savings accounts, etc. While it is a nuisance to collect all of this information, the resulting interest rate will usually be lower (and often, the maximum *LTV* will be higher).

If you have not been in the same line of work for at least two years, if you are self-employed, or if you are not currently working, you might try to use a *Stated Loan*. Here, you tell the LO what your income is and they take your word for it. As you would expect, this poses more risk to the lender and that will be reflected in a higher interest rate and often a lower maximum *LTV*. Before the last downturn, the number of Stated Loans exploded in growth and led to a lot of the troubles in the mortgage industry. It is now much more difficult to get a stated loan for an owner-occupied person, and virtually impossible to get for an investment property.

Ratio Analysis. A **full doc** loan will usually be evaluated with two **ratios** – front and back. The front ratio takes your monthly income before taxes and multiplies it by a ratio. For a loan that strictly conforms to Fannie Mae guidelines, it might be 40%. If you make $4,000 a month, you could spend as much as $1,600 ($4,000 x .40) on PITI and HOA fees, if any. (PITI is principle, interest, taxes and insurance. HOA is home owners association). This is the analysis you would use for purchasing a home in which you will live.

GLOSSARY

Construction Loan – A shorter term loan, often for 24 months or less, used to purchase a Fix and Flip on an *Apartment* that an investor wishes to *Convert* to *Condominiums*. Often the lender will loan 75-80% of *LTV* or *LTC*, whichever is lower.

If you are purchasing a rental property, they will usually add 75% of the rental income to your earned income. They assume the other 25% of the rental income is for property management, vacancy reserve and maintenance. For example, if your property currently has a tenant paying $1,000 per month, the annual income from the property is $12,000. After the 75% adjustment, there is $9,000, or $750 per month. This increases your overall income to $4,750 per month. Assuming you had no debt on that property, a strict loan would allow you to spend 50% of that, or $2,375 a month, on the mortgage for your personal residence and the investment property.

You'll also need to be tested with the back-end ratio. A conventional lender will multiply your total income by 50%, or $4,750 * 50% = $2,375 in this case. All of your debt service must be under this threshold. In addition to your two mortgages, this would include car payments, student loans, and the regularly scheduled servicing on credit card balances. As discussed earlier, even if you pay off your credit card each month, the Lender will often include the minimum payment onto your monthly debt as if you did not pay off the balance that month.

Portfolio Lenders are banks that plan to hold on to your mortgage and not immediately re-sell it. As a result, they have the flexibility to develop their own underwriting standards, including their own front and back ratios. You can expect higher ratios, which will make it easier to qualify, but you will usually also pay a slightly higher interest rate. Generally, it is worth it (often you don't have a choice!).

CASE STUDIES

Fixed versus Variable Doomsday Scenario
What if interest rates go through the roof? Imagine if you held on to your investment for five years, you decided to start with a three year ARM, and rates went up 3% (from 4.375% to 7.375%) in the fourth year.

Payment for the thirty year fixed rate loan is always: $946. Payment for the three year ARM is $799 for the first 36 months, then $1,105 in our doomsday scenario for the last twenty four months.

Total payment for fixed rate = $946 * 60 months = $56,760. Total payment for the three year arm = $799 * 36 months + $1,105 * 24 months = $55,280

In this case, you are still slightly better off with the three year variable rate loan. You can ask your Loan Officer to calculate how much a variable rate loan would have to go up to cost the same as your fixed rate loan. Then you can have a discussion about how likely such a scenario is for the holding period you anticipate for the investment. Whoever said investing in real estate was easy!?

Fixed versus Variable Rates: For owner-occupants that plan to live in a property for a very long time, choosing a long term fixed rate loan (e.g., a fifteen or thirty year fixed) can be a good choice. It certainly eliminates all uncertainty about your mortgage payments. However, people are moving in greater frequency, and the average duration in a typical home is now about 7 years. You will be paying a premium for locking in a rate for that long a period of time. Make sure you check though! We've often seen fixed rate loans at LOWER rates than variable rate loans. Do your homework and get the right loan product.

BEST PRACTICES

To get better terms, you could consider renting out your current personal residence and maintaining the existing owner-occupied financing, if the economics make sense. Then you could purchase a new personal residence and get a better interest rate. Ask your lender; most will require one year of owner occupation.

An alternative option is to get a variable rate loan with an initial lock-in period that is similar to the period of time that you are considering living in the home. For example, if you think you will live in a home for five years (which is close to the average amount of time for most people), you could get a "5/1 ARM." This interest rate would be fixed for five years, and then would float based on its index rate after initial lock up period.

The Truth About Owner Carry

"There ain't no such thing as a free lunch."
  -- Robert A. Heinlein

Real estate is not like the fairy tale with a magic lamp whose genie could grant three wishes. In most cases, sellers only grant one wish to buyers – a better price or better terms. It is rare to get both. If you are getting both, you are likely to be purchasing a property that was very difficult for the seller to get rid of… and unless you are going to make some significant changes to the root cause of that difficulty you will likely have a hard time selling it, too.

The number of sellers who will offer owner carry is quite limited. Most sellers do not have much equity in their property and could not offer owner carry even if they wanted to. Not coincidentally, the sellers who do have either the equity to carry or the financial ability to do so tend to be more sophisticated. They will, if it suits <u>their</u> needs, carry for you, but often the terms are not that attractive. However, even if the interest rate is higher than you could get elsewhere, you might find owner carry to be a great option – particularly if you are cash or credit constrained and could not otherwise purchase the property. It can be a viable alternative to Hard Money. Owner carry is most common in recessions and very rare during expansions.

GLOSSARY

Grant – A monetary gift, usually from a third party, such as a city or county government, or a non-profit agency. In most cases, the investor will actually pay for the so-called grant by rolling the cost into the mortgage for the property.

All About "Grant" Programs

Grant programs come in two main configurations – money you don't have to pay back, and money that you do pay back.

The government (city, county, state, federal) will sometimes offer grants that you do not need to pay back to spur investment in redevelopment areas. You will need to invest some time to learn about the fine details of how the grant works, or get a team member (likely your mortgage broker or real estate agent) that knows the red tape. Don't expect any free lunches; usually you'll be investing in a less-desirable part of town (otherwise there wouldn't need to be an inducement to get you to invest there). However, in a very small number of cases it can be worth the trouble and the hassle.

The majority of grants you will come across either need to be paid back, or you are somehow paying for the grant in the first place. The government, usually on the city or county level, will in some markets offer down payment assistance to people who make a certain percentage or less of the area's average income. This most commonly occurs in higher cost counties. The "grant" isn't a grant at all; usually it is in the form of a second mortgage on terms that are more favorable than the borrower can get from a traditional lender. The government's objective is to help teachers, nursing assistants, police officers, etc, afford to live in the high cost communities where they work. In most cases the investor will (surprise!) not meet the eligibility requirements, but it is worth

BEST PRACTICES

Most of the "grant" programs that investors will be eligible for will not really be a free handout. In the majority of cases, the money is simply rolled into the mortgage for the property you are purchasing. The "grants" can reduce your equity requirements without increasing your interest rate.

making a few calls to find out. The upshot is we've almost never seen an investor use a grant successfully. But that doesn't mean it can't be done, just that it's harder than it looks.

Chapter 4: How the Pros Manage the Buying Process

"Inequality of knowledge is the key to a sale."
        -- Deil O. Gustafson, real estate executive

If you know more than the other party, you can often get a better deal.

What's in this Chapter. Now that you have determined what sorts of investments are best for you, you have built your team, and you have arranged your financing, it's time to buy the property! This chapter reviews the steps that you will go through on your first purchase.

Executive Summary – Best Practices

These are some of the best ideas that we have seen our clients implement. Each one is reviewed in more depth in this chapter.

- Set goals and document your assumptions. Review them after the project is completed. Adjust your goals and assumptions with what you learned and your project profit forecasting will improve over time.

- Spend a reasonable amount of time thinking through which neighborhoods you want to target before you get in the car and start driving around. For most investment types, your choice of neighborhood will greatly influence how well your project will perform. This is most important if there is a lot of inventory for sale. If inventory is tight, don't worry as much about location.

- Be willing to drive another fifteen minutes to make an extra $10,000. Don't just focus on your own back yard because it is easy. Most neighborhoods will NOT be viable choices for fix up homes. Work with an agent who knows which neighborhoods will work well.

- Determine the typical discount (last list price vs. sold price) in your market and target neighborhoods. Use this as a guide to developing your initial offer price.

- Bid on homes that are below market price. Don't waste the discount you can negotiate (which is usually relatively small) getting a home from being overpriced to market average price.

- If you are going to give a low-ball offer to a Seller, it's a numbers game – be prepared to write a lot of offers. Don't be surprised if you find yourself writing 20 offers for every accepted contract.

- Before writing the offer, complete your profit and loss analysis and determine your *Walk Away* price. Assess the other party's level of motivation. Determine who has the upper hand and negotiate accordingly.

- After you write the offer, work with your Loan Officer to ensure he or she has everything they need to successfully close your loan. Your close attention to this will make the closing process smoother.

- Think through what you want to accomplish with the Inspection and pick an Inspector accordingly.

The Ideal Purchasing Process

Set Goals. Work with your real estate agent and friends you have met from your real estate investing groups to set some reasonable goals for the process and document the assumptions you are using to set these goals. After you complete the investment life cycle, we'll come back to review these goals and assumptions to assess your results. You will find that some of your assumptions were good, and some were not as close to reality. A few might have even been crazy! You can modify your goals and assumptions based on what you learned and your forecasting for future projects will be more realistic.

Be willing to drive another fifteen minutes to make an extra $10,000. The best deals are usually not in your immediate backyard.

Pick a Few Neighborhoods. Work with your real estate agent to determine which neighborhoods are most likely to have the types of homes that make sense for you. A big mistake we see many investors make is to shortchange this step of the process. They are so eager to get started, they want to go out and look at property right away. Some areas are better candidates than others.

<u>View properties</u>. With your project type, goals and neighborhoods now in mind, you can finally get in the car and see some properties. Your Castle Real Estate runs classes on this. Visit www.yourcastle.com.

MLS – Multiple Listing Service. The MLS is a regional organization that collects, compiles and distributes information about properties listed for sale by its members, who are Real Estate Brokers.

<u>Learn About the Neighborhood</u>. When you find a property that you are considering writing an offer on, spend a little time walking around the neighborhood – on foot. It won't take much time to do this, but it will give you time to spot things that you will miss if you are rushing to see six homes in two hours. Walk through the alleys. Talk to all of the people you see. If you kids, bring them. Ask if this is a nice place to live. How is it for kids (especially if you plan to rent the property and families are your target audience). How are the schools?

People LOVE to complain so expect to hear some whining. The first time you do this you will be convinced the area is about to slide into a dark sinkhole, never to return to civilization again. After you do this in a few neighborhoods, you will be able to calibrate your whine-o-meter to differentiate between a normal amount of complaining and a level you should be concerned about.

If you are planning a remodel job, think through what level of renovation would "fit" the area.

Writing Great Offers

There are many things you can do to differentiate your offer from all of the less experienced investors with whom you are competing. The first several ideas will apply to most situations. The final few ideas are appropriate when dealing with a novice listing agent.

Investigate Discounts. Your real estate agent can usually do some research for you to determine what the average discount (the difference between the asking price and the sales price) is for your market. Most MLS's track this information. Many MLS's are also starting to track sales incentives other than price discounts, such as seller-paid closing costs and seller contributions to grant programs. If that information is available, have your agent get that too. From this, you can estimate what the average discount is for your market place. Ideally, learn what it is for just this neighborhood. The typical discount range will be your guide for your offer price. Don't

Equity – The difference between net market value after closing costs and the mortgage amount. The amount of money the Seller clears after the closing.

get crazy and offer 40% below the asking price if the market average is only 2% off. Competent agents will stop working with you if you **insist** on wasting everyone's times doing this. The Your Castle team has those stats.

Bid on Below-Market Homes. Pull some comps on the home and make sure that it is either at a fair market price or, ideally, has a motivated seller so it is priced below a fair market value. Keep in mind that the below market price properties usually have sellers that are less willing to give discounts than properties that are priced above market. Generally, don't waste time bidding on over-priced properties.

Pick Homes with Equity. If you find a house worth $180,000, it is priced at $180,000, and the seller owes the bank $170,000, this seller is going to break even on the deal – he'll likely have $10,000 of closing costs and commissions to pay. If you offer $160,000 and he has $10,000 of expenses, he'll net $150,000 and have to bring $20,000 to the table. Not likely to happen. You are much more likely to have your request for a discount granted if there is some equity in the home or if the bank just needs to dump the property. In most marketplaces your agent will have access to this information. If not, your title company can usually find it for you.

Assign or *Assignment* – as in "*Assign a Contract.*" An investor who is interested in Assignments gets a property under contract for an attractive price then assigns the contract to another buyer (usually another investor). The first investor will be paid a fee for the work.

Agents at our firm have access to a custom-developed software package that can scour the entire market to identify the small number of properties that are good values.

Cash Offer. It used to be that you could write a cash offer (e.g., a contract with no loan contingencies) even if you planned to get a loan. Banks have caught on to this game though and now require "proof of funds" with a cash offer. This might be a bank statement showing a balance that can cover the purchase price. A HELOC statement (Home Equity Line of Credit; see glossary for more) will also suffice for proof of funds.

Don't add "or assignees" to the Buyer Name. This is a big red flag to the seller. Instead, set up a shell LLC (in many states you can do this on line, yourself, for a very small fee). The only thing the LLC owns is this contract. If you need to assign the contract to another party, sell the LLC to them instead.

Don't use "subject to review by my partner." This is a particularly poor excuse to get out of a contract. Most logical sellers would not even read such a contract – they'd tell you to bring in the decision-maker, since clearly you are not. And maybe to grow up as well. Here's a better approach: in most states, you have an inspection period – use this as the back door to get out of deal if you decide you don't want it for some reason.

Assess Your Competition. Have your real estate agent chat with the Listing Agent while discussing and explaining the contract to try to get a sense of how much experience the Listing Agent has. If possible, do a search in the MLS to see how many listings the Agent has had and closed in the last few years (this is possible in some, but not all, MLS systems). Go to the state regulatory site and look up the Listing Agent's license – sometimes it will tell you how long they have been active.

Specify Your Title Company. In many markets, the listing agent picks the Title Company that will perform the closing. Usually there is no preference on the part of the seller, and the Listing Agent just picks the company they always use. If you have a Title Company with which you do most of your business, specify that in the contract's additional provisions. This removes some of the variables about having your closing managed by an incompetent or inexperienced closing agent, and the location is assured to be convenient to you. This is doubly important if you plan to get a *Hold-Open Title Policy* because you will be re-selling the property relatively quickly.

Hold Open Policy – A title policy that costs about 10% more at the time of purchase (the difference is paid by the buyer). If the investor sells in two years or less (the time varies by Title Company), the investor doesn't have to purchase a new title policy – they only pay the difference in the value of the purchase price and the sales price. Usually this is a nominal amount and it saves the investor about $1000.

Right to Extend Close Date. If you are arranging financing and you did not write up your offer as a cash deal, consider adding a clause to the additional provisions that all of the dates in the contract can be extended by a week if your financing is delayed for some reason out of your control. Consider asking for the right to extend for up to thirty days if you give a month's mortgage payment to the seller. An experienced listing agent will quash this, but an inexperienced agent might not even think twice.

Managing Your Dates. If you are not writing a quick, cash offer, make sure you drag out all of your "weasel" dates as long as you can. Make the inspection for at least five business days, and ideally two weeks. Make the appraisal last at least twice as long as you should normally need. Why? Murphy's Law applies to real estate – anything that can go wrong often will, and it's nice to have more time to address problems.

See if you can get away with having the loan commitment deadline the day before the closing. An experienced listing agent will squish this, but a green one might not. Note that if a bank-owned property accepts your contract they will send you back an Addendum with a whole new set of dates. Don't panic! The dates are usually pretty fair. If for some reason a date is unacceptable, let the listing agent know and normally an accommodation can be made.

Lowball Offers

Your real estate agent should be able to determine the average discount (the gap between the final asking price and the sold price) for your city and usually even for the neighborhood(s) that you are interested in. The vast majority of properties will usually sell within a few percentage points of that average discount. If the average discount is 3%, plus or minus 2%, not many offers will be accepted that are more than 5% below the asking price.

Some investors will begin by offering 20 or 25% below the asking price. Usually this is a waste of time, as the majority of Sellers either will not respond or will simply counter at their asking price less a percentage point or two. It takes a LOT of offers to find the small number of motivated Sellers that can (mentally and financially) accept a low offer.

The Letter of Intent

If you ever take a real estate agent that focuses on listings out for a beer, you will hear a lot of stories about greedy sellers that list their home for more than it is worth. Some of the sellers know they are overpriced, but want to "test the market" to see "if some fool will pay this much for my house." The vast majority of the time they are very disappointed that the market works efficiently and their house does not, in fact, attract any fools. Once in a blue moon it works and those few lucky sellers tell everyone in the world, which encourages many other sellers to try to the same tactic. The mindset of many of the overpriced sellers is that "we are willing to negotiate" and "we know we're a *little* high on the pricing." This can happen even when they are motivated to sell.

> **GLOSSARY**
>
> *Letter of Intent* – also known as *LOI*. A letter that a prospective buyer can send to a prospective seller – whether the property is listed or not. Rather than using the formal state-regulated offer contract, this one page letter briefly outlines the important terms of a purchase contract in a non-binding manner. If the prospective seller has interest, the Buyer can then take the time to draft a complete contract.

A *Letter of Intent (LOI)* is a short letter that a prospective buyer can send to a prospective seller – whether the property is listed or not. Rather than using the formal state-regulated offer contract, this one page letter briefly outlines the important terms of a purchase contract in a non-binding manner. If the prospective seller has interest, the Buyer can then take the time to draft a complete contract.

While painstaking to do, we have seen investors send LOIs to lots of Sellers. The majority of the Sellers ignore the LOI, but a small percentage will respond to at least initiate a discussion. Occasionally the Buyers will find the motivated Seller and they'll get a much larger than average discount. It's a numbers game, but it can work. However, it will almost never work with bank-owned properties so don't waste your time.

Negotiation

Before you even pick up the pen to write an offer, sketch out the rough economics of your project. What is the maximum price you could pay to still have a viable deal? This is your *Walk-Away Price*. You should determine this value before you start negotiations and stick to it, unless you uncover material facts that change your assumptions. An example: You are purchasing a rental property and you believe that the Owner pays for the utilities. You develop a profit and loss forecast and determine that you have to purchase at price X to meet your target rate of return. During due diligence you discover that the Tenants pay the utilities. This lowers your expenses and increases your expected profitability. As a result, you can afford to pay somewhat more for this property and still meet your target rate of return.

Next, let's review the different levels of motivation that Buyers and Sellers might have:

- **Need to Buy / Sell.** Some will need to complete a deal and ideally they want to complete it quickly. They are motivated to get the deal done. Seller examples include businesspeople with an impending tax event that need to raise cash quickly, a pending foreclosure, a divorce, or a relocation that has forced a family to carry two mortgages. Buyer examples include commercial investors that have sold their property and have a 1031 exchange deadline (see glossary; this is a way for investors to legally defer their tax bill) to meet, or a relocation buyer that is moving their family and they need a new home to move into since the moving van is already on the way. Let's call these folks **Highly Motivated**. This is usually a small percentage of the overall market.

- **Want to Buy / Sell.** Some would like to complete a deal, and they certainly will be doing so *sometime* soon, but there is not the same level of urgency. A Buyer example: tenants in a month-to-month lease that want to buy their first home. They can wait until they find the right deal. A Seller example: An owner of a cash-flow positive rental who has located a replacement property they would like to buy, but don't have to buy. Let's call these folks **Modestly Motivated**. This is usually a considerable part of the overall market.

- **Would Buy / Sell, but Do Not Have To.** The classic residential example is the second or third trade-up home: the family has outgrown their current home but they could continue to live with it for several more years if they had to. They (usually both spouses) will engage a real estate agent to list it to "test the market" and if "someone is willing to pay *our* price" then "*maybe* we'll sell and trade up." The classic commercial example is the rental owner who is enjoying nice cash flow that doesn't need to sell, but thinks "anything is for sale at a high enough price" and they want to see if they can find someone who will pay. Let's call these people **Unmotivated**. This is usually a large part of the overall market.

- **Don't Want to Buy / Sell, but Have to Look Like They Are.** A residential example: Same as the residential example above, but Spouse #1 secretly doesn't want to move and Spouse #2 openly does want to move. Spouse #1 is assigned the task of finding the real estate agent and listing the house, while Spouse #2 does the fun work of hunting down the replacement home. If Spouse #1 has a passive-aggressive personality, they will surreptitiously do many things to sabotage the home sale including setting the price too high and never making the home available for showings. Alternatively, the home will be available for showings under ludicrous limitations. Don't laugh! This happens much more often than you would imagine! A commercial example: Spouse #1's hobby is managing their rental real estate, and Spouse #2 wishes Spouse #1 would spend more time at home. #2 nags #1 to "list that nasty rental and sell it." #1 complies (well, complies by listing it, at least), but does so in a way that it will never sell. Again, this happens more frequently than you would expect. Let's call these people **Passive/Aggressive**. This is usually a small part of the overall market, but it's a great source of water-cooler stories.

The main thing to keep in mind about real estate, especially residential real estate, is that this is an emotional sport as much as a rational one. A lot of stuff happens in the market that doesn't make sense. This is why many listings, even in hot Sellers' markets, don't sell. Obviously Buyers want to deal with Sellers in the Highly Motivated category. Sometimes it can be worth your time to work with people in the Modestly Motivated group. Usually nothing good comes from working with the last two groups.

Before writing an offer, ask your real estate agent to engage the Listing Agent to learn as much as you can about the Seller(s) and their situation. If you can develop a sense of their motivation it will help you greatly. Legally, the Listing Agent cannot reveal anything about the Seller's motivations or level of commitment to get a deal done, but you would be surprised how often (perhaps as much as a third of the time) you can get them to give you quite a bit of information (keep this in mind when you hire a listing agent to represent you!). If they are Passive-Aggressive or Unmotivated don't waste your time writing up an offer unless the asking price is under your *Walk-Away* price. Don't expect much negotiating room from the Seller.

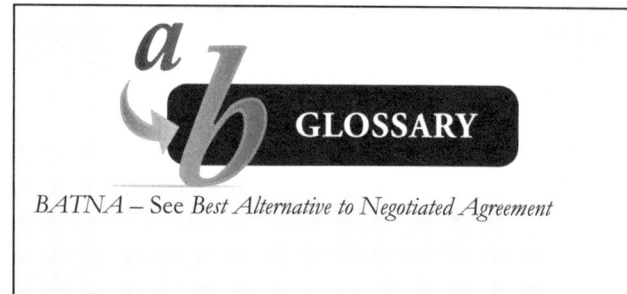

BATNA – See *Best Alternative to Negotiated Agreement*

When you find a Seller that is at least willing to discuss terms with you, spend some time thinking through the *Best Alternative to Negotiated Agreement,* or *BATNA,* for you and the other party. This will take only a few minutes and it will give you some insight on how hard to push.

If it is a Seller's Market, there are not enough properties to go around (and most of them will eventually sell), so the Buyers have fewer options than the Sellers. Therefore, the Buyers relative bargaining position is weaker. If it is a Buyer's Market, there are too many properties available for the current level of market demand (and most of them will not sell, or if they sell, it will be after a long marketing process). The Buyers have many options to choose from, so the Seller is in a weaker position.

If the property has been on the market for significantly less than average marketing time, the Seller is likely in a mindset that "it is still going to take a while, so I need to be patient. I can ignore low offers now since a better offer may come later." Most Sellers are less receptive to low offers at this time. It's rare to see a Seller accept a low offer if the property has been on the market for a short time, in either a Buyer's or Seller's market. If the property has been on the market for at least the market average number of days, then as time passes the motivated Sellers become more willing to consider lower offers.

If you are considering one type of investment (e.g., fix and flips or small apartment buildings) and there appear to be many choices that make sense for you to pick from, then you have a lot of power. On the other hand, if you have looked at fifty properties and this is the first that is even vaguely close to your requirements, either your requirements are unrealistic or the market just doesn't have much to offer that you will like. You have relatively less power in this situation, since you might need this deal to go through more than the other party does.

It is important to understand there isn't a mathematical formula that you can feed all of this information into. No Cray computer can tell you which property to buy and which not to. You'll be tempted to fill out a detailed Excel spreadsheet with every last data input you can think of and fancy 5 year IRR projections and think you have the answer. You don't! This business is at least 50% art and 50% science, so at best you have ½ the answer. This is one of the strange and wonderful characteristics of real estate investing.

The more elements of the deal that seem to be in your favor, the more likely you are going to be able to push to get a better price and/or terms. And if you don't get it from this Seller, there is another Seller just around the corner you can try instead. If you find yourself in this situation, consider narrowing down the market to the three properties you like the best and write somewhat aggressive offers on all three of them at the same time. If you really don't care which you buy, you can get the one where the Seller is the most motivated to meet your price and terms.

Don't disengage from the process once you are under contract – your active involvement will help to identify problems before they become big issues.

Things to Monitor During the Closing Process

Congratulations, you have your property under contract. From here to the closing you should (in theory) be able to relax somewhat since the hard work is largely done (at least until you close). You have several hand-picked advisors working for you to get the closing done. However, don't disengage from the process – your active involvement will help to identify problems before they become big issues. It will also make the whole process go more smoothly. Your first step is to communicate the specifics of the proposed deal to your Loan Officer so you can formalize your financing.

Underwriting. If you are purchasing a condo, have the Loan Officer get in touch with the HOA to determine what percentages of the units are owner-occupied versus rentals. Make sure that this ratio is consistent with the underwriting guidelines for your loan program. Most Lenders will want to see 50+% owner occupied. This will occasionally blow up a deal at the last moment if you don't check into it. Conforming loans require that the majority of the owners in the complex live in the complex.

Spend some time with the Loan Officer to see if there are other underwriting trip wires that can be managed up front to make the closing process as smooth as possible. Reconfirm what cash reserves you will need to document at the closing and make sure that you have them. Many Lenders want documentation of cash (or cash equivalents) for the down payment, closing costs, and six months of *PITI* (principal, interest, tax and insurance payments). Ask what ratios are applied to stocks and bonds – usually underwriters use only 70% of stocks and bonds, so be sure to ask about this early in the process to avoid delays the day before you close.

The Final Stretch. Once the appraisal is finished, you can usually get the underwriter to give final approval for the loan in a few days. Be sure to ask the Closer at the Title Company for the final settlement statements a few days in advance of the closing. Don't be surprised if you end up getting them a **few minutes** before closing, though! Review them carefully to check for errors. Make sure that loan terms match what you agreed to in the Good Faith Estimate with the Loan Officer.

Special Purchasing Circumstances

Short Sales. A short sale is a property that has not yet been foreclosed on…but the clock is ticking. Sometimes it is possible to negotiate with bank(s) that hold the mortgage(s) to arrange a payment amount that is less than the amount owed to fully satisfy the debt. This is called a "short sale."

Short sales can represent good values, but expect a longer and more frustrating purchase process than you would otherwise experience. The bank(s) will require a hardship letter from the Seller describing why the bank should accept less money than is owed to them, and there will be a considerable number of forms to be completed and hoops to be jumped through. Frequently a foreclosure attorney has already been engaged (who initiated the foreclosure process on behalf of the bank), and there is no incentive for them to help you. In fact, if you succeed in purchasing the property with a short sale, the property will not go to the foreclosure auction, and the attorney will have less work to do (and hours to bill). Expect a commensurate level of cooperation.

Bank-owned Foreclosures. On the other end of the process, the former owner has been removed from the property and the foreclosure process (which varies somewhat by state) has been completed. Now the Lender owns the property. Some Lenders hold onto the property as an *REO* (Real Estate Owned) property; other Lenders will bundle groups of hundreds properties across the nation and sell them off at a discount to investor groups. In 2012, about 40% of the properties sold in Denver Metro were REOs, short sales, and HUDs. It was a similar ratio in many other major markets across the US. As the market improved in the years after 2012 the number of REO's, short sales and HUDs plummeted. It is critical that you become very adept at this fast moving market. Most cities in Colorado in 2018 have very few REO.

Amazingly, the valuation set on these homes is frequently based on the analysis of an *AVM* (Automated Valuation Model, a complex computer-based assessment of a home's likely value) without the benefit of someone walking through the home to assess its condition. As a result, many foreclosure homes that are in poor condition (which is most of them – people tend to be pretty upset when being evicted from "their" home, even if they have not made a payment in a year… and they often take it out on the house). However, they are often priced as if they were in average condition. This makes them very poor values. Conversely, occasionally you will find a foreclosure home in wonderful condition that is priced as though it were in average condition and does represent a good value. This is the exception, not the rule. What this highlights is that you cannot invest in real estate from your desk – you need to see properties to find the deals.

The Lender, who can obviously borrow money at a lower rate than anyone else, has relatively low holding costs so they tend not to be in a hurry to lower their prices. Prices are sometimes lowered very slowly, and the marketing times for foreclosures can be long.

HUD Homes. When the government forecloses on an FHA loan, a government agency called HUD (Housing and Urban Development) is often assigned the task of getting rid of the home. Many HUD foreclosures represent good values, particularly for owner occupants. The government's mandate here is not to be greedy, but to help give an edge to owner occupants. To this end, investor (e.g., non-owner occupant) offers are not considered until the eleventh day after the property was put on the market.

Often the offers received in the first five days of the HUD auction are all considered as if they had arrived at the same time. This helps owner-occupants who have a hard time making up their minds to be able to compete with more decisive buyers. During the next five days (days six through ten), offers received from owner occupants are considered once a day. If the property has not sold by the tenth day, on day eleven HUD will begin considering investor offers as well. The best deals rarely last until day eleven, but occasionally they do. Our investors buy about ten bank-owned, or shortsale properties for every HUD deal they get.

This makes it tempting for an investor to misrepresent their intensions about living in a property so they can make a bid before other investors. **Don't do it. If you are caught you could face jail time.** There are enough good deals available in most markets that you don't need to run risks like this. And if there aren't, get into another business. One of the authors has repeatedly turned offenders into HUD's Fraud Prevention Hotline. Take it from us, HUD is only too happy to get these phone calls.

As with many government interactions, HUD has their own method for submitting offers and earnest money checks. If you decide to pursue HUD auctions be sure that your real estate agent has experience with HUD auctions and is currently registered to be able to submit offers (most agents are NOT registered), and that they have the HUD key (a physical key that opens all the HUD homes in a metropolitan area) to be able to show properties to you.

Chapter 5: Rental Property Fundamentals

"The Landlord is a gentleman ... who does not earn his wealth. He has a host of agents and clerks that receive for him. He does not even take the trouble to spend his wealth. He has a host of people around him to do the actual spending… His sole function, his chief pride, is the stately consumption of wealth produced by others."
      -- David Lloyd George (1863–1945), British Politician

"We wish!"
      -- The Authors

What is in this Chapter. The purpose of this chapter is to provide some insights that apply to all classes of rental properties, from single family homes to large apartment buildings to lease options. We'll start by examining if rentals are a good choice for you, based on several criteria. The criteria will help you determine which type(s) of rentals are likely to work the best for you. Next, we'll discuss which neighborhoods you should consider in your city. We'll then walk you through a sample analysis template for your rental's first year. You can use this template to compare multiple properties against one another. Then we'll look at the best property with a five year projection. These generic templates will work with any rental property, from a one bedroom condo to a forty unit apartment building. The specific chapters that follow fine-tune these models where needed. Visit www.yourcastle.com for lots of classes on this topic.

Executive Summary – Best Practices

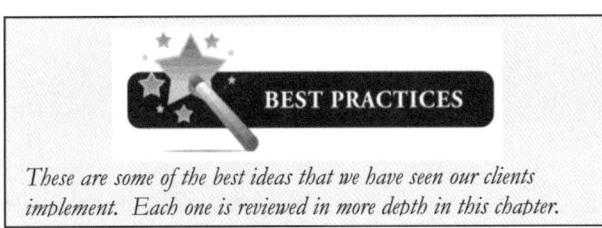

These are some of the best ideas that we have seen our clients implement. Each one is reviewed in more depth in this chapter.

- Begin by understanding where the rental buildings in your price range are located. In most cities they will be clustered into a relatively small number of neighborhoods; they will NOT be "just anywhere."
- Get a sense of how cash returns vary from nice areas to crummy areas. Usually the nicest areas have the lowest cash returns. Sometimes, but certainly not always, they will have better prospects for appreciation. Decide whether location or cash returns are more important to you to help focus your search.
- Review the advantages and disadvantages of each category of rental. This is explored in depth in this chapter. Some investors have a definite preference, and discovering this earlier in the search process will save you considerable time and frustration.
- When you have picked your desired type of rental building, consider the different tenant segments and their pros and cons. Make sure you are comfortable with the tradeoffs and characteristics of the types of people your target property might attract.
- Be sure to assess the competitors around your target building so you have a sense of your relative strengths and weaknesses. This will also help you validate the rent claims made by the seller.
- Get in touch with your local Apartment Association to learn about the typical rents and vacancy rates in your target neighborhood to provide a second check to the seller's rent claims.
- Don't be too concerned about the building's historical level of occupancy. This is frequently more of a reflection of the quality of the property management than the building itself.
- Do a one year quick projection of the building's P&L (profit and loss statement). You can use this to compare multiple buildings that you are considering. Use a more detailed five year projection for the small number of buildings that you are most interested in.

Categories of Rentals

Here is a summary of the types of rental properties you might want to consider. Refer to the initial Chapter "What Type of Investment is Best for You?" to help select among these options.

Rental Condo or Rental Home. Purchase of a residential property to be rented out to tenants, usually on a 12 month lease term. This is how most new landlords get started. You can hire out all of the property management functions, but in many cases you will do many of them on your own. The purchase process and financing process is very similar to what you experienced buying the home you live in now. It's great for beginners to get started.

Small (2-4 Unit) Apartment Building. Purchase of duplex, triplex or quadplex to be rented to tenants, usually for 12 month terms. Often what the rental home/condo landlords graduate into. In most markets they cost a little more than a rental home, but are more likely to cash flow. Less cash flow risk; if one unit is empty you have other tenants that still help you with the mortgage payment so it doesn't all come out of your pocket. Many owners will start to delegate some of the property management tasks to an on-site assistant (typically the most responsible tenant), such as yard maintenance and showing empty units. The financing process is only slightly more involved than a residential loan. The purchase process is also very similar to purchasing a home. Great for beginners.

Large (5+ Unit) Apartment Building. Still targeting tenants for 12 months at a time, buildings with more than four units are considered "commercial" property. The loans are somewhat more difficult to qualify for, and usually a larger down payment is needed. Less common for the new investor; this is usually what landlords with several years of experience "trade up" to. Cash flows on larger buildings are more stable than for smaller buildings, and the economies of scale make it practical (and desirable) to hire a property manager to take over most of the work for you. This takes away most of the hassles and less fun elements of the landlord process. We have had many successful new investors start with larger apartment buildings, but generally newbies will do something a bit smaller.

Lease Options. Again, you are seeking a tenant for a property, but usually for a slightly longer term (12-24 months) and frequently (though not always) with the goal that the tenant purchase the property from you at the end of the lease. If you purchase the property then it's an easier process; if you find a highly motivated seller to let you re-lease the property to another tenant, it can be a lot of work to set up. However, the re-lease method doesn't require any cash out of pocket and does not rely on your credit score, so it is appealing to many investors. Lease Options are great for beginners.

What Types of Investor Should Consider Rentals?

Equity Needed is how much in the way of liquid assets you and/or your investment team will need to have. Purchasing a large apartment building, for example, usually requires at least 20% down on a purchase price that might start at $500,000 in a small market like Pueblo. You would need $100,000 in cash to consider such an investment. You may need 2x that down payment in Denver or Northern Colorado (e.g. Fort Collins, Boulder, etc) A rental home or condo will also require at least 20-25% down but the numbers are usually smaller.

As in anything in life, however, more cash does make things easier. As you progress in your investing career and build up your funds, additional investment opportunities will become available to you. The following chart will give you a summary of the equity requirements for different types of rentals.

Investment Class	Equity requirements
Rental Condo Rental Home Small (2-4 unit) Apartment	**$25,000 and up**. 15-20% of the purchase price is generally required to be put down on the loan. Lenders will also require six months of operating expenses in reserves. For example, you might put 20% down on a $150k property and deposit $5k into your operating account. Three and four unit properties usually require 25%-30% down. Ex: Cos 1Br CND: $150K and 15% down + closing costs. Denver & Northern Co DSF: $300k and 20% down = $60k + closing costs
Large (5+ unit) Apartment	**$120,000-$225,000 and up.** Buildings over four units require a commercial loan. Sometimes a lender will loan up to 80% of the purchase price, requiring 20% down. Frequently 25% will be needed. You'll need to have a few months of reserves in your operating account as well. Most new investors start with smaller rental buildings to build experience and build equity. Prices for buildings will vary by market and neighborhood. Ex: Pueblo might have a 6 unit bldg. @ $100k/door or $600k total. 20% down = $120k. Denver & Northern Co more likely @$150k/door or $900k total. 25% down = $225k.
Lease Options (Owner Carry)	**$0 is typical.** Like Assignments, one of the appealing attributes of owner carry L/O's is that your credit score is not impacted by the transaction and neither is your checking account. However, also like Assignments, this tends to be a very competitive sector of real estate investing since the entry barriers are so low.
Lease Options (Investor Carry)	**$20,000 and up. $55,000 might be typical.** 20% of the purchase price down is typical. Since you are bringing some money to the deal, you'll have a lot more flexibility than the L/O investors that don't bring money. Can be a wonderful tool for the right investor in the right phase of the market. The typical estimate is for the investor that puts down 20% on a $250,000 property and deposits $5,000 to the operating account.

Credit Score will be important for some types of investments. Large apartment loans require nearly impeccable credit for the best terms. A small rental or fix and flip might require solid, though not perfect credit. If you can put down 10-20%, you can often purchase a small rental even if your credit is less than perfect. The following chart gives you an initial idea of the relative importance of your credit score with different types of rentals.

Investment Class	Minimum Credit Score Requirement
Rental Condo Rental Home	**Average.** You'll be purchasing the property, usually as a non-owner occupant (since you probably already have a primary residence). The mortgage companies will look at your credit score a little more closely than they will for your primary residence. As a rule of thumb, if you can qualify (even with a high interest rate) to buy a home to live in, you will be able to qualify to buy a home to rent out. However, the interest rates will be a little higher.
Small (2-4 unit) Apartment	**Average +.** The discussion for rental home and condo applies, but the standards, are a little tighter when you get a slightly bigger building.
Large (5+ unit) Apartment	**Average+/ Near Perfect.** You can get a commercial loan with a credit score that is a little better than the average, but you'll pay a higher interest rate. On larger buildings, the economics are very sensitive to your financing, so if you have just above average credit, not as many buildings will make sense for you. Conversely, if you have perfect or near perfect credit, you'll be able to get the most favorable commercial rates which will increase the number of buildings that are economical to invest in. Most investors believe only the building matters and their credit is not considered. That is very rarely true.
Lease Options (Owner Carry)	**Terrible.** You won't use your credit score for this type of investment, which makes it open to anyone.
Lease Options (Investor Carry)	**Average.** Same commentary as for "Rental Home" above.

As you can see, having terrible credit will not prevent you from getting involved in real estate investing, but it will reduce some of your choices and will make the choices you make less profitable than if you had better credit. Get started with a project and start learning, and while you do that take any steps you can to improve your credit score.

Experience with Contractors is not as important for rentals as it is for fix and flips or condo conversions. If you purchase a larger apartment building that already has a competent property manager in place, you won't need any experience with contractors.

This table outlines the relative importance of this skill for different types of real estate investments:

Investment Class	Importance of Experience with Contractors (or Willingness to Learn)
Rental Condo	**None / Very Limited.** Things will break in the rental units a little more often than they do at your home. If you overpay to get a deluxe contractor that holds your hand through every step of the process (e.g., go to Home Depot and hire their people), you are not going to significantly change the economics of your investment.
Rental Home	
Small (2-4 unit) Apartment	
Large (5+ unit) Apartment	**1-2 Projects.** As the number of units increases, you are going to have to fix more things more frequently. Getting good at managing contractors will make your building more profitable. As above, not getting it perfect will not kill your investment but you'll be leaving money on the table that an experienced investor would not.
Lease Options	**None / Very Limited.** See discussion for "rental condo"

Experience with Property Managers makes purchasing a rental property easier and more fun. It certainly is not essential though and you can learn by doing. Your experience will fall somewhere on this chart: As you review the chart below, you will see that extensive experience with property managers is not a requirement for any of these real estate investment groups

Investment Class	Importance of Experience with Property Managers (or Willingness to Learn)
Rental Condo	**None / Limited.** If you decide to hire a property manager you'll need to get some experience in managing them, but most investors for this size of a rental manage the properties on their own. For most investors, it makes more economic sense to do it on their own and they learn many lessons first hand that enable them to better select and manage property managers in the future on their larger investments.
Rental Home	
Small (2-4 unit) Apartment	**Limited.** For many investors, this is their follow-up rental investment, and they will start to experiment with delegation of at least some of the property management functions.
Large (5+ unit) Apartment	**Limited – Somewhat Important.** As your rental buildings get bigger, you'll be increasingly likely to outsource at least some of the elements of the management job.
Lease Options	**None / Limited.** See discussion under "rental condo" above.

Time Required Each Week varies on the project specifics, but we'll make some broad generalizations so you have a sense of the level of commitment you'll have to make to improve your chances of success. We break the discussion into the number of hours to get started, then the number of recurring hours of effort each week to keep the investment working well. Here is a rough guideline to what you can expect to get your project started. The table after that will outline your time commitments after the project is started (e.g., after you close):

Investment Class	What's required to *GET STARTED* (time you invest just once, up through and including the purchase of the property)
Rental Condo Rental Home Small (2-4 unit) Apartment	**20+ hours.** You will want to spend time with your real estate agent discussing your needs, then hunt for properties, then manage the closing process. Once you close, there will be some one-time set up activities (set up checking account for building, notify tenants of new landlord and payment procedure, etc).
Large (5+ unit) Apartment	**20+ hours.** Similar to the smaller rental buildings but the allocation of the time is different since you probably have purchased a rental building before. It will take less time to assess your needs and you will probably be more efficient at finding a building. However, the change-over process once you close takes longer since there are more tenants to be managed. You'll probably have a property management firm helping with at least some of the tasks, and they will need set-up time (involving your input) to get up and running.
Lease Options (Owner Carry)	**Can be extensive (60+ hours).** Usually you will start by finding a motivated seller, then negotiating the lease terms. Depending on the conditions in your market, this can takes some time. Once you have located the property, then you need to find a tenant to match to the property. Again, depending on the market this can also take time. Once you have located all of the parties there is some paperwork to fill out on a one-time basis (the leases, the option).
Lease Options (Investor Carry)	**Can be extensive (40+ hours), though significantly easier than L/O Owner Carry.** Often you will start with finding the tenant (it depends on what is currently going on in your market). Once you find the tenant, matching an appropriate home usually doesn't take as long as the L/O Owner Carry method. Once you have located all of the parties there is some paperwork to fill out on a one-time basis (the leases, the option).

Investment Class	What's required to *KEEP GOING* (time you invest every week, after you close on the purchase)
Rental Condo Rental Home Small (2-4 unit) Apartment	**0 – 5 hours / week.** For the months when the building is full, you'll just have to mow the grass, shovel snow, or deal with the occasional tenant question. If you get someone on site to do the yard work you'll have many weeks where you do nothing at all. When you have a vacancy you'll have to run an advertisement, answer some phone calls and do some showings (again, you might hire someone to do much of this for you), but it should not take too much time once you are in the rhythm of doing it.
Large (5+ unit) Apartment	**0 – 20 hours / week.** If you hire a property management company this should be very close to zero hours. If you elect to do it on your own, it still might not be much if you have a person on-site to do yard work and show vacant units for you. If you do it all yourself it will depend on the size of the building, but will generally be among the least time intensive real estate investments.
Lease Options (Either Type)	**0 – 5 hours / week.** Very similar to the "rental condo" above, and if done properly, it can be even less work than working with a traditional tenant, since the lease-option tenant often does their own minor repairs.

The **Number of Monthly Interactions** is also important to some people. They are happy spending one or two long sessions on the property, but would be highly annoyed to have twenty very short interactions. Other people, due to home or work requirements, might have the opposite preference. We'll help set your expectations. In addition to understanding the number of hours required to be invested to be successful, some investors have different preferences for the number of interactions they will need to have.

Due to the balancing act of work and family, some prefer to have a smaller number of longer interactions, while others prefer many interactions of shorter duration. Which do you prefer?

Investment Class	Typical number of monthly interactions (e.g., phone calls, meetings, on-site visits)
Rental Condo Rental Home	**Average 1 – 5.** Should not require much on-going effort for the months when the unit is occupied; more effort when you are filling a vacancy. Less if you have management assistance. Most of the interactions will be very brief (e.g., following up on why rent is late, answering questions about a vacant unit).
Small (2-4 unit) Apartment	**Average 1 – 10.** Similar to "rental condo" above; you just will have vacancies more frequently.
Large (5+ unit) Apartment	**Average 1 – 20+.** Similar to "small apartment"… if you hire out all of the property management it can be very easy. You'll have some longer discussions with your property manager on a monthly "status call".
Lease Options (Owner Carry)	**Average 1 – 5.** Similar to "rental condo"; likely to have even fewer interactions (longer durations for the tenants than typical rental, they handle many small maintenance issues for you).

Perception of Hassle varies as much by individual as it does by project, but again, we can offer some broad guidelines. This is the toughest area to assess – what annoys one investor might be a challenging and fun puzzle to solve for the next. However, there are some broad observations we can share:

Investment Class	How Much Hassle is Required
Rental Condo Rental Home Small (2-4 unit) Apartment	**Very Low – Moderate.** You will have the occasional person that never pays on time, irritates other tenants, or is the one complaining about every possible issue. Hopefully it is the exception and not the rule. Unless you are in a dreadfully bad renter's market, keeping your building occupied usually will not be too much of a problem if you work hard and pay attention.
Large (5+ unit) Apartment	**Very Low – Moderate.** Most investors don't buy a larger building until they have some experience with a smaller building – for a very good reason. They've already learned many lessons on tenant selection, and hopefully how to get a property manager to help them. A good property manager will make this score "very low". If you do a lot of the work yourself, you'll make more money, but you'll have more headaches, too.
Lease Options (Owner Carry) Lease Options (Investor Carry)	**Before "closing": High – Very High.** If you don't bring a credit score or cash, you are going to have to bring your time and willingness to deal with a lot of nonsense to find a good deal. The seminars and infomercials make it sound easy, but it can be frustrating. **After "closing": Very Low – Moderate.** Looks like "rental condo" but sometimes even more favorable.

Risk Tolerance is the level of comfort that you and the key people that influence your decisions have with risk and ambiguity. If you are going to be awake at 3AM every morning worrying about this decision, it may not be the right asset category for you. This chart will give you an initial orientation to the degree of risk that you are accepting with different types of real estate investments.

Investment Class	Relative Degree of Risk and/or Uncertainty
Rental Condo	**Very Low.** The investment is easy to assess, easy to purchase, and easy to sell if you don't like it. A small condo is probably the easiest category of rental to manage. Like all rentals, the returns are fairly easy to predict and are not too volatile.
Rental Home	**Low.** Similar to rental condo, but you'll have to make arrangements for outside maintenance on your own… but you won't have HOA fees, either.
Small (2-4 unit) Apartment	**Low.** Less risky than rental condos and homes since you have more than one unit, so it's unlikely you would ever have to make a mortgage payment completely on your own. A little more risky than a condo or rental home since it (typically) costs more to purchase, and might take a little longer to sell.
Large (5+ unit) Apartment	**Low – Medium.** Less risky than other rentals in that the cash flow should be the most stable of any rental group. More risky since they cost more, require more equity, and take longer to sell than other types of rental buildings. In the hands of a landlord seasoned with experience from smaller buildings there's a relatively low degree of risk. Returns are certainly more predictable and controllable than the stock market!
Lease Options (Owner Carry)	**Low.** The owner is still accountable to the bank for the mortgage payments (not you!).
Lease Options (Investor Carry)	**Low - Medium.** You are accountable for the mortgage payments, which is similar to the rental house category above. However, the number of tenants you have to work with is quite a bit smaller since you have more particular requirements in seeking a lease-option tenant that a traditional landlord.

Where Should You Buy?

In most cities, some neighborhoods tend to have a much higher concentrations of rentals than other areas. This chart shows an example of the locations of two, three and four unit buildings in Denver:

2, 3 and 4 unit buildings

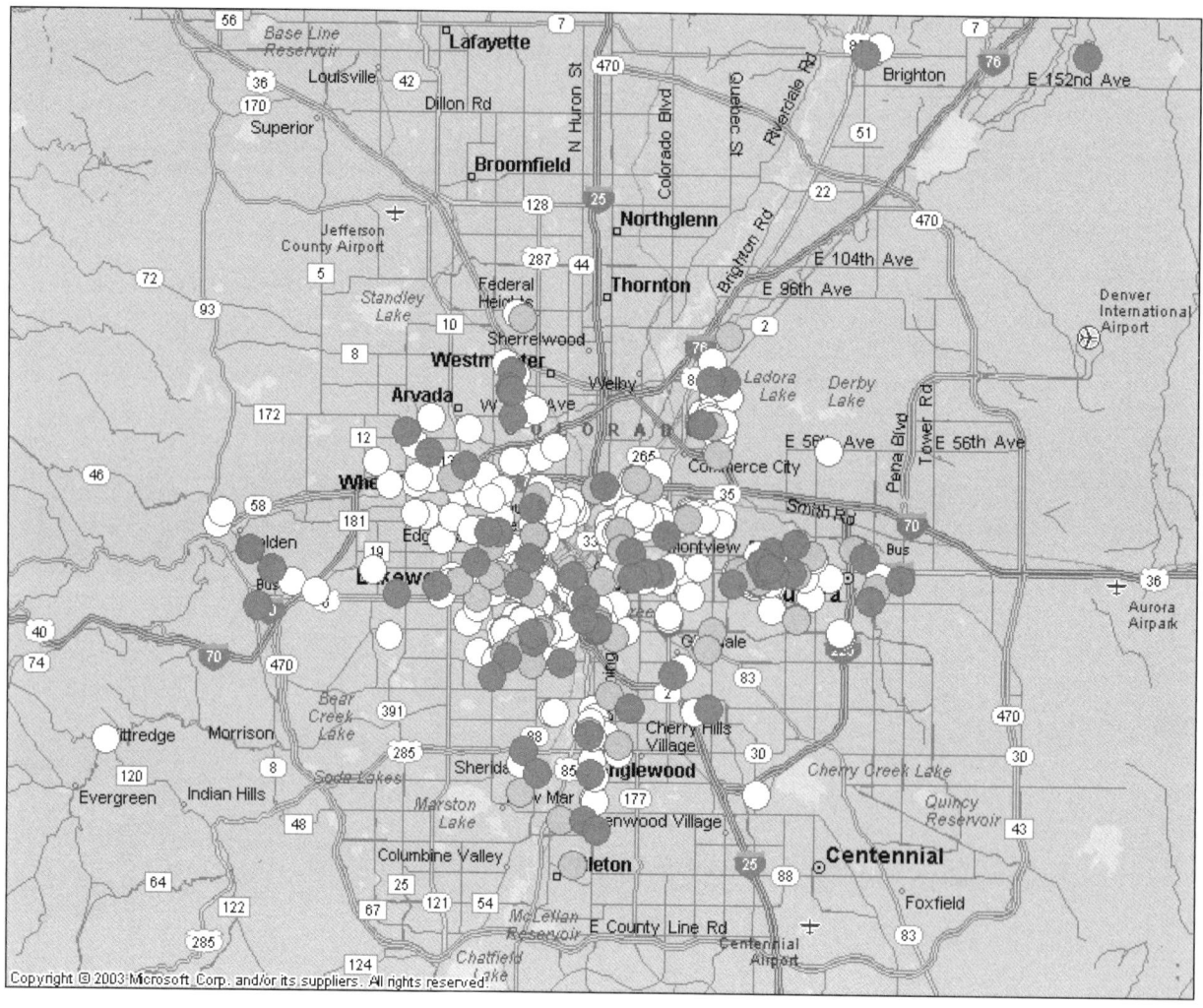

Source: Your Castle Real Estate analysis; Metrolist data

Dark dots are four units, light dots are three units, and white dots are two units. You will notice that almost all of the buildings are in the central part of the city, and the suburbs further from the city center do not have any small rentals.

If you were to zoom in to just examine Denver County, you would see this pattern:

2, 3 and 4 unit buildings

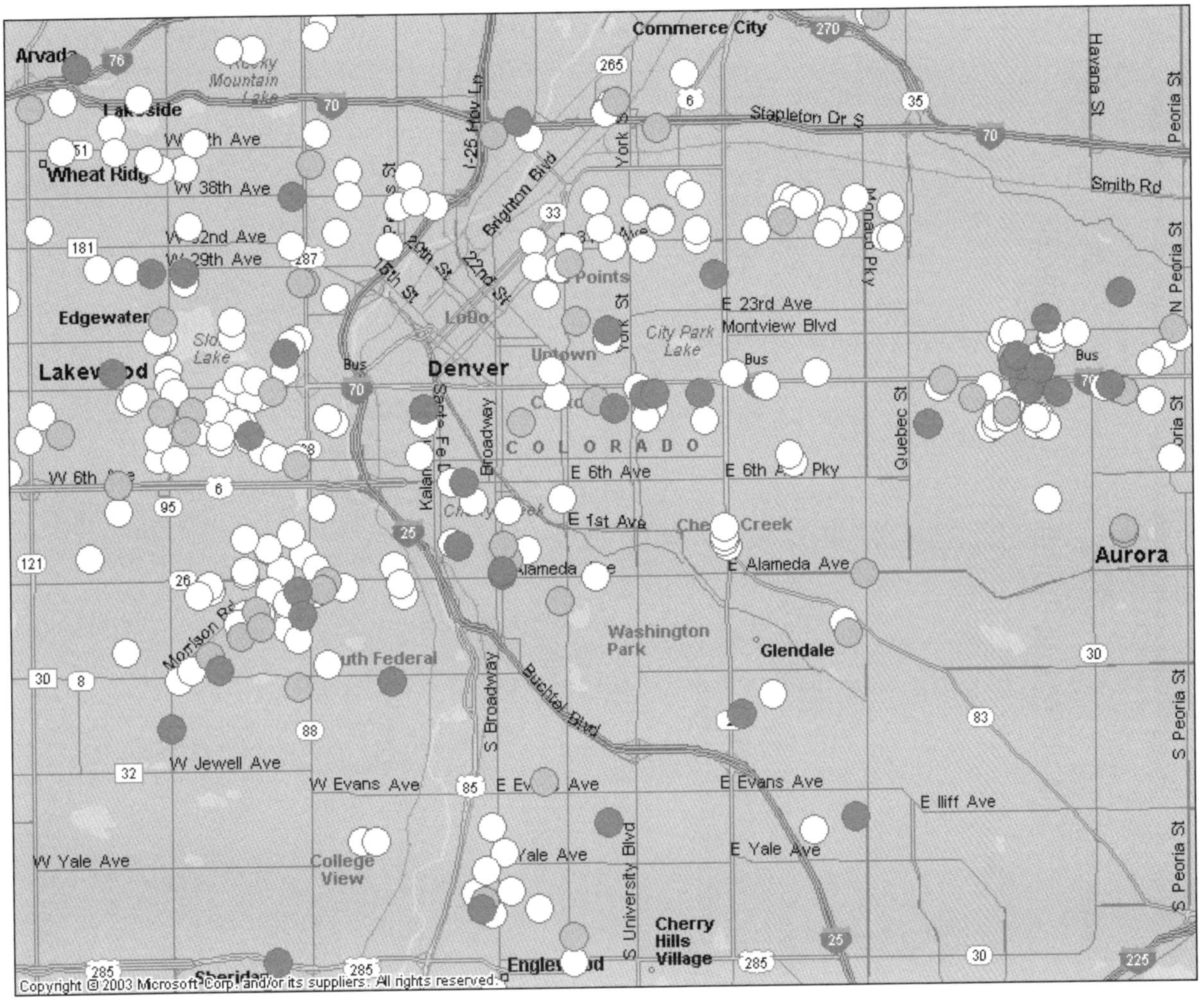

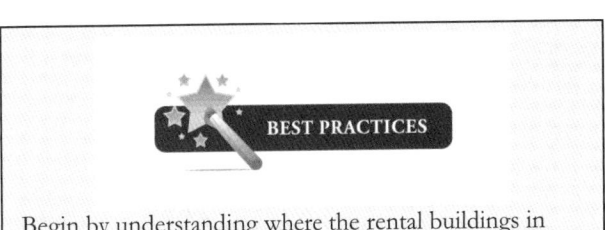

Source: Your Castle Real Estate analysis; Metrolist data

Notice that some neighborhoods have a much higher concentration of rental property than others. This will be true in most major markets.

BEST PRACTICES

Begin by understanding where the rental buildings in your price range are located. In most cities they will be clustered into a relatively small number of neighborhoods; they will NOT be "just anywhere."

If you were to examine the location of mid-size apartments (from 5 to 25 units) you will see they are distributed in about the same pattern as the two to four unit buildings. The white triangles are the buildings between two and four units and the dark squares are the buildings between 5 to 25 units.

5 to 25 unit buildings

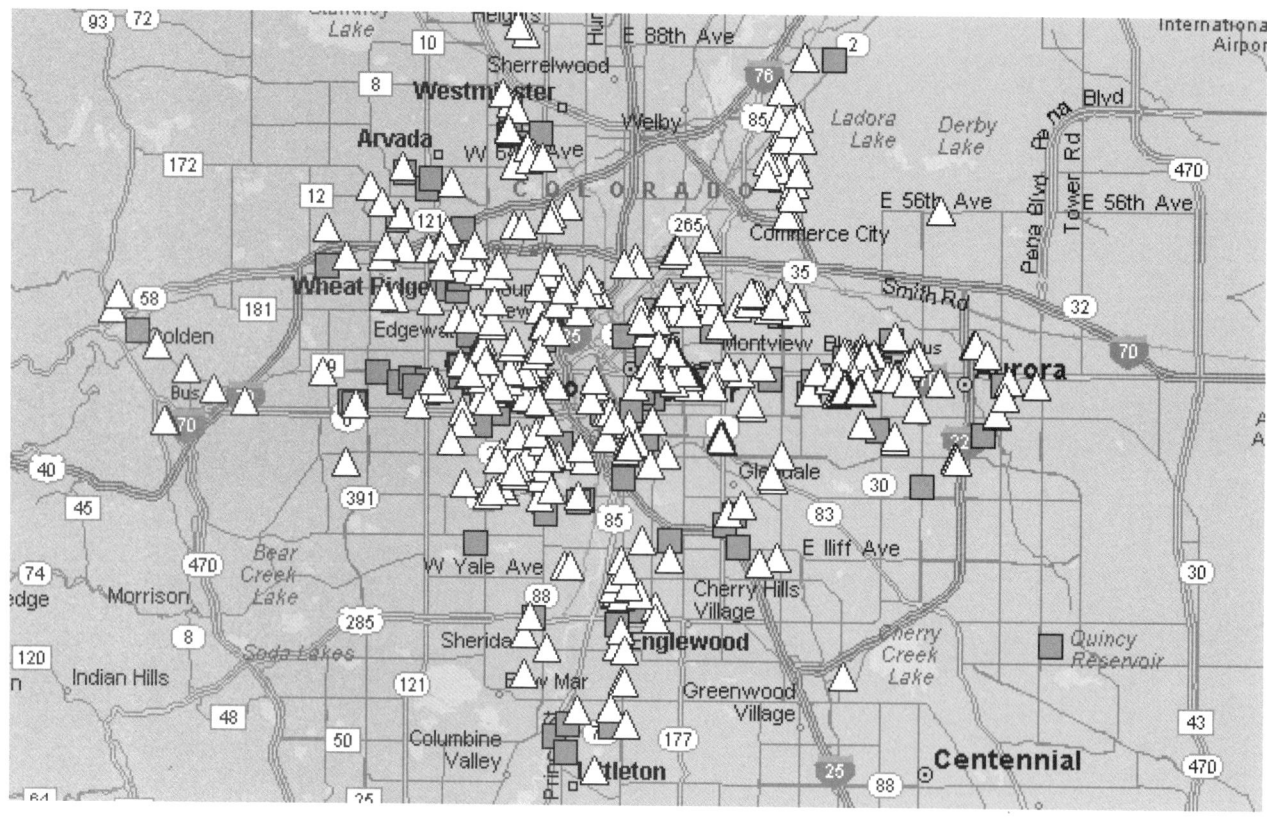

Source: Your Castle Real Estate analysis; Metrolist and Loopnet data

If you were to look at the locations of large complexes of 100 or more units (not plotted here), they would be at the outskirts of the city in the newer suburbs. The price of these developments, in the multiple millions of dollars, is outside the scope of this book.

On the other hand, if you want to look for rental homes, you might seek out 3 bedroom, 2 bath homes under $425,000. It is easier to have positive cash flow when the home costs under $425,000. They are more widely distributed across the metro area:

Homes with 3 bedrooms, 2 baths and under $425,000

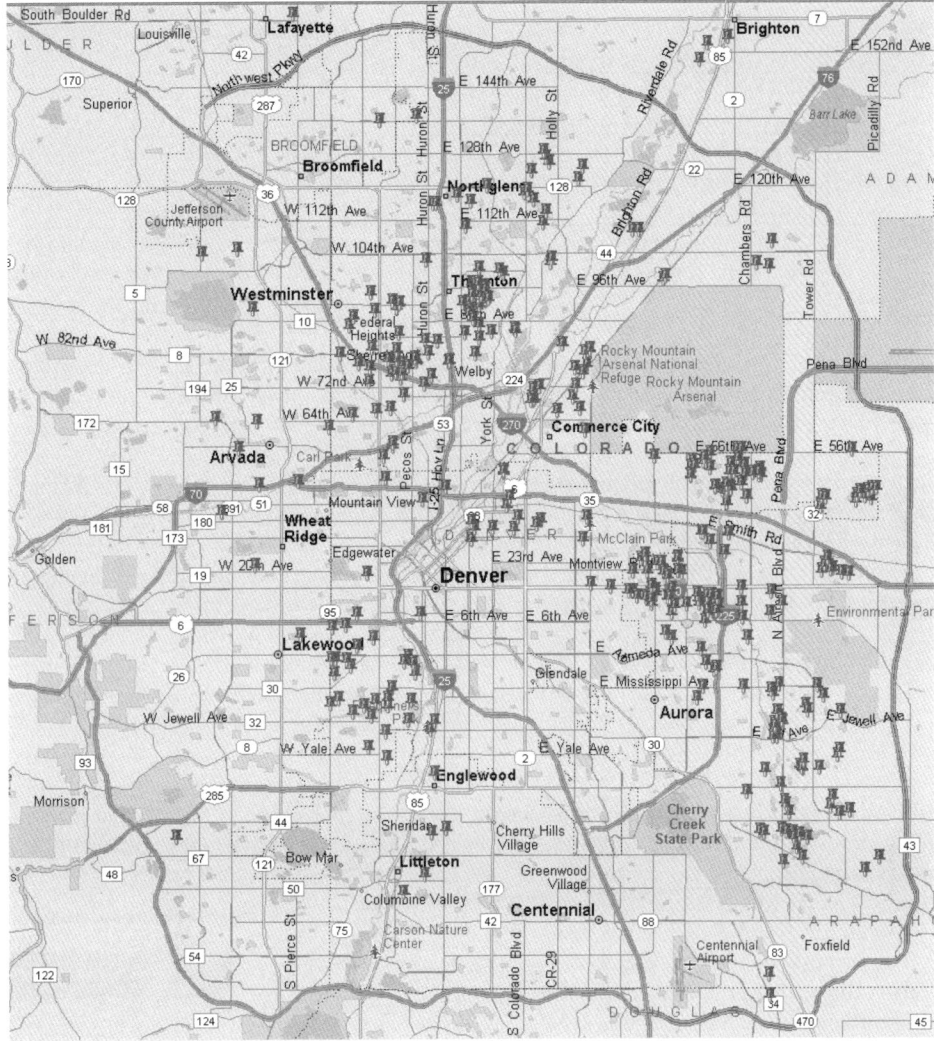

Source: Your Castle Real Estate analysis; Metrolist data.

Even so, you can see that there are large parts of the metro area with little inventory of homes and some neighborhoods with lots of inventory.

Different Classes of Buildings. You could segment the population of rental buildings into three buckets, from "A" to "C" quality, based on the size of the development and its build date. Different people (and markets) will have different cut-offs for the segments, but for a discussion aid, let's use these criteria for the sake of our discussion:

Property Class	Units	Location	Build date	Condition / Amenities
A	100 or more	Outskirts of town, newer and nicer suburbs; often near very major streets	Last 10 – 15 years	Usually excellent; often with pool(s) and clubhouses
B	12 – 50	Usually closer to the city center; may or may not be near major streets	Last 10 – 25 years	Mixed condition depending on owners, usually do not have many amenities
C	2 – 12	Often much closer to the city center; can also be in "run down" areas of the city	Often 25+ years	Mixed condition; usually the lowest level of maintenance; few or no amenities

"C" properties are what most new investors can afford to buy. They are generally under $1,000,000 or around $150,000/door in Denver metro. As they gain experience and equity, many will trade up to "B" properties. "A" properties are usually owned by REITS (Real Estate Investment Trusts) and sell for well over $30,000,000 or $300,000/door in metro Denver.

With this in mind, you can see that a small rental building may not be in your backyard, particularly if you live in a new suburb far from the city center. Your real estate agent will be able to give you good insight into what neighborhoods are appropriate for you in your city. The natural inclination for most new investors is to choose the area that is closest to their home in order to make the management of the property easier. This is certainly a factor, but you should spend some time evaluating how cash on cash returns and projected appreciation rates vary by neighborhood as well. We'll examine how to calculate cash returns in a later chapter.

If you are planning on hiring a property manager to do most of the on-site work for you, you might be much better off making the financial returns a more important part of the overall decision process than the distance from your home.

Nice Guys (and Buildings!) Finish Last. The other broad rule of thumb to keep in mind is that nicer neighborhoods will usually have a lower cash flow than nastier neighborhoods. This is because the marketplace is efficient. If you could buy a building with a 7% first year return in a great area, or a building in a lousy area with that same 7% return (the price, of course, would be lower, but your hypothetical return would be the same), which would you buy? The vast majority of investors would pick the nice area. As a result, the prices in the nice area increase (and the returns decrease), and the prices in the nasty area decrease (and the returns increase) until some sort of market equilibrium is achieved. Work with your agent to investigate how big the premium or discount is for various neighborhoods and you can make a good choice on what is the best fit for you. Most new investors pick nicer areas and settle for lower returns. As they gain experience, they tend to migrate to rougher areas with higher returns.

BEST PRACTICES

Get a sense of how cash returns vary from nice areas to crummy areas. Usually the nicest areas have the lowest cash returns. Sometimes, but certainly not always, they will have better prospects for appreciation. Decide if location or cash returns are more important to you to help focus your search.

Role of Appreciation. Determining (uhhhh, making an educated guess) which neighborhoods are going to appreciate the most is as difficult as picking next year's highest-returning stocks. Your agent will be able to provide you with some ideas, but it's a guess at best. In general, keep these things in mind:

- A run-down area with a significant level of political support for redevelopment is likely to do better than a similar run-down area without the redevelopment.
- Very nice neighborhoods tend to maintain their values well, but they don't always have the best appreciation. They will tend to be average. They generally have less downside risk and less upside opportunity. Go figure.

- If you can find an area that is undergoing gentrification, that might be a good bet if you are early in the cycle. If you have missed the majority of the renovation work in the area, investigate the neighborhoods immediately on the perimeter of area with recent above-average appreciation.
- Don't be a momentum investor. A neighborhood that has had several years in a row of above-average returns is not automatically destined to have another year of the same results. The same holds true for under-performing areas.

The research team at Your Castle Real Estate took a look at the long term price trends in the Denver market to try to gain some insight into this topic.

Average price of a single family home, in thousands, in Denver Metro, from 1971 - 2017

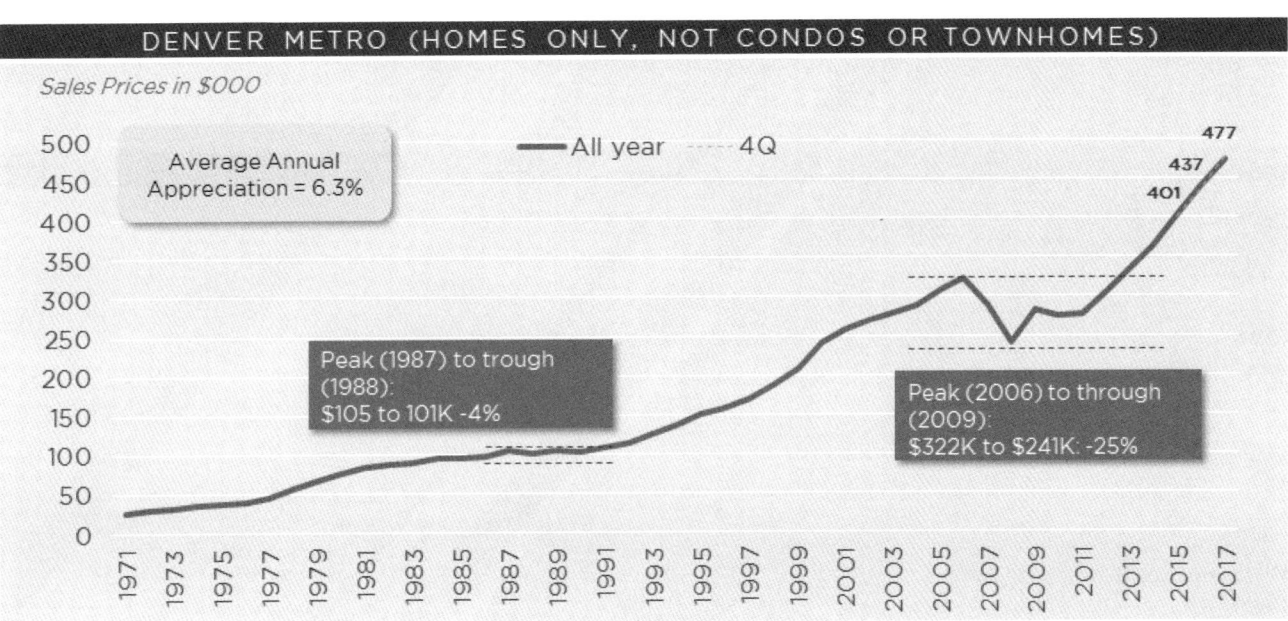

Source: Your Castle Real Estate analysis; Metrolist data

You can see that real estate prices, on average, go up in most years. The average is 6.3% per year, between 1971 and 2017. However, since inflation averaged 4.6% per year during that time span, actual prices after inflation increased about 1.7% per year, on average.

Note that there was a recession in the Denver market in 1987 – 1989. A lot of foreclosures came with the job losses and the average home price in Denver metro dropped a bit. It took three years for prices to pop back.

We hit another peak for home prices in 2006. Home prices dropped around 25% in the years that followed. After 2009 the prices came roaring back.

Note that during the last foreclosure boom in the late 1980's, the northern part of Aurora dropped quite a bit more than the overall Denver market. This is partially due to the fact that homes in North Aurora are less expensive than the metro average. Many of the buyers in the mid-1980's were first time buyers and didn't have large down payments or large savings accounts. As a result, when the economic conditions got difficult, these families tended to be the first to lose their homes.

On the other hand, more affluent neighborhoods generally tended to have families with larger down payments at the time of purchase and larger savings accounts. If these households were hit with a job loss, they were more likely to be able to ride out the economic storm without losing their home. Their larger savings accounts enabled them to make their mortgage payments while looking for a new job. If worst came to worst and they had to sell their home, there was enough equity in the house (since they had larger down payments at purchase), so they could sell.

What does this mean to the investor?

If you want to purchase a small home as a rental property, buying near the bottom of an economic cycle is a great time to do it. The smaller, less expensive homes fall in value more during a downturn and rise more in value during strong economic times.

Let's look at how an investor of a small home in North Aurora would have done in the late 1980's.

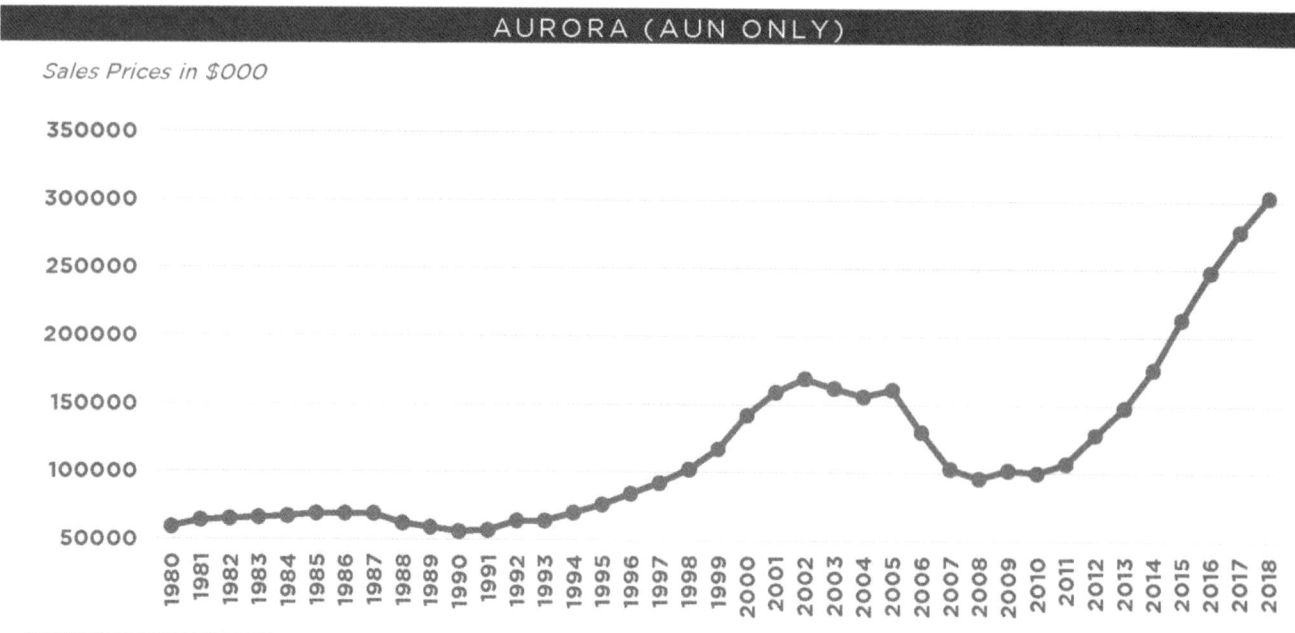

AURORA (AUN ONLY)

Sales Prices in $000

Data Source: Recolorado.com, YCRE analysis

Less expensive markets (e.g., SW Denver, S. Westminster, North Aurora) have more volatility in downturns. Traditionally they offer more potential upside in a recovery. Buying after the downturn in 1991 resulted in a 70% annual return just from appreciation.

The market bottomed out in 1990, when the average home price in North Aurora was $49,000. Let's imagine you are a very cautious, conservative investor. You wanted to wait to buy until you saw clear evidence the market was past the bottom. You waited a year, until 1991, and then purchased at the average market price: $50,000. You put 10% down, or $5,000. If you waited two years, the average home price appreciated to $64,000. Your gain from appreciation would have been $64,000 - $50,000 = $14,000. Since you put $5,000 down, that would be an excellent return - 280%!

Note that this is just the return from appreciation. There are also other benefits to real estate investing. You should earn some positive cash flow each month while you own the property. As you make your mortgage payment each month, you pay down the balance of the mortgage a bit. And you get a lot of tax benefits from real estate. When you sell, the capital gains are handled in a favorable manner if you owned the property for more than a year. Talk to your CPA; you will be amazed at how much more favorable the taxes are for real estate versus stocks or most other types of investment.

If you take a look at the right side of the exhibit, you can see that the average home price in North Aurora dropped about 40% from 2003 (peak = $167,000) to 2008 ($99,000). This foreclosure boom has been more severe (40% drop) than the last foreclosure boom in the late 1980's (25% drop). Are we at the bottom? No one has a crystal ball to say for sure, but we think the evidence in many neighborhoods suggests we are actually a year or more **past** the bottom.

If you were to buy the average priced home in North Aurora, in 2001, you'd pay around $160,000. You would likely need to put 20% down, or $32,000. If the prices continue to rise to say $200,000 you would have a $40,000 return on a $32,000 investment. This is what we call a solid single.

Another idea to keep in mind is that not all neighborhoods increase or decrease in price at the same time. The research team at Your Castle Real Estate does a lot of work on this topic. We wrote a custom software package that takes Denver Metro and segments it into over 400 small neighborhoods. We can calculate the foreclosure intensity and the price change (among other things) in each neighborhood. This information helps our clients make better decisions.

This chart shows you that information for East Denver County and North Aurora. Look at the left side, about half way down. You can see the Montclair neighborhood. You see the average home price was $442,000 with a 14% rise in prices over the previous year.

Metro Denver Price Change Map

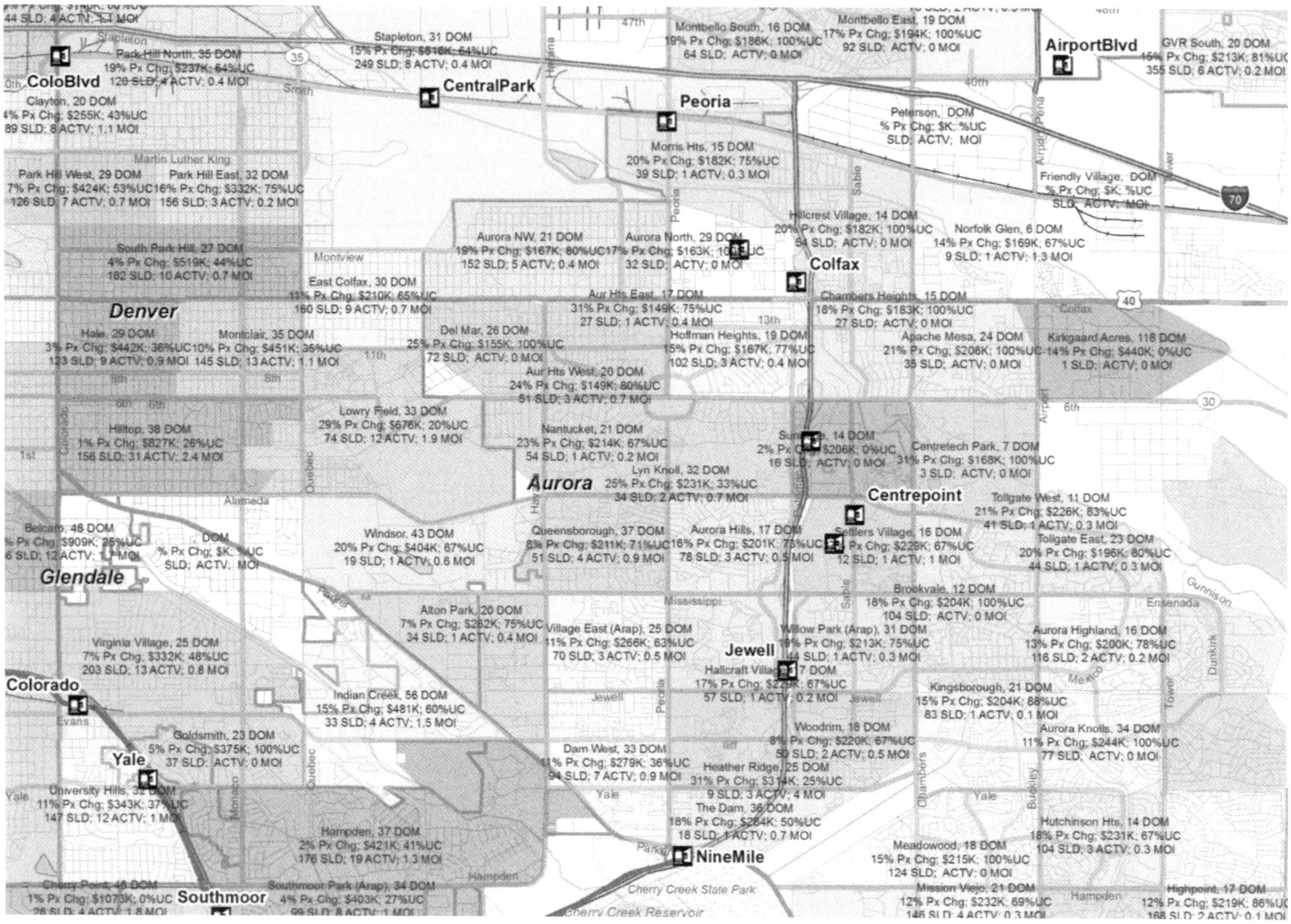

Source: Your Castle Real Estate analysis; Metrolist data

DOM (Days on Market) was 37 days. This is the time between when the property was listed in the MLS and when it went under contract. The long term average days on market in a balanced neighborhood is about 90 so this neighborhood is selling well which explains the 14% price rise.

Compare and contrast to the neighborhood immediately to the South of Montclair: Hilltop. Here the average price was $800,000 and the yearly price change was only 2%.

Remember the old adage of what matters in real estate? "Location, location, location." It has never been more true than today.

Review the advantages and disadvantages of each type of rental. Some investors have a definite preference, and discovering this earlier in the search process will save you considerable time and frustration.

Pros and Cons of Different Rental Types

Detached Single Family Homes (DSF)
Advantages:
- Easy to understand
- Easy to sell if you don't like it
- Easy loan process
- Relatively easy to manage yourself
- Available in most parts of town; some areas will cash flow much better than others

Disadvantages:
- Hardest to get a property manager
- No HOA, so you or your tenants have to do all of the maintenance work, inside and out
- Generally the hardest type of rental with which to achieve positive cash flow unless you buy under $150,000
- If you have a vacancy, you are paying the entire mortgage out of pocket – more volatility of cash flow. Consider having a higher percentage of reserve cash.

Condos.
Advantages:
- Easy to understand
- Inexpensive, easy loan process
- Easy to sell if you don't like it
- Easy to manage yourself
- HOA handles the outside maintenance for you, and often some common area cleaning
- Available in many parts of town; some areas will cash flow much better than others

Disadvantages:
- Hardest to get a property manager relative to ease of finding apartment property managers
- HOA can eat up a lot of the cash flow; particularly on the smaller units
- If you have a vacancy, you are paying the entire mortgage out of pocket – more volatility of cash flow. Consider having a higher percentage of reserve cash.

Duplex – Triplex – Quadplex
Advantages:
- Relatively easy to manage yourself
- Easier to get a property manager (or an on-site helper)
- Easier to achieve positive cash flow
- Down payment requirements are slightly higher than single family or condo, but less than larger buildings (5 or more units); generally easy loan process
- If you have a vacancy, you are not paying the entire mortgage out of pocket – less volatility of cash flow. Smaller reserve cash requirements.

Disadvantages:
- Somewhat harder to sell if you don't like it
- Available in select parts of town; some areas will cash flow much better than others; you will probably have to drive a bit further to get there.
- You are responsible for cleaning and maintenance, or hiring it out.

Five units and up (B and C class properties)

Advantages:

- Easiest to get a property manager (or an on-site helper)
- Easiest to achieve positive cash flow
- High/medium return and few hassles once it is set up properly
- If you have a vacancy, you are not paying the entire mortgage out of pocket – less volatility of cash flow.

Disadvantages:

- Hardest to sell if you don't like it; especially in a recession.
- Large down payment requirements; somewhat more difficult loan process
- Available in select parts of town; some areas will cash flow much better than others; you will probably have to drive a bit further to get there.
- You are responsible for cleaning and maintenance, or hiring it out.

Lease Option (L/O) - Single Family Homes.

Advantages:

- Easy to understand
- Easy to sell if you don't like it (you don't even have to sell if you don't take title)
- Small (or no) down payment requirements; easy loan process
- Your L/O tenants will do some of the on-site maintenance and yard work in most cases
- Relatively easy to manage yourself
- Available in any part of town; some areas will cash flow much better than others

Disadvantages:

- Hardest to get a property manager (especially at an affordable price)
- Lease option tenants are much more difficult to locate than traditional tenants
- If you have a vacancy, you are paying the entire mortgage out of pocket – more volatility of cash flow. Consider having a higher percentage of reserve cash.

Types of Tenants

Very Short Term (0 – 3 months). A small segment. Many of these tenants will have excellent credit, employment history and cash reserves. Examples include executives on out-of-town assignments and families that have recently relocated to an area. The families might prefer a rental home to an apartment unit. Condos in downtown areas close to where executives work would be great, also.

Features:

- Might need fully furnished rooms (as an alternative to an extended stay hotel).
- Usually pay premium rates to compensate for higher management intensity of high tenant turnover.
- You can probably develop a relationship with a real estate agent that specializes in relocation to get a steady stream of referrals.

- You could talk to corporate HR departments, particularly at the professional services firms (e.g., accountants, consultants, attorneys, engineers) to get referrals. Try the corporate relocation companies as well. Lets be real, though, that's easy to say and hard to do!

Short Term (3 – 6 months). A small segment of the overall tenant marketplace. Many of these tenants will also have excellent credit and employment history. You will find more relocation buyers, and some families that have sold their current home while they are waiting for their new home to be built. Features are very similar to the very short term group. You should consider talking to real estate agents that specialize in new construction and Builders to see if you can get referrals.

Traditional (6 – 12 month) – Pre-Up and Coming Segment. A medium to large segment. These are often (but not always) young adults who have recently left their parents' home and/or are college students. They are young enough that they have not had much work experience or employment history. Most will eventually become home owners, but "that is a long time from now" in their minds. Some are amazingly responsible, some are shockingly irresponsible. Don't always trust your "gut feel" to tell the difference – they can and will fool you. They have not "settled down" yet. Strongly consider trying to get a responsible adult (e.g., their parents) to co-sign the lease, since they will not have much credit history. It's almost impossible to generalize about this group. The authors and our clients have had some wonderful experiences working with these young people and we have had some teeth-chattering horror stories. Most of our renter experience is somewhere in the middle. A group that churns frequently; not many will be renting from you for long (e.g., over a year) no matter how nice your property is or how nice you are to them as a landlord. They just tend to move around a lot as their life situations change rapidly. Don't take it personally.

Good screening and collection of damage deposits, if you can get them in your market, are important for this segment. They'll be more receptive to an offer of a "free iPad" to get them to move in than other groups – particularly when Mom and Dad are paying the rent for them. It's an important group of renters for "B" and "C" properties, as these people will be much more willing to deal with the tradeoffs of older, and frequently less well maintained properties, in exchange for charm, a great location, and/or less money for rent. To find them:

- If you are near any type of school or set of employers that tends to focus on younger workers with lots of turnover, this would be a great place to advertise and/or put up fliers to advertise your rental.
- Most markets will have a newspaper oriented to young adults. Advertisements in this publication should target this audience.
- CraigsList

Traditional (6 – 12 month) – Up and Coming Segments. A medium size segment. These renters have excellent credit, employment, and reserves. They are the folks in the Pre-Up and Coming Segment after a few years of maturation. Often they are just out of school but not ready to buy. Overall in America, between 60% and 70% of people own their own home (the ratio varies by market, mainly on housing affordability). This is a future owner group, and they'll be owners soon. They tend to treat your rental very nicely. They are pickier than the prior segment. They will want very clean housing that has been well maintained that appears to be safe. Note that appearance of safety and actual safety are, of course, different things. Generally these renters will want "A" grade space, but for the people for whom drive time is important, they could end up in nice "B" and "C" properties that have outstanding locations. Homes and condos would also work well for this group. To find them, try:

- University employment placement departments
- The HR departments of large employers
- Craigs List

Traditional (6 – 12 month) – A-Paper Transitional Segments. A small segment. Very similar to the Up and Coming Segment. A classic example is people who have recently divorced and they have sold their own home, and they are sorting out their situation before purchasing their own, smaller home. These people have been owners and will be owners again. They will generally treat your property well. More likely to prefer homes over apartments if they have children. To find them, try:

- Church groups
- Counseling groups

- Craig's List

Traditional (6 – 24 month) – C-Paper Transitional Segments. Small segment. The classic example is the two income couple that really needs both incomes, and then one of them loses a job. They fall behind on their payments, temporarily ruin their credit, and lose their home. They are now renters again. The spouse that lost their job gets through the medical crisis or whatever precipitated the problem, and they are both working to "get back on their feet again." This is an ideal segment for lease option candidates. Also good for rental homes, as they likely just left a home and the idea of going back to an apartment is really disquieting. To find them, try:

- Church groups
- Targeted mail to pre-foreclosure homes
- Craig's List

Traditional (6+ months) – Lifetime Renters with Jobs. Large segment. About a third of Americans rent their housing, and a large fraction of them are lifelong renters. Some of them lurch from one credit problem to the next, and never truly build the credit score they need to buy. Many others have weak credit, but it is good enough that they could purchase if they wanted to… but since their friends all rent, and their parents probably rented, they have a "renter's mentality" that they will rent their entire lives. As a landlord, these tenants can be wonderful, since they churn (e.g., move) a lot less that most other groups, once they settle down to a place they like. The authors and many of our clients have experiences purchasing a building with a few tenants that had been there for over a decade. In most situations, those tenants were still in the building five years later when we sold the buildings. You want to be careful not to be taken advantage of, but this group generally tends to respond well to respectful treatment and maintenance of their rental home. If you are good to them (but not a push-over) you should see longer rental durations that are relatively hassle-free.

As with the pre-up and coming segment, the enormous variety of people that you will meet in this group makes it impossible to generalize. They usually cannot afford "A" properties, and end up in "B" and "C" buildings. They are much less likely to be in condos and homes. They are not your ideal candidate for lease options since its unlikely they will purchase.

When you have picked your desired type of rental building, consider the different tenant segments and their pros and cons. Make sure you are comfortable with the tradeoffs and characteristics of the types of people your target property might attract.

Traditional (6+ months) – Lifetime Renters without Jobs on Assistance Programs. Large segment. Very similar to the previous segment, except these folks generally don't work, or if they work, it is for cash and not declared to the government. No credit score, or if they have a score, you are not going to be happy when you see it. They often have a poor or inconsistent employment history. But it doesn't matter too much, as they participate in one of the many social programs that pay for most or all of their rent each month. Often the agency automatically direct deposits it into your checking account! There will be some red tape you'll have to work with to get your building eligible for the program, and usually each renter comes with a stack of forms, too. There might be some inspections from the government agency. If you have just one unit to rent, this paperwork might be more hassle than it is worth. However, if you have multiple rentals that are likely to appeal to this segment, then it is likely to be worth your time to learn how the programs work. Your mastery of them will give you an edge over the landlords that do not invest the time.

Which Tenants are Best Suited for Each Type of Building?

In summary, the type of building you have will influence the types of renters that are likely to be a good fit for you. It also will give you a bit of prediction of the level of turnover you might expect from one type of investment property to the next:

	DSF Home	Condo	Duplex / Quadplx	Apt Bldg B	Apt Bldg C	L/O Home
Very Short Term (0 – 3 months) Short Term (3 – 6 months)	**Yes**	**Best**, if strong location	**Maybe**, depends on location	**Maybe**, depends on location	**Maybe**, depends on location	No
Traditional (6 – 12 month) – **Pre-Up and Coming** Segment	**Yes**, if lower end	**Yes**, if lower end	**Yes**, core group	**Yes**, core group	**Yes**, core group	No
Traditional (6 – 12 month) – **Up and Coming** Segments	**Yes**, if nicer	**Yes**, if nicer	**Yes**, if nicer	**Yes**, if nicer	**Yes**, if nicer	No
Traditional (6 – 12 month) – **A-Paper Transitional** Segments	**Yes**	**Yes**	**Yes**, if nicer	**Yes**, if nicer	**Yes**, if nicer	No
Traditional (6 – 12 month) – **C-Paper Transitional** Segments	**Yes**, if lower end	**Yes**, if lower end	**Yes**, core group	**Yes**, core group	**Yes**, core group	**Yes, Ideal**
Traditional (6+ months) – **Lifetime Renters with Jobs.**	**Yes**, if lower end	**Yes**, if lower end	**Yes**, core group	**Yes**, core group	**Yes**, core group	No
Traditional (6+ months) – **Lifetime Renters on Assistance Programs**	**Yes**, if lower end	**Yes**, if lower end	**Yes**, core group	**Yes**, core group	**Yes**, core group	No

Analyzing Your Investment – One Year Projection

"Get your facts first, and then you can distort them as much as you please."
    -- Mark Twain

Now that we have spent some time reviewing the types of rental properties and tenant segments, and which tenants do the best in each type of building, let's review the generic analysis template for evaluating rental properties. If you hate math, be sure to find a real estate agent that is good at this so they can do much of the heavy lifting for you. But really, it's not that hard.

This section will discuss the cash flow model for year one. It's concise and ideal for comparing multiple properties against one another. The research team at Your Castle Real Estate develops this cash flow projection for every rental building on the market with more than three units. When we have an investor that wants to purchase a rental, we can rank the buildings in their price range by projected return. This saves a lot of search time, as we look at only the buildings that make economic sense.

After we review the one year projections, then in the next section we'll look at a multiple year model to see how the investment performs over time.

Unit 1: 1BR	1,075
Unit 2: 1BR	1,100
unit 3: 2BR	1,400
Gross Rent (Monthly)	**$3,575**
Gross Rent (Annual)	**$42,900**
Square Footage	3,600
Rent $/Foot	$0.99
Rent reasonable-ness	Low
Prop Mgmt (10%)	358
Gross income (monthly)	**$3,218**
Annualized	$38,610
Vacancy @4.5%	$1,931
Net Income (annual)	**$36,680**

Quick Analysis: A quick, simple analysis of potential investment properties is often a valuable tool when considering a number of prospects. Rather than attempt an in-depth analysis of each property we have found the following technique to be very effective.

We are looking for the ratio of the monthly gross income to the price of the property. For example, a property selling for $ 100,000 that has gross income of $ 1,000 per month would have an income ratio of 1% ($1000 / $ 100,000 = .01 = 1.0%). In our experience any property with a ratio of 0.75% or **higher** is worth another look in our current (Denver) market. Again, this is for properties where we are considering **cash flow** as the significant factor. This is only applicable to any specific market at a specific Time. You will need to talk to experienced investors in your market to determine the norms for your area.

Once the list has been reduced using this quick filtering device you will want to do further analysis of your candidate properties based on operating expenses, deferred maintenance, etc. Again this can be a very practical tool for sorting through lots of available properties to help identify that "needle in a haystack".

Sample Building. The sample property we are examining here is a triplex. It's in good condition in a desirable neighborhood. It was built about 50 years ago, which is typical for this neighborhood which is less than ten minutes from downtown.

Email us at croberts@yourcastle.com and we'll email you a copy of this analysis template. Check out our investor training classes on the web site at www.yourcastle.com, too.

Income Overview. The first unit is an upstairs two bedroom one bath unit with about 800 square feet and rents for $1075 per month. The second unit is identical, but it is on the garden level and gets $1,100 per month. The separate house in the back of the lot, which is separated from the first building by a pleasant garden area, is $1,400 per month for a two bedroom, one bath unit that is about 1,000 square feet. This particular property does not have a garage to rent, nor does it have an on-site laundry, though one could probably be added. The Gross Monthly Rent is the potential income the building could generate if every unit were full every month.

SAMPLE CHECKLIST

Competitive Assessment. If you are seriously interested in the building you should ask to see a copy of every lease so you can confirm the rents. You may not be able to get this until you go under contract on the building, but you can certainly get it after you are under contract. You should also drive through the neighborhood and call on other properties that are for rent to inquire about their terms. Pretend "your sister from Cleveland" is moving to your city, and you are doing some advance scouting work for her. Would it be possible for you to see the unit? This will give you a good idea of how your potential investment stacks up against the competition in terms of …

- Quality of property management
  - How quickly did they respond?
  - Did they have good sales and closing skills?
- The building
  - Is it clean?
  - Does it have more or fewer amenities than the property you're considering?
  - Does it have parking, storage, or an on-site laundry?
  - Are the common areas clean?
- The unit itself
  - It is clean?
  - How is the layout? Efficient or lots of wasted space?
  - Does it have special features like a deck or a fireplace?
  - Is it about the same size?
- The terms
  - Are utilities included?
  - How much is the security deposit?
  - Is there an application fee?
  - How much is the rent?

BEST PRACTICES

Be sure to assess the competitors around your target building so you have a sense of your relative strengths and weaknesses. This will also help you validate the rent claims made by the seller.

Rent Reasonableness. We like to compare the rents to the size of the building to calculate the rent per square foot. Most larger cities will have an Apartment Association that gathers rent and vacancy statistics by neighborhood. They will also usually collect the information on a rent per square foot basis. We compare the pro-forma rent per foot to the average from the Apartment Association to test for reasonableness.

BEST PRACTICES

Get in touch with your local Apartment Association to learn about the typical rents and vacancy rates in your target neighborhood to provide a second check to the seller's rent claims.

Ideally, the building cash flows well with the existing low rents. When tenants move out, you will have no difficulty replacing them at the same levels of rent. In some cases you will raise the rents and further improve your cash flow. If the building is struggling to meet your cash flow objectives and the rents are high relative to the market place, then you may have a difficult time getting the cash flow to increase over time unless you have a strong opportunity to reduce the operating expenses.

CASE STUDIES

Increasing Income Case Study #1 – Raising Rents

We had a client that purchased a four unit building. All of the tenants had been there for multiple years. The owner, who had had the property for over a decade, had a very low mortgage and liked the tenants, and had not raised the rents as much as the market dictated. The building had solid cash flow with the clearly below-market rents. Our client raised the rents to get them in line with the market over a two year period and dramatically increased the building's value and his cash flow.

If the rent per square foot seems too high, we will make a negative adjustment to the rents to get the ratio to a reasonable level. Conversely, if the rents are significantly below market, we may adjust them upwards modestly to see what impact it has for the investor's bottom line.

Increasing Income Case Study #2 – Finding Other Sources of Revenue

We have had clients add garages to buildings in neighborhoods where the parking is tight. We have also seen clients add coin-operating washer and driers to boost revenue. In some markets you might be able to convert unused space in the basement to secure storage space and charge for it. Other owners have added wireless Internet to buildings. Be creative.

Property Management. We assume that investors will not be managing the rental and that they will hire a property management firm to help them. Ten percent of gross rents is a typical fee for property management. You can do it for less if you have an on-site person that does some of the work for you, and if you do some of the work. We'll review this in more detail in the chapter on property management. If you plan to do all of the work yourself your bottom line will look much better.

Vacancy. Not every unit in your property will be occupied with a rent-paying tenant every month. You will want to include a *Vacancy Allowance* for the months you don't have tenants. Your local Apartment Association should have a sense of what a reasonable vacancy rate is for your market. Often they can tell you the vacancy rate by the type of building and the neighborhood to provide even more detail. You'll want to model this at the current rate so you can estimate what your cash flow will be when you take over the property.

You will also want to model it with the five year average rate. If you are in a booming time in your market, the rate might be lower than the historical average. When the market cools off and the tenants start to get the upper hand, you can get a sense of how that change in the vacancy rate impacts your cash flow. Conversely, if you are in a slow market (from the landlord's perspective), the gloom can't last forever (though some days it might feel like it). Run the numbers with the high vacancy rate you are currently experiencing to see if you can make your mortgage payments, but also check it with the

BEST PRACTICES

Don't be too concerned about the building's historical level of occupancy. This is frequently more of a reflection of the quality of the property management than the building itself.

average to see how much better the cash flow will be when things get back to normal in a year or so.

Many times our clients will be curious about the historical occupancy levels of a building they are considering. It's nice to get this information, but make it a small part of your overall evaluation process. The vacancy rate of the building is more a function of the quality of the property manager (which will usually be the seller, especially for smaller buildings) than it is of the building itself. For example, if the current property manager is hard to reach on the phone, you can expect that the building will have a higher than average vacancy rate.

Net Income. This is the adjusted income that your property can be expected to produce after paying for your property manager and accounting for the vacancy rate. Next year, hopefully you will be able to increase the rents modestly and your income will increase.

Net Income (annual)		$27,670
Insurance		$700
Property taxes		$1,396
Repairs	7%	$2,352
Electric	$400	tenant
Gas	$400	tenant
Water + Sewer		$600
Advertising		$150
Operating Expenses (annual)		**$5,198**
Expense as % net income		19%
NOI Net Operating Inc		**$22,472**
Transcation price		$310,000
Cap Rate		**7.20%**

ANALYTICAL TEMPLATES

Expense Overview. Now that we know how much money is coming in, we need to estimate how much will be going out each month.

Insurance. This includes hazard insurance to protect your Lender. You might also want to consider liability insurance and lost rent insurance as well. You can call your current insurance provider to get a quote – most companies that write owner-occupied insurance policies also can insure rental property. Ask you real estate agent for recommendations as well.

Reducing Expenses Case Study #1 – Increasing Deductibles

In many markets, insurance companies have started to track the claims that a building has over time. When you sell the building, if it has a history of claims, the insurance rates could be significantly higher for the new owner. Be sure to investigate the rates before you purchase. After you purchase the building, you don't want to make claims on your insurance unless they are for substantial incidents. As a result, it might make sense to raise your deductibles to the maximum to reduce your insurance payments.

Property Taxes. You can usually get this information from the Listing Agent, but you will want to confirm it at the County web site. They will usually have a link to the assessor's office for your city where you can look up the tax amount.

Reducing Expenses Case Study #2 – Reducing Property Taxes

A client purchased a large building that was assessed at $2.66 million. The purchase price was only $2.0 million. The client followed the assessor's dispute process, and with a few hours of work was able to reduce the property tax bill by several thousand dollars per year. This does not always work, but is worth trying.

Repairs and Cleaning. We assume that our clients will hire out most of the repair and cleaning work. If you are a hands-on person who is good with tools and want to do the work yourself, you can probably cut your repair estimate in half. We typically use 7%. This sets aside a little extra to replace appliances, hot water heaters, carpets, etc.

Utilities. In most properties larger than a single family house, the owner will be responsible for water and sewer charges. You might also have to pick up the tab for garbage collection if the city does not provide it. The electric and gas bill will vary by building. Be sure you understand whether the rents include the utilities or not, and budget accordingly.

Reducing Expenses Case Study #3 – Reducing Water Bill

We had a client that was considering purchasing a five unit apartment building. As part of the due diligence, we reviewed several years of profit and loss statements. The water bills were several times higher than we expected for a building of its size. All of the other numbers made sense and the building had solid cash flow. She purchased the building, then had the water department come out to audit the water use. It turns out there was a major leak between the water meter at the street and where the water line entered the house. The city repaired the leak and the water bill dropped from $300 per month to $60 per month, which improved her cash flow almost $3,000 per year.

This case study illustrates how a savvy investor can increase the value of a building. The research team at Your Castle Real Estate gathers a lot of information to help our clients make more profitable investing decisions. Here's an example. We gather the operating costs for each of the buildings that help clients assess and we maintain a database of income and cost benchmarks.

In the chart below, for example, we have the average water and sewer bill for a number of different apartment buildings in Denver County. Since the water bill rates vary from one county to the next, it's important not to mix apples and oranges! To normalize the spending information, we divided the annual water bill by the number of doors (e.g., the number of units) on the left hand side. You can see the building with the greatest water usage was around $370 per year per unit.

On the other end of the spectrum at 1151 Colorado, the owner is spending only around $120 per year per unit. The average spent was $215 per unit, and the 1Q (top quartile) was $150. To show an example, an investor was considering buying a building at 1201 Clarkson. The spending on water there is $120 per door, or best in class. There is no savings opportunity here.

Imagine instead that the spending was $315 per unit per year, and it was a ten unit building. The potential savings would be $315 - $215 (average spending) = $100 per year per unit savings * 10 units = $1,000 per year potential savings.

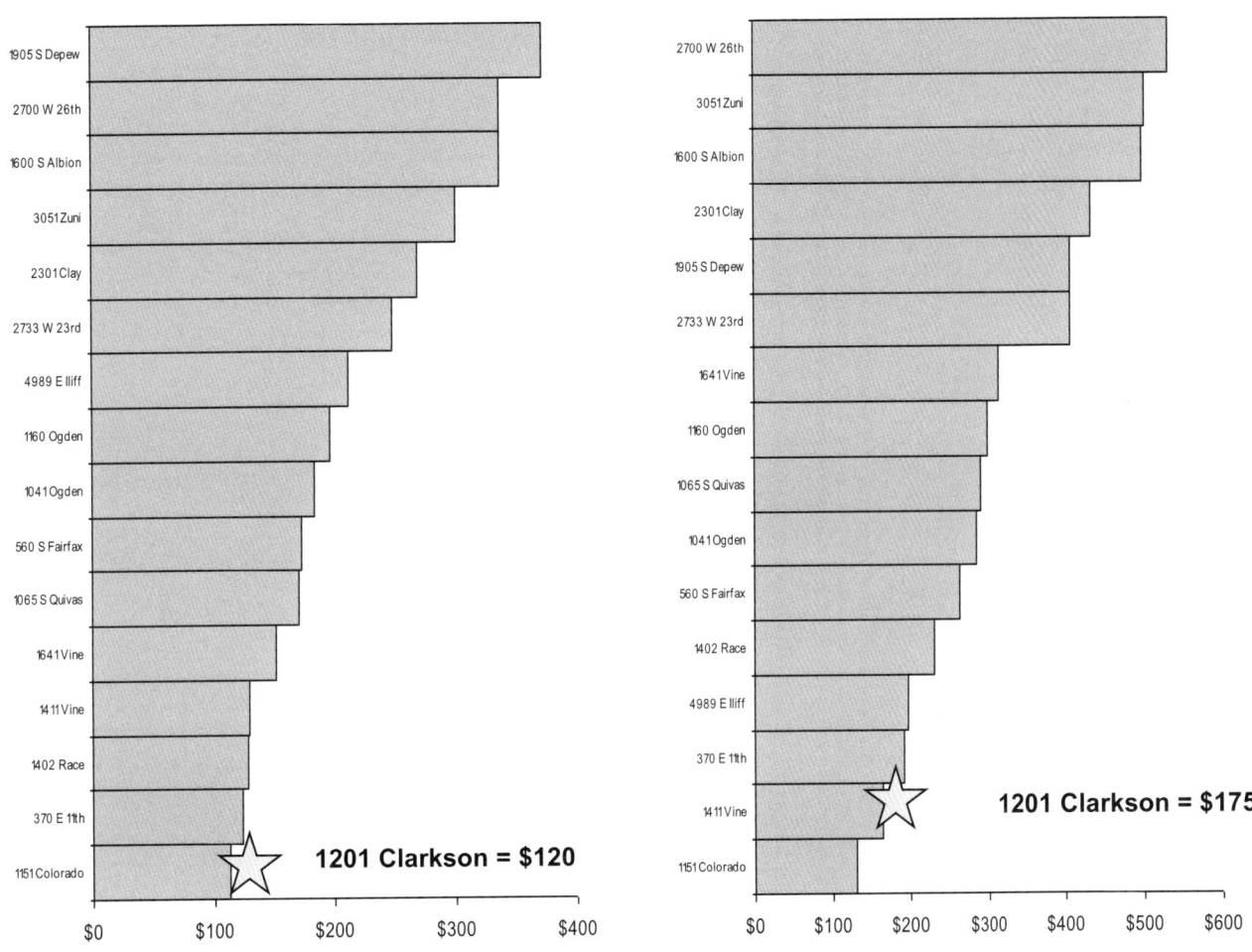

Source: Your Castle Real Estate Analysis

As a rough rule of thumb, take your annual savings and multiply by 15 to get a sense of how much value you can add to your building. In this hypothetical example, our client could increase the building value by $15,000 by getting the out-of-control water bill down to normal levels.

The chart of the right side of the page shows the water bill dividing by the size of the building. It's important to look at it this way, too. One of the reasons why the 1201 Clarkson building has such a low water expense is because most of the units are studios, which tend to attract single tenants. It has effectively no yard to water. Fewer showers, fewer loads of laundry, fewer dishwasher runs. On the other hand, a building with large three bedroom units in a family-oriented neighborhood may have four people per unit, with a commensurate increase in water usage. A large yard will also skew the numbers. Examining water use based on the building's size helps to normalize for this.

Reducing Expenses Case Study #4 – Reducing Water Bill

A client was considering purchasing a 38-unit building that was approximately forty years old. When performing the inspection, we noticed most of the sinks and shower heads did not have low-flow adapters. After the client purchased the building, they replaced the inefficient fixtures and reduced the water bill significantly. This was done during a drought, and the city water department gave incentives that covered most of the labor and material costs to improve the building's efficiency.

Advertising and Other. If the building you are considering is on a busy street, you may not need to run advertisements – a sign in front might do the job. If not, be sure to include some money for this. We've had tremendous success with Craigslist.

Total Operating Expenses. Your real estate agent and/or your Apartment Association should be able to give you a sense of what a typical expense ratio (the total operating expenses divided by the income) should be for a building of a given age in your market. If it is running higher than average, you might have an opportunity to create value by fixing a problem.

Net Operating Income. Subtract the operating expenses from the net income to get *Net Operating Income* or NOI. If you paid cash for the building, or someday when the loan is paid off, this is all for you! An important ratio is to divide the NOI into the transaction price to get the *Cap Rate*. This is your return on the investment. The target Cap Rate will vary on many factors which are highly specific to your marketplace.

Financing. Since most investors don't pay all cash for their buildings, you will want to consider the impact of financing. Here, the spreadsheet is taking the proposed LTV and interest rate to calculate the loan amount you will need to take out to purchase the building, and how much equity you will need to invest. In this case we are assuming an interest-only loan, then we're calculating how much cash flow will remain after all expenses and interest payments.

Total Return. The annual cash flow divided by the amount of equity that you have invested is your cash-on-cash return. This is today's reward for purchasing and managing the property. The larger reward comes when you refinance it some years down the road or sell it – the appreciation. If you purchase with 25% down, and the property appreciates 4% per year, you will get a 30% per year return in addition to the cash-on-cash return. This is why people invest in real estate!

Rate (5yr fixed)	5%
Purchase Price	$310,000
Proposed LTV	75%
Loan Amount	$232,500
Cash Invested:	$77,500
Annual Interest	$11,625
Annual Cash Flow (fx)	**$10,847**
Cash on Cash Return (5yr)	**14%**
Property Apprec %	4%
Property Appreciation	$12,400
Total Return (5yr fx)	**$23,247**
Total Annual Return (5yr fx)	**30%**

Analyzing Your Investment – Five Year Projection

After analyzing and visiting several buildings, you will eventually settle on a favorite. Make some quick modifications to the one year analysis template to see how your investment performs over time.

	2019	2020	2021	2022	2023	Change
Unit 1 3BR/2 Bath	$1,862	$1,936	$2,014	$2,094	$2,178	4%
Unit 2 4BR/2 Bath	$2,106	$2,190	$2,278	$2,369	$2,464	4%
Unit 3 2BR/1 Bath	$1,789	$1,861	$1,935	$2,012	$2,093	4%
Unit 4 2BR/1 Bath	$1,506	$1,566	$1,629	$1,694	$1,762	4%
Gross Rent (monthly)	**$7,263**	**$7,554**	**$7,856**	**$8,170**	**$8,497**	
Gross Rent (annual)	**$87,156**	**$90,642**	**$94,268**	**$98,039**	**$101,960**	
Prop Mgmt/Mo (10%)	$726	$755	$786	$817	$850	
Gross Income (Monthly)	**$6,537**	**$6,798**	**$7,070**	**$7,353**	**$7,647**	
Annualized	$78,440	$81,578	$84,841	$88,235	$91,764	
Vacancy@4.5%	$3,530	$3,671	$3,818	$3,971	$4,129	-1%
Net Income (Annual)	**$74,911**	**$77,907**	**$81,023**	**$84,264**	**$87,635**	

Income. The income for your units in the first year is from your current rent roll. If you have vacant units, estimate the market rent for when they are filled. Then, increase the rents by an inflation factor each year. If your local Apartment Association tracks this information, consider taking the average rental growth rate for your market over a long period (such as ten or fifteen years) to use as your assumption.

The **Property Management** percentage will be constant over time. If your **Vacancy Rate** is currently unusually high or low (relative to the historical average) you might consider adjusting it slightly over several years to get it to the historical average. In this example the vacancy rate is 4.5%. The historical average for this market is 5.5%, so the model adjusts the rate down 1% each year for three years.

BEST PRACTICES

Do a one year quick projection of the building's P&L. You can use this to compare and contrast multiple buildings that you are considering. Use a more detailed five year projection for the small number of buildings that most interest you.

		2019	2020	2021	2022	2023	Change
Insurance		$1,129	$1,163	$1,198	$1,234	$1,271	3%
Property Taxes		$2,777	$2,860	$2,946	$3,035	$3,126	3%
Repairs	8%	$4,809	$5,194	$5,609	$6,058	$6,543	N/A
Electric	$400	Tenant	Tenant	Tenant	Tenant	Tenant	4%
Gas	$400	Tenant	Tenant	Tenant	Tenant	Tenant	
Water & Sewer		$1,351	$1,392	$1,433	$1,476	$1,521	3%
Advertising		$125	$125	$125	$125	$125	N/A
Operating Exp (annual)		$10,191	$10,733	$11,311	$11,927	$12,584	
Exp as % net income		14%	14%	14%	14%	14%	
NOI Net Operating Inc		**$64,720**	**$67,174**	**$69,712**	**$72,337**	**$75,050**	
Transaction Price		$940,000					
Cap Rate		**6.89%**					

Next, increase the operating expenses each year. Many of these will grow with inflation, but historically they grow at a rate just a little bit less than the rental inflation rate. Insurance, property taxes, and utilities need this adjustment. If something specific is going to happen in your area that will cause your prices to adjust significantly in the future, make that adjustment. Repairs, which in this case are 8% of revenue, will grow automatically each year as the rents grow.

Capitalization Rate, or Cap Rate: Used by investors to evaluate income properties, the NOI divided by the Cap Rate gives an estimate of the building's value. Similar to return on investment for other types of investments, this is the return that you would get from investing in a building if you paid all cash. Cap Rates are roughly tied to interest rates - as rates go up, Cap Rates usually go up

The **Net Operating Income** grows quite a bit each year – this is also reflected in the **Cap Rate**.

	2019	2020	2021	2022	2023
Interest Rate (5yr Fixed)	5.50%	5.50%	5.50%	5.50%	5.50%
Proposed LTV	75%	75%	75%	75%	75%
Loan Amount	$705,000	$705,000	$705,000	$705,000	$705,000
Cash Invested	$235,000	$235,000	$235,000	$235,000	$235,000
Annual Interest	$38,775	$38,775	$38,775	$38,775	$38,775
Annual Cash Flow	**$25,945**	**$28,399**	**$30,937**	**$33,562**	**$36,275**
Cash on Cash Return	**11.04%**	**12.08%**	**13.16%**	**14.28%**	**15.44%**
Property Apprec %	4.00%	4.00%	4.00%	4.00%	4.00%
Property Appreciation	$37,600	$37,600	$37,600	$37,600	$37,600
Total Return	**$63,545**	**$65,999**	**$68,537**	**$71,162**	**$73,875**
Total Annual Return	**27.04%**	**28.08%**	**29.16%**	**30.28%**	**31.44%**

Next, let's review the impact of financing. If you thought you were going to own the property for five years, you might select a five year fixed rate that adjusts after the fifth year. If you had an interest only loan (depicted here for simplicity), the interest bill would be constant each year. All of the improvements in Net Operating Income all fall to the bottom line. As a result, your cash-on-cash return each year improves from 7.6% in year one to 22.6% in year five.

The property is appreciating each year, too. If it grows in value by four percent (again, you might consider taking the average appreciation rate in your area over the last ten to fifteen years), appreciation will constitute most of your return if you have a high LTV.

We can pull all of this together into a final scorecard. If the property appreciates 4% per year, the value at the end of year five would be $648,000 (actually, it would be a bit higher due to compounding interest, but this is a simple calculation to make the example easier to follow). This is $108,000 higher than the purchase price. The total of the cash flows each year is $40,400. The estimated sales costs (title work, real estate agents, escrow fees, etc) are $18,900. The total project return is $129,500.

If you had to put $54,000 of cash down to purchase the building, your total return would be 240% over the five year period, or 48% per year. Better than the stock market any day!

Your actual returns would likely be a bit higher, as you probably would have enjoyed some tax write-offs during the five years that you held the building, as well. You can tinker

Value of property, year five	$648,000
Purchase pric	$540,000
Five year appreciation	$108,000
Total Annual Cash flows	$40,406
Sales costs @ 6.5% year 5	-$18,900
Total project return	$129,506
Downpayment	$54,000
Return, five year	240%
Annual retrun after all expenses	48%

with the model to see what the impact of changing various assumptions does for your overall return. In most cases the important variables are:

- Property appreciation rate, since this drives most of your return.
- LTV… higher LTV will result in higher overall project returns. Be sure to increase the interest rate as the LTV goes up, since the Lender will charge a higher interest rate as you put less money down.
- The spread between the Cap Rate and the borrowing rate. The bigger the spread, the larger the project return.
- The gap between the annual rent increases and the expense inflation rate.

Chapter 6: Buy a Great Rental Home, Condo or 2-4 Unit

What's in this Chapter.   Let's say you have decided that a small rental building is the place to start – a logical choice. We'll review the different types of small rentals and some of the characteristics needed to succeed. We'll then walk you through a quick analysis of how much you can afford to pay for a given unit and still break even on cash flow. This isn't perfect analysis, so we help you evaluate the range of likely price points that will be attractive to you. Next, we'll consider some criteria to keep in mind as you evaluate the individual properties. Finally, we'll help you customize the generic analysis template from the "Rental Property Fundamentals" chapter to the specific needs for smaller rentals.

Executive Summary – Best Practices

- Consider starting the screening process by gathering the average rents and back-solving for how much you can afford to pay to break even.
- Don't forget to set aside 6-10% of the revenues for maintenance, repairs and cleaning, and another 4-6% for vacancies.
- Keep in mind that nicer units and/or more amenities (e.g., a pool) will command higher rents… and you can afford to pay more for such a unit and still break even (or better).
- It's OK to want to buy a nice property with nice tenants in a nice area. The cash flow will be lower than the other alternatives on the market, but you can still do well financially. Your comfort level should be a major factor in the decision process, not just the financial returns.
- Don't expect to steal the property. Be willing to pay a fair price for the condition it is in.
- If you don't like the property, the worst thing that could happen is that you will sell it. You'll probably break even or make a modest amount of money, and you will have learned a lot from the experience.
- 10% is a reasonable starting estimate for property management, when all of their fees are included
- Be sure to document all of your assumptions and why you selected the values. Check on your results six or twelve months after purchase to see where you guessed correctly and where you can improve (in other words, where you were wrong!). Figure out which variable really drove your results. Use this information to improve the quality of your forecasting for your next purchase.

What Types of Investor Should Buy a Small Rental?

Let's briefly review what we learned in Chapter 1. Below is a summary of the types of rental homes, apartments, and small buildings under five units you might want to consider. All of these investment types share the common feature that they are much easier to finance than their commercial brethren. Refer to the initial Chapter "Which Investment is Best for You?" to help select among these options.

Residential Property.   To be rented out to tenants, usually on a 12 month lease term. This is how most new landlords get started. You can hire out all of the property management functions, but in many cases you will do many of them on your own. These buildings usually have smaller down payment requirements than larger rental buildings. The purchase process and financing process is similar to what you experienced buying the home you live in now. It's a great way for beginners to get started.

Small (2-4 Unit) Apartment Building. Our goal is the purchase of a duplex, triplex or quad to be rented to tenants, usually for 12 month terms. In most markets they cost a little more than a rental home, but are much more likely to cash flow. There is less cash flow risk: if one unit is empty you have other tenants that still help you with the mortgage payment so it doesn't all come out of your pocket.

Many owners will start to delegate some of the property management tasks to an on-site assistant (typically the most responsible tenant), such as yard maintenance and showing empty units. The financing process is only slightly more involved than a residential loan. The relatively small down payment requirements make it accessible for first time investors. The purchase process is also very similar to purchasing a home.

Equity Needed is the liquid assets you and/or your investment team will need to have. A small rental home or condo will usually require 20% down. What is needed: **$10,000 and up**. **$20,000 would be typical.** 20%-25% of the purchase price as well as 6 months of PITI in reserves.

Credit Score will be important for some types of investments. If you can put down 20%, you can often purchase a small rental even if your credit is far less than perfect. What is needed for condos and homes: **Average.** You'll be purchasing the property, usually as a non-owner occupant (since you probably already have a primary residence). The mortgage companies will look at your credit score a little more closely than they will for your primary residence. As a rule of thumb, if you can qualify (even with a high interest rate) to buy a home to live in, you will be able to qualify to buy a home to rent out.

What is needed for 2-4 unit buildings: **Average.** The discussion for rental home and condo applies, but the standards, not surprisingly, are a little tighter when you get a slightly bigger building.

Experience with Contractors is not as important for rentals as it is for fix and flips or condo conversions. What is needed for four units or less: **None / Very Limited.** Things will break in the rental units a little more often than they do at your home. Even if you overpay to get a deluxe contractor that holds your hand through every step of the process (e.g., just go to Home Depot and hire their people), you are not going to significantly change the economics of your investment.

Experience with Property Managers makes purchasing a rental property easier and more fun. It certainly is not essential and you can learn by doing.
- What is needed for condos and homes: **None / Limited.** If you decide to hire a property manager, you'll need to get some experience in managing them, but most investors for this size of a rental manage the properties on their own. For most investors, it makes more economic sense to do it on their own and they learn many lessons first hand that enable them to better select and manage property managers in the future on their larger investments.
- What is needed for 2-4 unit buildings: **Limited (2–4 Projects).** For many investors, this is their follow-up rental investment, and they will start to experiment with delegation of at least some of the property management functions.

Time Required Each Week varies on the project specifics, but we'll make some broad generalizations so you have a sense of the level of commitment you'll have to make to improve your chances of success. We break the discussion into the number of hours to get started, then the number of recurring hours of effort each week to keep the investment working well.

What is needed to get started: **20+ hours.** You will want to spend time with your real estate agent discussing your needs, then hunt for properties, then manage the closing process. Once you close, there will be some one-time set up activities (set up checking account for building, notify tenants of new landlord and payment procedure, etc).

What is needed to keep going: **0 – 5 hours / week**. For the months when the property is full, you'll just have to mow the grass, shovel snow, or deal with the occasional tenant question. If you get someone on site to do the yard work, you'll have many weeks where you do nothing at all. When you have a vacancy you'll have to run an advertisement, answer some phone calls and do some showings (again, you might hire someone to do much of this for you), but it should not take too much time once you are in the rhythm of doing it.

The **Number of Monthly Interactions** is also important to some people. They are happy spending one or two long sessions on the property, but would be highly annoyed to have twenty very short interactions. Some people, due to home or work requirements, might have the opposite preference. We'll help set your expectations. In addition to understanding the number of hours required to be invested to be successful, some investors have different preferences for the number of interactions they will need to have.

Due to the balancing act of work and family, some prefer to have a smaller number of longer interactions, while others prefer many interactions of shorter duration. What is needed for condos and homes: **Average 1 – 5.** Should not require much on-going effort for the months when the unit is occupied; more effort when you are filling a vacancy. Less if you have management assistance. Most of the interactions will be very brief (e.g., following up on why rent is late, answering calls about a vacant unit).

What is needed for 2-4 units: **Average 1 – 10.** Similar to "rental condo" above; you just will have vacancies more frequently.

Perception of Hassle varies as much by individual as it does by project, but again, we can offer some broad guidelines. This is the toughest area to assess – what annoys one investor might be a challenging and fun puzzle to solve for the next.

What is needed: **Very Low – Moderate.** You will have the occasional person that never pays on time, irritates other tenants, or is the one complaining about every possible issue. Hopefully it is the exception and not the rule. Unless you are in a dreadfully bad renter's market, keeping your building occupied usually will not be too much of a problem.

Risk Tolerance is the level of comfort that you and the key people who influence your decisions have with risk and ambiguity. If you are going to be awake at 3AM every morning worrying about this decision, it may not be the right asset category for you. This is a critical factor that most new investors fail to assess.

Investment Class	Relative Degree of Risk and/or Uncertainty
Rental Condo	**Very Low.** The investment is easy to assess, easy to purchase, and easy to sell if you don't like it. A small condo is probably the easiest category of rental to manage. Like all rentals, the returns are fairly easy to predict and are not too volatile.
Rental Home	**Low.** Similar to rental condo, but you'll have to make arrangements for outside maintenance on your own… but you won't have HOA fees, either.
Small (2-4 unit) Apartment	**Low.** Less risky than rental condos and homes since you have more than one unit, so it's unlikely you would ever have to make a mortgage payment completely on your own. A little more risky than a condo or rental home since it (typically) costs more to purchase, and might take a little longer to sell.

How Much Can You Pay and Break Even?

Here is a quick analysis that you can perform before you go out into the field. It will give you a sense of what you can afford to pay for a unit to break even in your first year. It certainly is not perfect but it will give you a starting point. It is written from the perspective of analyzing a condo, but **the same template can also be used for a home**. Just eliminate the HOA line.

If there are dozens of condos for sale in the area in which you are interested, you can use the break even analysis here to quickly screen down the candidates to the handful that make the most sense for you. A few minutes invested here should save some time in the car driving around looking at properties at random.

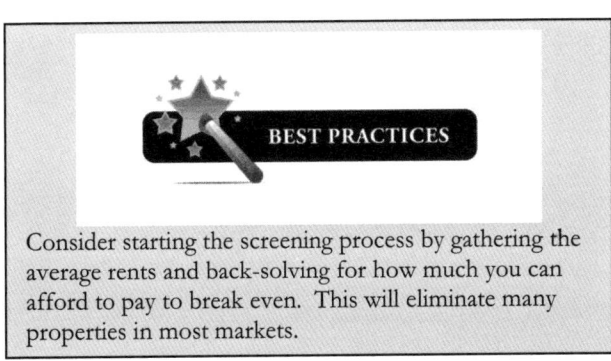

BEST PRACTICES

Consider starting the screening process by gathering the average rents and back-solving for how much you can afford to pay to break even. This will eliminate many properties in most markets.

If you hate math, be sure to find a real estate agent that is good at this, so they can do much of the lifting for you. Delegation should not be abdication – you should still take the time to understand the assumptions and the results from this analysis. Do not outsource your decision making. You, and only you, make the final decision.

Condo Rental Analysis Template

	1BR 1 Bath	2BR 1 Bath	2BR 2 Bath	3BR 2 Bath
"Average" rent for area / month	$1,100	$1,400	$1,500	$1,800
"Average" rent for area / year	$13,200	$16,800	$18,000	$21,600
Typical Vacancy Rate	5%	5%	5%	5%
Income after vacancy	$12,540	$15,960	$17,100	$20,520
Property Management	10%	10%	10%	10%
Income after property mgmt	**$11,286**	**$14,364**	**$15,390**	**$18,468**
HOA (annual)	$2,340	$2,621	$2,935	$3,288
Utilities (paid by tenant)	-	-	-	-
Maintenance @ 8%	$1,056	$1,344	$1,440	$1,728
Insurance if not in HOA	-	-	-	-
Advertising	$60	$60	$60	$60
Property taxes (annual)	$600	$700	$800	$900
Operating Expenses	**$4,056**	**$4,725**	**$5,235**	**$5,976**
NOI Net Operating Income	**$7,230**	**$9,639**	**$10,155**	**$12,492**
Down Payment %	25%	25%	25%	25%
Interest rate %	5.50%	5.50%	5.50%	5.50%
Maximum amount to pay	**$111,231**	**$148,295**	**$156,225**	**$192,189**

Email us at croberts@yourcastle.com to get a copy of this analysis template. Be sure to visit our web site at www.yourcastle.com to see what upcoming classes are available for investor education, too.

The first line is the **Average Rent Per Month** for the neighborhood you are considering. You can get this from your local Apartment Association if they collect rent and vacancy statistics. If they don't have what you need for your specific sub-area, drive around the neighborhood and write down the phone numbers on the for-rent signs that you see. Call and get a sense of the terms (and ideally, take a look at the units). Try www.zillow.com or www.rentometer.com. A third method to get the values would be from the classified advertisements in the newspaper. If you have a hard time getting a sense of the average rental value after trying all three methods, perhaps this neighborhood is primarily occupied by owners. That isn't necessarily a bad thing, but it is a good input to your decision process.

The next line is the average rent per month multiplied by twelve months in a year. Next, back out the **Average Vacancy Rate** for that area. Again, the Apartment Association will be the best source for this important information. Next, back out an allowance for **Property Management** if you plan to hire out that task. This gives us the expected **Income** for properties of different sizes.

Now we'll review expenses on an annual basis. If you are considering condos, ask your real estate agent to pull some active listings in the area that you are considering and take an average of the **HOA Fees** for each size of unit you would be willing to purchase. Be sure to adjust them, as some will be reported annually, some might be quarterly, and some (most) should be monthly. If you are considering a rental home, then the HOA will be zero in most cases.

Include a **utility estimate** if the owner is responsible for anything that is not included in the HOA. For condos this usually will be nothing, but for homes you will want to include a value. If you are not sure what the average utilities are for this area, try calling the utility providers. Many times you can give them an address or a zip code and they can provide you with a range.

Estimate the **maintenance expense** that you want to set aside each year. For a condo, the HOA will be responsible for common areas and exterior maintenance in many cases, but the owner will still pay for all interior maintenance. Somewhere in the 6 – 10% range for a small unit is normal. If you are considering a home, include periodic exterior maintenance and yard work, if the tenant is not going to be responsible for it.

In many cases the **insurance** will be covered by the HOA, but you can call a few of the HOAs to find out what they include and what they don't.

Set aside a small reserve for **advertising.**

Finally, in most cases, you can get the **property taxes** from the MLS system. The sample active listings from your real estate agent will give you a good range of the expected taxes for a unit or home of a given size in a given area. Total these expenses to get your estimated **Annual Operating Expenses.**

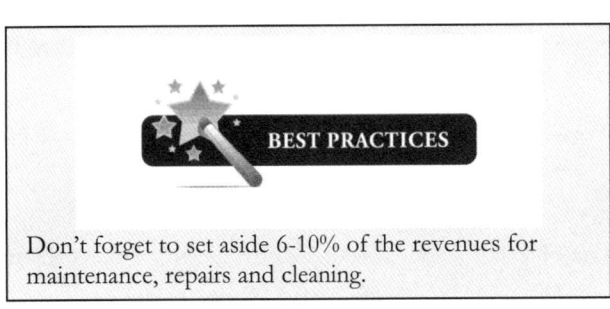

Don't forget to set aside 6-10% of the revenues for maintenance, repairs and cleaning.

The income after property management, less the annual operating expenses, gives you the **Net Operating Income,** or NOI. This is the money that would be left for you if you paid cash for the building. In most cases you will have a mortgage. Estimate what percentage of the purchase price you will put down in cash and the interest rate that will be required with a down payment of that size. Your Loan Officer can help you with the tradeoffs on this. As always, the larger the cash down payment percentage, the lower the interest rate will be.

Keep in mind that nicer units and/or more amenities (e.g., a pool) will command higher rents… and you can afford to pay more for such a unit and still break even (or better).

To find **your maximum purchase price**, you can ask your Mortgage Broker to calculate it for you, or you can do it yourself with a spreadsheet or a financial calculator. If you have Microsoft Excel on your computer, you can use the following formula to calculate how much you can afford to pay:

$$= PV \text{ (Interest Rate } / 12, 360, \text{ - Net Operating Income } / 12) / (1 - \text{Down payment \%})$$

The first part takes the annual interest rate and divides by twelve to get a monthly interest rate. The "360" is the duration of the loan in months (12 months per year for 30 years). The third part is the amount you can afford to pay each month (the annual NOI / 12). The final part makes an adjustment for your cash down payment percentage.

Congratulations! Now you know the maximum that you can afford to pay for a given unit and break even on your cash flow in the first year. In this example, you could afford to pay $57,300 for an "average" one bedroom one bath condo (putting 20% down) and you could reasonably expect to break even in the first year. If you bought the average unit for less than that, you should have some positive cash flow. If you pay more, you might need to subsidize the unit for a period of time. Subsidizing can be desirable if you believe that the appreciation potential of the area is strong.

In the second year, your rents will (hopefully) go up slightly, as will your expenses, due to inflation. Rents often go up a little faster (say, 1%) than expenses. Additionally, since the expenses are quite a bit smaller than your rents, the net effect of inflation for most rental properties is that the cash flow (NOI) increases quite a bit. Since your mortgage payment does not change (assuming your rate is fixed for the first few years), the cash flow that you get to spend increases significantly. Woo-Hoo!

Impact of Property Condition on Rents and Cash flow

Nicer units in better condition, larger units, or the units that include a reserved parking space, will command more than units on the garden level, units with shoddy levels of cleanliness or maintenance, or that are smaller. Condo complexes that are newer with more amenities (e.g., a nicer swimming pool, work out room, or club house) might get higher rents than the older condo complex next door without these amenities.

You could do the same analysis for one size of unit at the low rent, at an average rent, and at a high rent to see how the condition of the units and the features of the community impact the potential price that you could pay.

Our objective from this exercise is to get you thinking about:
- The average rent in an area, and its range
- The impact of features and conditions of the property on those rents
- How the condition of the property might impact some of your expenses, such as the HOA and your unit's maintenance budget

Condo Rental Analysis Template

Condition	Poor	Average	Excellent
	1BR	1BR	1BR
	1 Bath	1 Bath	1 Bath
"Average" rent for area / month	$900	$1,100	$1,300
"Average" rent for area / year	$10,800	$13,200	$15,600
Typical Vacancy Rate	5%	5%	5%
Income after vacancy	$10,260	$12,540	$14,820
Property Management	10%	10%	10%
Income after property mgmt	**$9,180**	**$11,220**	**$13,260**
HOA (annual)	$2,340	$2,574	$2,830
Utilities (paid by tenant)	-	-	-
Maintenance @ 8%	$864	$1,056	$1,248
Insurance if not in HOA	-	-	-
Advertising	$60	$60	$60
Property taxes (annual)	$550	$600	$650
Operating Expenses	**$3,814**	**$4,290**	**$4,788**
NOI Net Operating Income	**$5,366**	**$6,930**	**$8,472**

You will often find that the condo communities with fewer features will have a lower HOA – they may not have a pool or a clubhouse to maintain. The nicer condos will have more features and command higher rents, but have slightly higher HOAs. As you look at the alternatives in your target neighborhood, you will get a sense of these tradeoffs, and they will certainly be inputs to your decision.

Similarly, rundown units that have not had much maintenance or renovation work will be likely to have a higher level of maintenance spending in the near future than units that have been well cared for. Finally, the nicer units that cost a bit more to purchase will likely also have higher property taxes.

Looking at Potential Properties

Selecting the Right Type of Property. Before you jump in the car to look at properties, take some time to read and reflect on the "Rental Property Fundamentals" chapter. We review a number of types of properties that you are likely to come across. We also outlined different types of renters, and which types of renters are likely to be the best fits with different types of buildings. Hopefully, you have a sense of some categories that sound appealing to you and some that you really are not interested in. It might make sense to spend a few hours with your real estate agent to see one or two examples of each type of property in the markets that you are still willing to consider. Narrow it down by property type and neighborhood. This will reduce your set of properties to consider from an overwhelming number of choices to a very reasonable number.

It's OK to Want Something Nice. Keep in mind for many of the types of properties, you won't be renting out to people just like yourself and your friends, and the properties you are considering are places where you might not ever want to live. That is OK as long as the property's features are consistent with what the likely renters will want for features. If you just are not comfortable with that – that's OK! Most first time landlords don't want to buy in a "slum area"; they tend to be most comfortable with nicer neighborhoods renting to people they like and can relate to. That's absolutely fine, and it is, in fact, how most successful investors get started.

It's OK to want to buy a nice property with nice tenants in a nice area. The cash flow will be lower than the other alternatives on the market, but you can still do well financially. Your comfort level should be a major factor in the decision process, not just the raw financial returns.

Questions to Keep in Mind. When you are looking at properties, think about:
- What types of tenants live here now?
- Are these types of tenants likely to be the best types of people for this type of building?
- Would I be comfortable working with these types of people?
- Does this property need a lot of work? Is it the kind of work that I would enjoy doing (or would at least like to try to learn how to do?). If not, would I feel comfortable hiring people to do it for me?
- Do the pro-forma numbers we have assembled look realistic?

Don't Expect the Deal of the Century. We'll often see first-time investors get obsessed with finding the deal of the century. This is often due to unrealistic (uh…moronic) expectations they get from seminars, books, and infomercials. The deal of the century comes just about that often. Your goal should be to pay a fair price for a solid property. It'd be nice to get it at a slight discount but don't be fooled by appraised values, tax assessments, listing material hogwash, etc. The gurus rarely mention this, but rental buildings (duplexes and up) are much less commonly foreclosed on than single family homes and condos. It's very rare for large apartment buildings to go into foreclosure. People smart enough to build the capital over years to be able to afford an apartment building are usually too smart to let an investor get a "great deal" purchasing from them. Gurus, however, make millions of dollars convincing new investors otherwise.

If you are buying a property that has a problem (e.g., high vacancy) or needs maintenance work, the price should be discounted enough to compensate you for your time to correct the issue.

Don't expect to steal the property. Be willing to pay a fair price for the condition it is in.

You Don't Have to Do This Forever. About the worst thing that could happen is that you buy the property then decide that you don't like it. And then you sell it. You'll likely still get all of your principal back and might even still make a little bit of money. And you will have learned a lot of in process. This isn't like a marriage commitment that you have to keep for the rest of your life!

The Easiest Approach for Newbies

If you are completely new to rentals and want to get involved with the least amount of trauma, you are what real estate agents call a "Retail" investor. You will want to pick a neighborhood where you are comfortable, or perhaps like so much that you would even consider living there. You will want to work with tenants that you can relate with easily. And you will probably want the minimum of maintenance headaches. You can make a great living investing in properties like this. For a great review of just this section of the market, please see Suzanne P. Thomas' book, *"Rental Houses for the Successful Small Investor."* The material in this section is a synthesis of material from her book and from our observations working with hundreds of investors.

BEST PRACTICES

If you don't like the property, the worst thing that could happen is that you will sell it. You'll probably break even or make a modest amount of money, and you will have learned a lot from the experience.

Buy a Condo or Single Family Home. The types of tenants you will most enjoy working with are going to want a single family home or a condo. They will have jobs, which you can relate to, and they are more likely to work in a field like you are involved in. They will be quite a bit more affluent than the tenants you find in apartment buildings, as discussed in the "Rental Property Fundamentals" chapter. If you decide after a period of time that you are not really enjoying being a landlord, these types of investments will be slightly easier to sell than a small apartment building (and significantly easier to sell than a large apartment building).

Focus on Newer Properties. Your tenants, just like other people, want a nice place to live. Most of the design features that have been incorporated into homes in the last ten to fifteen years will be appealing to them as well. Examples include larger windows, open floor plans, larger closets and larger bathrooms. Newer properties will have the additional advantage of requiring less maintenance than older properties. Finally, if you are living in a newer property yourself, you are likely to live relatively close to several potential housing developments that could be good rentals. Older buildings tend to be located in specific, older parts of the city, usually closer to the downtown area.

Focus on Price Point. You will need to use the break even analysis described earlier in this chapter to determine which homes are most likely to have positive, or at least break even, cash flow.

ANALYTICAL TEMPLATES

How to Analyze Your Potential Investment's Return in Year One

After you have found a specific unit that interests you, you and/or your real estate agent can run the specific number for the property to see if it is a good deal for you. Earlier in this chapter, we looked at a generic analysis template and a discussion of how to analyze a generic investment. Now, we'll review some specific considerations for the smaller building – condo, home, or two- to four-plex.

Warning! All too often we see first-time investors get locked into "analysis paralysis." Some are not good at math but feel they have to make an effort at running the numbers. Others are good with math and want to analyze the property with ninety different what-if scenarios. It's important to spend some time with the numbers to get a sense of whether the project is viable or not. But you will also have to listen to what your gut is telling you and determine your comfort level with the risk of real estate investing. Don't skip the numbers, but don't make it an exercise in overkill, either.

Unit 1: 1BR	1,075
Unit 2: 1BR	1,100
unit 3: 2BR	1,400
Gross Rent (Monthly)	**$3,575**
Gross Rent (Annual)	**$42,900**
Square Footage	3,600
Rent $/Foot	$0.99
Rent reasonable-ness	Low
Prop Mgmt (10%)	358
Gross income (monthly)	**$3,218**
Annualized	$38,610
Vacancy @4.5%	$1,931
Net Income (annual)	**$36,680**

Email us at croberts@yourcastle.com to get a copy of this analysis template.

Rents. The top few lines for income are either the actual values from the leases currently in place, or the estimated market rents you gathered from your research if the building is currently vacant.

Property Management. Let's assume you will not be managing the rental and will hire a property management firm. Ten percent of rents is a reasonable estimate. Smaller buildings and condos will tend to have a higher percentage fee than larger buildings, as there are some fixed cost elements to providing a property management service. The smaller the number of units to spread the costs, the higher the percentage fee has to be. You can do it for less if you have an on-site person that does some of the work for you, and if you do some of the work as well. We'll review this in more detail in the chapter on property management. If you plan to do all of the work yourself, then 0% is your value and your bottom line will look much better.

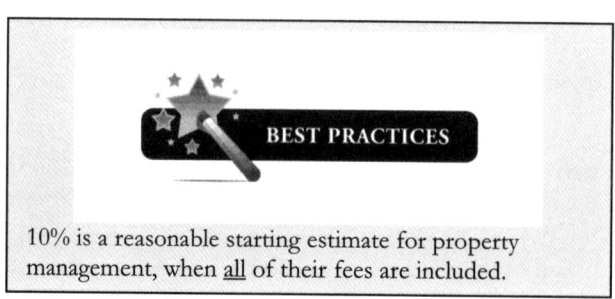

BEST PRACTICES

10% is a reasonable starting estimate for property management, when all of their fees are included.

Rate (5yr fixed)	5%
Purchase Price	$310,000
Proposed LTV	75%
Loan Amount	$232,500
Cash Invested:	$77,500
Annual Interest	$11,625
Annual Cash Flow (fx)	**$10,847**
Cash on Cash Return (5yr)	**14%**
Property Apprec %	4%
Property Apprecation	$12,400
Total Return (5yr fx)	**$23,247**
Total Annual Return (5yr fx)	**30%**

Financing. Since you most likely won't pay all cash for your property, you will want to consider the impact of financing. Financing requirements change all the time, but let's assume you put 25% down and finance at 75% LTV.

Evaluating Your Project. Six months or a year after making the purchase, check how you are doing and compare it to your assumptions to learn which assumptions were good and which were not. The next time you make a purchase, your projections will hopefully improve.

BEST PRACTICES

Be sure to document all of your assumptions and why you selected the values. Check on your results six or twelve months after purchase to see where you guessed correctly and where you can improve. Figure out which variable really drove your results. Use this information to improve the quality of your forecasting for your next purchase.

Chapter 7: Short Sales

In the ever changing real estate market short sales have developed into a great opportunity to acquire properties. A short sale is defined by the U.S. Department of Housing and Urban Development as the process that allows the mortgagor in default to sell his/her home and use the net sale proceeds to satisfy the mortgage debt even though these proceeds are less than the amount owed. A foreclosure is a legal procedure that occurs when the borrower defaults and the lender exercises its right to get its money back or take possession of the property. The foreclosure is an action taken by the lender when the terms of the contract (the Deed of Trust) are not met and the borrower is in default. The contract that the borrower signs with the lender does require the borrower to follow certain contract terms or the lender can repossess the property. If the borrower violates this contract the lender can accelerate the loan and make the full amount of the loan principle and any fees due immediately. In many cases, the house is not worth the amount that is due to the lender and therefore will not sell at an amount that will cover all loans on the house. The borrower may then try to "short sale" the property and negotiate a new amount owed to resell the property at the new market value. Short sales are common in a recession and rare in a solid market.

There are many common terms that are used in the pre foreclosure process. We have defined a few of these below.

- Notice of Election and Demand (NED)

    - A notice indicating the time, date, and other particulars or a proposed foreclosure sale date.

- Intent to Cure

    - A notice advising the lender or trustee of the intent of a borrower to bring a defaulted loan current or to otherwise cure a pending default.

- Redemption

    - A legal right afforded to foreclosed borrowers that gives them the post-foreclosure right to reclaim foreclosed property after the foreclosure sale upon the payment of all defaulted amounts, costs, and fees.

- Deficiency Judgment

    - Imposition of personal liability on a borrower for the unpaid balance of mortgage debt after a foreclosure has failed to yield the full amount of the debt which was due and owing at the time of the foreclosure.

- Loss Mitigator

    - Person that is assigned by the lender to negotiate any sales before the foreclosure sale.

- BPO – Broker Pricing Opinion

    - An estimate of the value of real property based on recent sales research by a real estate broker or real estate agent, typically ordered by a bank, lender, or investor to determine the market value of the property.

Colorado Foreclosure Protection Act:
- Once the NED is filed and until the foreclosure is discharged, compliance with the requirements of the law is **mandatory**
- Defines and regulates actions of groups
- Foreclosure Consultant – charges a fee for service/advice
- Equity Purchasers – acquires ownership interest in the property
- Associate – 3rd party to the transaction (friend, shill, partner)
- Specific requirements, including specific disclosures and rights of cancellation for the homeowner, must be followed
- Penalties include up to one year in jail, fines of $25,000, and contracts may be void if the law is not followed (including font size requirements!)

- Contracts must be written in English, or written by a Certified Translator into the language "Principally spoken by the homeowner" = whatever language is spoken at home
- Specifically affects transactions where the Seller is living in the house, it is their primary residence, and the buyer is not going to occupy the home
- The language of the law is broad and untested...it is STRONGLY RECOMMENDED to seek the counsel of a qualified attorney before getting involved in any transaction in which the property is in foreclosure (after the NED is filed and before redemption period had expired for all parties)
- At time of publishing this is the web address with the actual language of the Colorado Foreclosure Protection Act: http://www.leg.state.co.us/CLICS2006A/csl.nsf/fsbillcont3/D270FC0D5FFAE9AC872570AF007E3BEC?Open&file=071_enr.pdf
- Foreclosure Consultants: who is exempted under the Colorado Foreclosure Protection Act.
    - Lawyers
    - A lender, or its attorney, who has a lien or deed of trust on the property while performing services in connection with that lien or deed of trust
    - Anyone who is operating under the banking, trust, insurance, or escrow laws
    - The person originating or closing a loan if the loan is subject to RESPA
    - A judgment creditor where the judgment is recorded and any corresponding legal action started before the foreclosure
    - Title insurance companies or agents while performing services
    - Licensed real estate agents and brokers so long as they are performing real estate services within the normal scope that they are licensed for
    - A non-profit that only gives advice unless that non-profit is associated with someone who is deemed a foreclosure consultant

Who is NOT an equity purchaser:
- People buying for their personal residence to be used for at least 1 year
- Holders of debt, and their associates, who get a deed in lieu of foreclosure and the lien was recorded before the foreclosure began
- Holders of Public Trustee or Sheriff's deed after the sale
- If a court transfers ownership to you
- If you get the deed from your spouse, close relative, guardian, conservator or personal representative
- If you obtain the property while performing normal business activities, duties, or services under any banking, trust, insurance, title, or escrow regulation

So, an equity purchaser is basically an investor that purchases the home for the purposes of making a profit from the purchase.

Foreclosure Timeline At-A-Glance:

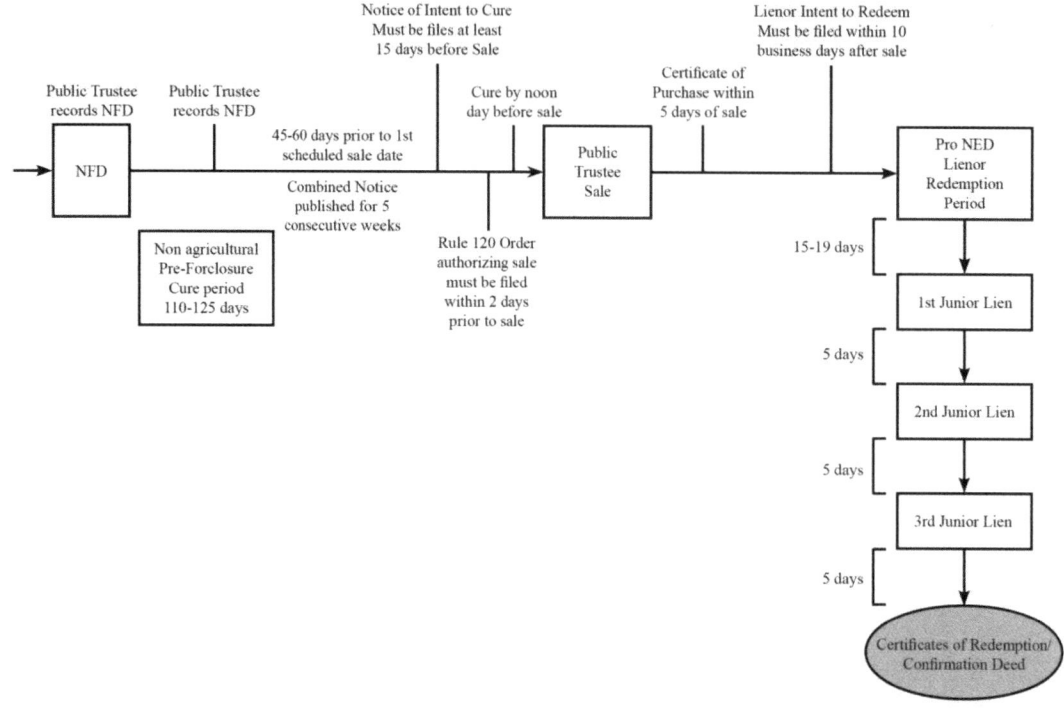

1. Lender notifies the Trustee of the default; this is the official beginning of the foreclosure process.
2. Trustee files a notice of default with the county courthouse or recorder's office. This document identifies the Trustor, Trustee, and Beneficiary. This notice also includes amount of loan and amount of default. A copy of this default is sent to all interested parties including any lien holders, homeowners, and any other entity identified on title.
3. A sale date is set no less than 110 days from Notice of Election and Demand. This is the cure period and where short sale negotiations take place.
4. The public Trustee sale is advertised.
5. Property is sold to highest bidder or taken back by lender at the Public Trustee auction.
6. Only junior lien holders whose liens were recorded prior to the Notice of Election and Demand have redemption rights and must file intent to redeem within 8 days of Public Trustee Auction.

What are the options the homeowner has if facing a foreclosure? The homeowner can cure the default in full; this would include any back payments, fines, and late fees. Loan modifications are a very popular option for many homeowners that qualify. A deed in Lieu of Foreclosure is an option where the homeowner can hand over the deed to the house in an agreement with the lender to stop the foreclosure process. In some rare cases the homeowner can still refinance the defaulted loan. If there is some equity still in the house the homeowner can sell the property and pay off all the debt including back payments and penalties. Negotiating a short sale is also a viable option for many homeowners that are behind in payments and the current value of their home is less than what they owe. The final option, which is certainly not recommended, is to do nothing and let the foreclosure process go through completion. It is best to speak with an expert in each of these fields to see which option is best for the homeowner. Ultimately the homeowner will need to take action and try one or all of these options if facing a foreclosure.

Many homeowners believe that filing a bankruptcy will stop a foreclosure. Unfortunately, this is a common myth that is wrong. In the State of Colorado a bankruptcy filing only delays the foreclosure process. For example, if the NED had been filed with the county public trustee and the foreclosure was at day 30 when the homeowner filed bankruptcy, the lender and the public trustee would stop the foreclosure process at the time of the bankruptcy filing. This usually delays the foreclosure by 3-6 months while the lender requests the home be pulled out of the bankruptcy procedures. Once the house is pulled from the bankruptcy filing the foreclosure process begins right where it was. So if the bankruptcy filing was on day 30 and the lender gets the house released from the bankruptcy, the foreclosure is now in day 31 of the foreclosure process with the public trustee. Filing bankruptcy may only delay the inevitable for the homeowner and the homeowner should talk to a qualified attorney before considering this option to delay the foreclosure.

So, now that we have an understanding of the foreclosure process in Colorado, who the stakeholders are in the process, and the options a homeowner has, how do many investors purchase homes for profit that are in pre-foreclosure? The most common and probably easiest way is to work with a realtor that will represent you, the investor, as a buyers' agent. As an investor you will need to identify what your target market is because investors have varying requirements based on price, location, condition, rentability, etc. After you have determined this with your real estate professional you will need to identify those properties that have been described in the MLS as a possible short sale property. Unfortunately, there is no standard way in the metro area regarding how a listing agent describes a short sale. Many of the common terms used for short sales are as follows:

- Short Sale
- Preforeclosure
- Lender approval required
- 3rd party approval required
- SS Pending Lender approval
- Bank approval required

The key to purchasing a short sale is twofold. First, as an investor you must use the correct contract that has all of the verbiage approved under the Colorado Foreclosure Protection Act. An astute real estate professional can help ensure that all interested parties are following the correct procedures. Second, you must be very patient. In many ways time is on your side. If an investor can put in a very qualified offer and wait out the prolonged timeline you will outlast most of your competition. Many homebuyers do not have the time or the patience to wait an extra three to six months (or longer) for a short sale to be approved. Unfortunately, many lenders have so many short sale requests that the process can be long and drawn out. So, if you can hang in there you can probably get some great deals simply by outlasting the competition. Another tactic you can take is to find short sales that have been on the Multiple Listing Service (MLS) for a prolonged period and contact the listing agent to see if there are any buyers that are still hanging around. Many times if the process has taken a very long time they may be close to an approval and all of the buyers that were around nine months ago have decided to move on. Again, the key is to learn the process thoroughly or use a real estate professional that understands the process and can counsel you on the intricacies of a short sale negotiation.

As an investor, you may prefer to find homeowners in distress before they have listed the property with a real estate professional and work with the homeowner directly. Next, we will discuss the tried and true method of finding, negotiating, and purchasing these homes. This is very much the hands-on method of purchasing pre-foreclosure properties. Beware, though, that this may not be for the faint of heart, as this involves much more time, work and expertise. However, there is potential to find great deals!

The first step to working with a distressed homeowner is finding a homeowner that needs your help. The list below are some of the most common ways.

- All NED filings must be published, so a great source of homeowners and addresses are listed in daily newspapers.

- Since the NED is a public notification, many counties have the NED lists published on their websites or publish those lists to public in various ways. The best way to figure out how the county publishes the NED lists is to call the public trustee or the clerk and recorder with the county and simply ask.

- Solicit homeowners in need. This can include

- We buy houses signs – check with your local municipality on the legality of posting these signs.

- Mailers to geographic areas or by obtaining address lists of homeowners.

- Hanging flyers door-to-door letting homeowners in that area know you are an investor interested in purchasing distressed properties

- Leads from local businesses, neighbors, postal workers, real estate professionals, mortgage professionals

- Knocking on doors. Many times you can get the NED list and knock on the doors of the people that are on that list.

- There are also commercial for-profit list providers that will send you the NED list, recent divorces, deaths, tax liens, etc.

After you have been contacted by the homeowner by using your advertising or referral base you must perform a little background information on the property. It is best to have your title company pull an owners and encumbrances (O&E) report. This report will notify you of who is on title, what liens are attached to the property, and any other information that has been recorded with this property. The first and most important thing you must do is make sure that you are actually going to go meet with a person that is qualified to sell the home. You will not get anywhere if you are talking to the wrong person! After you have determined that you are talking to the correct person, take a look at how many lenders you will be dealing with. Note that you must negotiate some type of amount with each lien holder (e.g., lenders, HOA, Mechanic's liens, city/county, IRS). Now that you know what types of negotiations you will be up against you need to sit down with the homeowner and make sure that they will be willing to work with you. Remember, it is not only up to the lien holders to accept your offer, you must also work with the homeowner during this entire process.

When you prepare to meet with the homeowner it is best to gets some comparable sales of the area. Make sure to get comps of homes that are both distressed and non-distressed so you can go to the homeowner with a qualified offer that you believe will be accepted by the lender(s). It is best to bring both the Owners and Encumbrances (O&E) report and the comps so you can have an intelligent conversation with them about the real value of the home and what they currently owe. Many times the homeowner is already so far behind or has no idea of what liens are attached to the home. When you first meet with the homeowner get to know them a little and LISTEN. Listen to how they got into their situation and let them tell you what they would like the ultimate outcome to be. You are there to help them solve a major crisis in their lives. One thing that you must make very clear is that if this is their primary residence, under the Colorado Foreclosure Protection Act, you cannot take over their loan and make payments and that they will not be able to rent the house back from you after the completion of the short sale. After this sometimes very tough conversation you must do your due diligence while in the property. You will need to take a property worksheet where you can go through the house and mark what deficiencies exist in the home. This worksheet will help you craft the amount you would be willing to pay and some negotiating points you have with the lenders. A great example is if the house has a roof problem with obvious leaks, you will need to take pictures and send this into the lender with notations on the amount anticipated repairs will be. Also, note the neighborhood and the condition of this home as compared to other homes on the block. If this property is in pristine condition the BPO that the bank orders may come in high. If the home is the "ugly duckling" on the block you may have more room to negotiate a lower price. Many times you can get all the information you need with one visit with the homeowner. However, each situation is different and you may need to have multiple meetings with some homeowners. After your walk through you must sit with the homeowner and discuss what you would be willing to pay for the house. Many times this will be lower than what the homeowner thinks their house is worth. You must be prepared with your information on where you derived that value based on comps, condition of the home, and general market conditions.

After you come to an agreement with the homeowner on price you must gather the following documents from them. Every lender has different requirements, but the list below has common documents that every lender we're worked with requests in their short sale packets.

- Recent mortgage statement or coupon showing balances, phone numbers, contact information for all mortgages and liens
- 2-3 Most recent bank statements
- 2-3 Most recent pay stubs

- 1-2 years tax returns/W-2's
- Home Owner's Association (HOA) Management Company/Phone
- Letter of Authorization
- Purchase contract with short sale addendum
- Hardship letter
- Financial worksheet

The Hardship letter is simply a letter to the lender that describes how the borrower ended up in their current situation and why they can no longer make payments. Many times major life events have caused their irreversible situation. Common hardships are medical, job loss, job placement in a new city, divorce, etc. The hardship letter is not meant to be a book on the borrower's entire life, rather it is one to two pages that summarize what has happened.

The financial worksheet describes what they currently make as well as all of the bills and payments to other sources that they are obligated to pay. For example, if the borrower purchased a home with a two income household and there was a job loss, many times the single remaining income will not allow them to make payments on all of the debt owed. Remember to include all payments, including but not restricted to all lien holders, food, gas, car payments, taxes, credit cards, child care, alimony, medical, insurance, tuition. Many times after going through this exercise with a borrower they come to the conclusion quickly that there is no way that they will be able to stay in the property. It is usually a very eye opening experience.

Now that you have successfully negotiated with the homeowner and they are willing to go forward with you, the hard work begins. Negotiating with lenders and lien holders is a laborious process that takes a lot of patience and diligence on your behalf. Since you have all of the lender information you collected from the homeowner, you should first call the numbers on the payment stubs and confirm the number where you're sending the short sale packet. The first person you talk to will never be the final decision maker so just get the fax number and send in your completed packet.

Below is the list of documents that most lenders require to begin a short sale. We recommend that you send in the documents in the order below. Remember to put the name, address, and loan numbers of the borrower on every document.

- Cover Letter
- Sellers Authorization
- Listing Contract
- Purchase Contract
- Short Sale Addendum
- Hardship Letter
- Financial Statement
- Copies of Pay Stubs (or Alternative)
- Copies of Bank Statements (or Alternative)
- Copies of Tax Returns (or Alternative)
- Appraisal or Comparables
- Repairs Worksheet
- HUD-1 Settlement Statement
- **<u>HAVE CLIENTS NAME, ADDRESS, AND LOAN NUMBER ON EVERY DOCUMENT!!!!!</u>**

More than likely, you will need to submit this information more than once. Why? Lenders are notorious for losing information - if they lose the information just send it in again and follow up. Follow up often with lenders; do not let your file go to the bottom of the pile. Many times the first 15 to 30 days are spent shuffling paper back and forth with the lenders. It usually takes 7 to 10 business days for the lender to get all of the paperwork into their system. After the first 7 to 10 days they should have your letter of authorization on file so you can talk with the lender about moving forward with negotiations. The first few layers of contacts you have with the bank will be employees that have very limited and specific tasks. These first contacts you have with the lenders usually have no decision making capabilities. These employees are normally tasked to make sure all documents are there and in order. They can then usually escalate the file once all of the initial paperwork meets the criteria that has been set.

After working with the lender to get the paperwork in order you will then be assigned a contact, usually in the loss mitigation department. After the file has been assigned to a loss mitigator, the next step is for the bank to order either a BPO or an appraisal. This will be one of the most important steps in the negotiations with the bank. Depending on who actually owns the debt, the BPO will define the amount that the lender will approve. There is really no formula that an investor can use to guess what will be approved by various lenders. Every lender and debt holder has their own criteria on what they will take as an offer. Some lenders may take 50% of the BPO value while others will not take a penny less. It is important to keep following up with the lender during this time to see what the BPO amount is. Once an approved amount has been determined, the lender will wither accept, reject, or counter your offer. If the lender rejects your offer it is up to you to determine how much you would be willing to pay for the property. Many lenders will not tell you their "magical" number, instead they will want you to keep submitting until you reach the approved amount.

Usually, the most important lien holder that you will negotiate with is the lender in first position. However, your negotiations must be made with all lenders and lien holders on the property. Even though the lender in the second lien position may not recoup any money if the property were to go to foreclosure you still must get an approved short sale with them. Same with HOA, city and county, IRS, and mechanics liens. It is crucial that all lien holders give written approval of a short sale before you can close the transaction. The process is basically the same with all lien holders. The lenders want to see why the borrower is in default. Lenders want to see what the borrower's current situation is and verify they truly will not be able to make payments going forward. There are a couple of lien holders that are exceptions to this rule. Many times Home Owner Associations are owed up to 6 months of dues. Most HOA's will negotiate with you if you can prove to them that you have a successful short sale negotiation with the banks in progress. The IRS can be a little tougher. However, they are like many other lien holders - they do want to get paid and the file off their books. Finally, Mechanics liens can sometimes be very hard to find. Many times if the lien holder does not have current information on the recorded lien it is very difficult to find that person. The lien holder will be notified in the NED filing from the county but may not respond. In this case you will need to work with your title company. If you do get in touch with the mechanics lien holder you can usually explain the situation and negotiate with that party as well. Remember to get everything in writing before going to closing.

Now that you have successfully negotiated with the homeowner and all of the lien holders you must coordinate the closing with the title company. The banks will give you a payoff and a short sale acceptance letter that is usually on good for a limited amount of time. Hopefully, you have been communicating with the homeowner during the negotiations process and they are aware that you will be closing the transaction in the next few weeks. Be sure to use a title company that is experienced in working with lenders on short sales. The transaction does require more work and coordination for the title company. Many deals have been lost at the end of the process so make sure you have everything in order. The next step is to set the closing up and once again verify with all lien holders, the title company and the homeowner that all documents are ready to go at the closing table.

Now that you know a little about how to purchase short sales, let's go over some frequently asked questions that may occur during the short sale process. Please note that the answers below are answers that the authors have been advised to tell clients. Consult with your attorney and tax advisors with your specific questions and concerns.

1. When does the foreclosure process begin?

    a. The Official start date of the foreclosure process in the State of Colorado is when the NED is filed with the county.

2. What will show up on my credit if we successfully negotiate a short sale with the lien holders?

    a. Both short sales and foreclosures may show negative facts as delinquent payment history, a balance remaining owed on an unpaid mortgage, or charge off. The main difference between a short sale and a foreclosure is that a foreclosure will be a public record on credit for 7 years, while the short sale is not listed as a public record.

3. Will I have to pay the lender the difference between the amount owed and the accepted short sale amount?

a. The short sale will result in a deficiency owed to the lender. The deficiency may result in collection of the debt owed, tax consequence, neither, or both. The final terms with the lender will determine how the lender handles the deficiency. Three of the most common options for the lender are; lump sum payment at closing, a pre-determined payment plan, or forgiveness of debt. Obviously the third option is preferred. This is the option that you will try to get for the borrower and it must be clearly stated in the short sale acceptance letter. Always advise the borrower to seek consultation from a CPA or tax professional.

4. What are the tax consequences of short sales?

a. If the lender discharges the debt the lender may issue a 1099-c. Advise the borrower to seek professional tax counsel to determine how to handle the discharged debt. There have been many laws passed by Congress to help troubled homeowners in this situation. Every situation is unique.

5. Why would a lender accept a short sale as opposed to going through with the foreclosure?

a. Believe it or not, lenders save a substantial amount of money by successfully negotiating a short sale. It is very expensive for the lenders to use attorneys to file paperwork, take control of the property, and then resell the home as a Real Estate Owned (REO) property. Short sales save the lender many of these costs and banks prefer not to hold properties as REO.

6. How long do I have before I have to move out?

a. The foreclosure process for residential properties is 110 - 125 days from the NED filing to the foreclosure sale in the State of Colorado. The process can be extended by the lender if they chose to do so in order to allow for more time for negotiations.

7. What are my options as a homeowner?

a. Paying the defaulted amount in full, loan modification, selling the property for what you owe including fees, deed-in-lieu, short sale, nothing.

8. Can I stay in the property?

a. If the homeowner is using the property as their primary residence the answer is clearly no. The Colorado Foreclosure Protection Act will not allow the seller to have the buyer occupy the property after closing.

9. As the homeowner, will I make any money in this transaction?

a. No, the lender is taking less than what is currently owed. The HUD-1 must clearly state that the borrower will get nothing from the transaction. Money settled outside of the HUD-1 would be a RESPA violation.

10. Do I need a real estate agent to do a short sale?

a. A licensed real estate agent is not required to complete a short sale transaction. However, many lenders do require a listing agreement and want proof of an MLS listing. If the seller chooses to use a real estate agent it would be advisable to use someone that has experience with short sales. This is not a normal transaction and expertise in short sales will benefit the homeowner. Also, the buyer must use the correct clauses in the purchase contract that coincides with the Colorado Foreclosure Protection Act.

Chapter 8: House Hacking

(Thank you to Chris Lopez for your input on this Chapter!)

House hacking is a term used to describe a number of different ways to invest in real estate beyond the traditional means. It usually involves buying a primary residence, living at the property, and in addition renting out the extra rooms or units to tenants. After a period of time (often one year later for tax purposes), the investor may buy another property, move into it, and turn the original property into a rental. The concept is decades old but the phrase "house hacking" is a new term which has taken on enormous popularity with millennials looking to build wealth with real estate. It's a phenomenal way to start investing but of course it's not everyone.

Here are common house hacking examples we have seen around Denver:
- House/Condo/Townhome - Live in the master bedroom and rent out the additional bedrooms individually and share the living space.
- Duplex, triplex, or fourplex - Live in one unit and rent out the other(s).
- Duplex, triplex, or fourplex - Live in one unit, rent out the other(s) and also rent out the additional bedroom(s) in the unit the investor occupies.
- House with carriage house or accessory dwelling unit (ADU) (another house on the lot) - Live in one house and rent out the other.
- Ranch style house with basement unit or mother-in-law suite - Live in the main house (or basement suite) and rent out the other unit.
- Short term rental (Airbnb) or long term rental - Find a long term tenant or rent it out on Airbnb for higher rents.
- And on and on and on. There is no limit, just your creativity and willingness to live with or near your tenants!

Favorable Financing

One of the main advantages to house hacking is that since you're living in your house hacked property, you're eligible for the incredibly favorable owner-occupied financing options. Why? Let's say Mr. Homeowner owns a nice house where his spouse, two kids, and Fido live. He also owns a rental property across town. What happens when Mr. Homeowner loses his job and can only afford one mortgage payment? Which one does he stop paying? Of course, he stops paying on the rental property!

Lenders realize this and offer stricter terms for investment loans. That's the basic reason why investor financing has higher interest rates and requires more money down than owner occupant financing – it's more risk for the banks. You can a buy primary residence for as low as 0% down (see below). The typical investment loan requires 20% down. The lower down payment for an owner occupied property, compared to an investment loan, is a significant amount of cash to the would-be investor. The down payment savings by house hacking allows investors to buy a property right away rather than waiting years saving for a 20% down payment.

Loan Type	Down Payment %	Down Payment for $300k Property
Investment	20% or more	$60,000
VA	0%	$0
FHA	3.5%	$10,500
Conventional	3%	$9,000

One thing to keep in mind is that typically, lenders will not consider the potential rental income from your Denver house hack for loan qualifications. You must qualify for the loan based on your income and creditworthiness without taking into account the rent you plan to make from the spare rooms or additional units. Make sure you discuss your various options with a qualified mortgage professional!

House Hacking Financial Model

To help you better understand the incredible opportunities available with house hacking we built a spreadsheet model to show you the numbers. Here is how the spreadsheet model works:

- You buy a property, live there, and rent out the bedrooms or other units.
- 2 years later, you buy a second property, live there, and rent out extra rooms/units. You keep Property 1 and turn it into a traditional rental property. Now you own 2 properties and live in the second property.
- 2 years later, you buy a third property, live there, and rent out extra rooms/units. You keep property 2 and turn it into a traditional rental property. Now you own 3 properties and live in the third property.
- 2 years later, you buy a fourth property, live there, and rent out extra rooms/units. You keep and turn the third property into a traditional rental property. Now you own 4 properties and live in the fourth property.

Note that there are numerous variables (property type, buying the next property faster or slower than every 2 years, AirBNB'ing vs long term rentals, etc) that have a big impact on the returns, the amount of work you do, the number of properties you buy, the risk you take, etc.

The financial model discussed over the next few pages is a real example of a client of ours . It's based on a 3 bedroom, 2 bath, move-in-ready condo that sold for $235,000 . The deal was found on the MLS. The client's plan was to live in the master suite and rent out the other two bedrooms to friends, allowing him to live for free. Let's look at the numbers.

Property #1 - 3/2 Condo for $235,000

He purchased the first condo with an FHA loan with 3.5% down.

- Taxes: $835/yr
- Property insurance: $250/yr
- HOA dues: $2,640/yr
- PMI: $1,500/yr
- Repairs and maintenance: $1,100/yr

End of Year	Personal Savings	Property #1		Total Property Cash Flow	Cash in savings account	Net Worth
		Cash Flow	Equity			
1	$12,000	$0	$23,969	$0	$12,000	$35,969
2	$12,000	$0	$40,462	$0	$24,000	$64,462

Column descriptions

Personal Savings - The personal savings column represents the money the client is putting into savings, since he is not paying rent or mortgage. He figured he's saving $1,000/mo.
Cash Flow - This is the monthly cash flow from the individual property. It's zero as of now since he's living for free.
Equity - Equity in the property.

End of Year	Personal Savings	Property #1		Property #2		Total Property Cash Flow	Cash in savings account	Net Worth
		Cash Flow	Equity	Cash Flow	Equity			
1	$12,000	$0	$23,969			$0	$12,000	$35,969
2	$12,000	$0	$40,462			$0	$24,000	$64,462
3	$12,000	$3,688	$57,742	$0	$29,879	$3,688	$22,743	$110,365
4	$12,000	$4,447	$75,846	$0	$47,635	$4,447	$39,190	$162,671

Total Property Cash flow - The total cash flow from the entire portfolio.
Cash in Savings Account - The accumulation of the monthly personal savings and excess cash flow from the properties.
Net Worth - The sum of the equity and total cash in the savings account.

Property #2 - 3/2 Condo for $259,000

For simplicity, we'll assume he purchases the exact same condo for his second property. To be realistic with the numbers, we're factoring in price appreciation, expenses increasing, and rent growth with the historical averages. The same condo that cost $235,000 two years ago, now costs $259,000. It's financed with a conventional loan with a 5% down payment. A 0.5% increase in the mortgage rate is also assumed (we're figuring interest went up over time). The down payment ($12,954) and other acquisition costs ($5,000) are subtracted from the "Cash in Savings account" column in year 3. What is so cool is the money saved on living expenses buys property #2!

Property #2's cash flow is zero, representing that he is living for free. Property #1 is cash flowing over $3,000 a year!

Property #3 - 3/2 Condo for $285,000

Again, we're assuming the exact same condo is purchased with the appreciated price, expenses, and rent. Another 0.5% increase in the mortgage rate is also assumed. It's financed with a conventional loan with a 5% down payment. The down payment ($14,282) and other acquisition costs ($5,000) are subtracted from the "Cash in Savings account" column in year 5. As you can see, a nice cash reserve is getting built up too!

End of Year	Personal Savings	Property #1 Cash Flow	Equity	Property #2 Cash Flow	Equity	Property #3 Cash Flow	Equity	Total Property Cash Flow	Cash in savings account	Net Worth
1	$12,000	$0	$23,969					$0	$12,000	$35,969
2	$12,000	$0	$40,462					$0	$24,000	$64,462
3	$12,000	$3,688	$57,742	$0	$29,879			$3,688	$22,743	$110,365
4	$12,000	$4,447	$75,846	$0	$47,635			$4,447	$39,190	$162,671
5	$12,000	$5,238	$94,814	$3,256	$66,261	$0	$32,568	$8,494	$41,412	$235,054
6	$12,000	$6,061	$114,686	$4,084	$85,800	$0	$51,773	$10,145	$63,557	$315,816

Property #3's cash flow is zero, representing that he is living for free. Property #1 and #2 are both cash flowing! Life is getting better and better!!!

Property #4 - 3/2 Condo for $315,000

Ok, let's do it one more time! Again, we're assuming the exact same condo is purchased with the appreciated price, expenses, and rent. A 0.5% increase in the mortgage rate is also assumed. It's financed with a conventional loan with a 5% down payment. The down payment ($15,750) and other acquisition costs ($5,000) are subtracted from the "Cash in Savings account" column in year 7. Between the monthly personal savings and cash flow, the savings account still grows, even with the new condo purchased subtracted!

End of Year	Personal Savings	Property #1 Cash Flow	Equity	Property #2 Cash Flow	Equity	Property #3 Cash Flow	Equity	Property #4 Cash Flow	Equity	Total Property Cash Flow	Cash in savings account	Net Worth
1	$12,000	$0	$23,969							$0	$12,000	$35,969
2	$12,000	$0	$40,462							$0	$24,000	$64,462
3	$12,000	$3,688	$57,742	$0	$29,879					$3,688	$22,743	$110,365
4	$12,000	$4,447	$75,846	$0	$47,635					$4,447	$39,190	$162,671

5	$12,000	$5,238	$94,814	$3,256	$66,261	$0	$32,568			$8,494	$41,412	$235,054
6	$12,000	$6,061	$114,686	$4,084	$85,800	$0	$51,773			$10,145	$63,557	$315,816
7	$12,000	$6,918	$135,507	$4,945	$106,299	$2,387	$71,943	$0	$35,522	$14,251	$70,071	$419,342
8	$12,000	$7,811	$157,322	$5,843	$127,803	$3,288	$93,126	$0	$56,313	$16,942	$99,013	$533,577

The total property cash flow and net worth are looking very impressive!

The Next Property

At this point, the investor how has four cash flowing rental properties and has built a solid foundation for further real estate investing. Now it may be time for him to buy a property for himself to enjoy without having roommates. When he moves out of Property #$, he'll have over $20,000/year in cash flow and a net worth over a half a million dollars! Amazing, huh?

Seriously. It sounds incredible but s at the spreadsheets, study the numbers, understand what he did. It may be the most valuable use of your time ever. It's worked for many investors in our market, it can work for you too.

Build Your Own House Hacking Model

There are an infinite number of variables (property type, buying the next property faster or slower than every 2 years, AirBNB'ing vs long term rentals, etc) that have a big impact on your returns. Download a copy of this financial modeling spreadsheet for free at https://www.denverinvestmentrealestate.com/HHSpreadsheet. Instructions and video tutorials are also provided. Touch base with us, we love this stuff and will be happy to walk through it with you.

Property Management and Tenant Screening

There's no way around it, if you're house hacking you're living with your tenants and you're also a landlord. This is exactly why most people don't do it. That idea either excites you (incredible wealth building opportunity!) or scares you (ugh, living with your tenants!), or perhaps both. Regardless, you'll gain incredibly valuable experience as a landlord because you'll be one. Aside from wanting someone that pays rent on time and treats your place well, you probably have an idea of who want living there... and who you don't.

In the eyes of the government, you're a landlord. The government knows the rules, your prospective tenant may know the rules, so you need to know the rules and laws as well. The federal government and State of Colorado have numerous rules and laws to protect tenants and home buyers from being discriminated against.

Here's a description of the Fair Housing Act from HUD's website:
> "...as amended, prohibits discrimination in the sale, rental, and financing of dwellings, and in other housing-related transactions, based on race, color, national origin, religion, sex, familial status (including children under the age of 18 living with parents or legal custodians, pregnant women, and people securing custody of children under the age of 18), and disability."

For example, a woman might be comfortable with another woman of similar age and interests as her tenant. However, according to the Fair Housing Act text above, that could be considered discrimination based on sex ("No men. Only women.")

Fortunately, the government understands that there is a difference when the landlord is living with their tenant under the same roof. This is known as Mrs. Murphy's exemption and the government won't apply the same fair housing standards and force the landlord/owner to live with someone that he or she does not want to.

States can modify Mrs. Murphy's exemption. Colorado exempts landlords from fair housing laws when it's an owner-occupied single family residence (not duplexes, triplexes, etc.) However, if you're a practitioner of real estate, own multiple properties, or hire a property management company to find a tenant, then Mrs. Murphy's exemption does NOT apply. Regardless, you can never advertise with discriminatory language.

Confused? You should be. Many real estate professionals don't understand these rules. Don't let it stop you from house hacking. Just realize you'll need to do a little extra homework.

Do You Need a Lease?

Do you need a lease to rent out a room or unit? No, legally you do not. However, you don't need a lease until you do need one! It means you don't need a written lease agreement when everything is going smoothly. But what happens when it's not going great? A written lease will answer those questions. If you have ever talked with experienced landlords, you've heard that eventually something goes wrong! Hope for the best, but plan for the worst. You're using house hacking to launch your real estate investment career. So, treat it like a business. No handshake deals, verbal agreements or grabbing freebie leases off the internet.

Long Term vs Short Term (Airbnb) Rentals
With the explosion of Airbnb you now have more options for generating rental income for your Denver house hack. Is renting out for the long term or short term better? Well, as with most things, it depends! Let's compare and contrast.

Furnishings

Long term rental: None.

Airbnb rental: It needs to be fully furnished. Look at Airbnb's website at places near where you want to house hack to see the quality of the furnishings.

Rental Income

Long term rental: Steady income month to month. Look on Craigslist and Zillow for rent comparables.

Airbnb rental: Typically, Airbnb income is higher than a long term tenant. However, it really depends on how many nights a month it is occupied. You'll need to actively manage the rent rates. In the beginning, you'll charge lower rents to get people in your place to leave good reviews, which will then allow you to increase the rent. Location and seasonality play a role as well. Do your homework and look on Airbnb for comparable rents.
How many nights a month can you rent out your place? 2 days a month vs 22 days a month is a big difference. Don't forget the old landlord adage that if "your occupancy is 100%, it means you're not charging enough!" Don't worry about perfection with your rents. Time and experience are the big factors for optimizing your rent.

Expenses

Expenses are hard to estimate and never a fixed amount each month. Don't worry about trying to get the perfect estimate, just do the best you can.

Long term rental: Many investors estimate 5% to 10% of rent to cover expenses. Another simple rule of thumb is to use one month's worth of rent. The age and condition of the property are the biggest factors in expenses. Talk with a property manager for help on specific properties.

Airbnb rental: Your location and class of guests will have a big impact on the expenses. Have a cool pad that is perfect bachelor parties and close to the bars? Well, you're going to have a lot of wear and tear and items breaking. Most Airbnb hosts supply consumable amenities (toilet paper, shampoo, laundry detergent, coffee, etc). Those items add up! Guests steal things as well. Ask any Airbnb host.
Don't assume that you can get your Airbnb guests to fix or payback for repairs of theft. Is it worth the time of going through Airbnb's mediation process or filing an insurance claim?

Time

No matter how your rent your property, a large part in the time spent managing depends on your ability for putting systems and procedures in place for handling issues. Don't worry about having a perfect process in place before you buy. Managing your time and creating procedures is part of the learning curve. Plus, are you the handyman or hiring someone?

Long term rental: Compared to an Airbnb rental, time invested will be minimal. Keep in mind that you're only a few feet and door knock away from your tenants.

Airbnb: You're running a hospitality services business now. It's a combination of hotel operator and concierge. How much time will you interact with your guests? Some hosts are a super host and enjoy spending time recommending things to do around time. That's fun, but it takes time.

Are you cleaning the place between guests? Who is scheduling the cleaner? How often are you running to Costco to buy new toilet paper?

Laws

Recently Denver passed a short term rental law that bans people renting out their property as a short term rental (30 days or less), unless it's their primary residence. According to the law, if you live in a multi-unit (duplex, triplex, or fourplex), you cannot rent out the other units on Airbnb. You can rent out the extra bedroom in your unit, but the not the others. ADU's and mother-in-law suites can be rented on Airbnb.

Surrounding areas are keeping an eye on Denver's new law. Some will most likely follow their lead. Short term rental laws are quickly evolving all over the country. Make sure you know the rules for your property before you buy. As a backup plan, make sure you're good with the long term rental numbers in case the laws change while you own it. Some Denver investors had to sell their units once Denver passed the law.

Greatest ROI

You may be asking, "Well, bottom line, which one will make me the most money?" There is no clear-cut answer because it really depends on a number of factors. Typically, Airbnb will generate the greatest amount of income and profit. However, don't assume that will be the case for your house hack. The location of your property will have a big impact on Airbnb rental income. The majority of Airbnb guests are on vacation want a good location.

Married?

Here's a typical scenario for a married couple: The guy is excited and sold on the concept of house hacking. He's ready to go! The wife is too until she sees the neighborhood, the condition of the property, and how close your tenants are living to you. In our experience, **the wife has vetoed the idea of house hacking more often than not**.

We're telling you this NOT to scare you away, but to make sure everyone's expectations are on the same page. When people buy a home, especially their first one, they have a picture painted in their mind of the 3-4 bedroom home in a nice neighborhood. They aren't dreaming about living in the basement unit while tenants are living in the bigger, nicer space above.

Remember, house hacking is a phenomenal way to get your start in real estate investing, even as prices continue to rise in Denver.

Case Study: A Launching Pad for Investing

Travis Sperr started his real estate investing career with a triplex house hack. At 26 years old, he and his wife purchased their first property, a triplex for in Aurora in 2010. The triplex cost $165,000. They financed it with a FHA 203k, which provides for rehab costs. Total loan amount was $195,000 (165,00 for purchase and $30,000 for rehab.) After fixing it up, they lived in the smallest unit and rented out the other two units. They lived for free and cash flowed a couple hundred dollars a month. After one year, they moved out with a total rental income of $3,000/mo. The mortgage payment is $1,250/mo.

Take a minute and really absorb those numbers and what Travis and his wife did. Was living in a triplex what they wanted to do? No, but they knew that some short term sacrifice would pay dividends down the road. It absolutely has for them because they are full time real estate investors now in their thirties.

"You're not going to live in the neighborhood that you WANT to live in, it'll be what you NEED to live in." - Travis Sperr
Was one year of sacrifice worth it? ABSOLUTELY! In 2017, Travis did a $30,000 remodel of the property. Now the property is worth over $400,000 and brings in over $5,000/mo of rent.

RESOURCE: Charles Roberts interviewed Travis on a podcast episode. Listen to the full interview at www.denverinvestmentrealestate.com/podcast11

It's a Balancing Act

There is no best way to house hack. Please don't try to create the perfect plan or exactly copy what others have done. You're balancing real estate investing and your personal living situation. Finding a return that you're happy with and a living situation that you're happy with requires a balancing act. You'll more than likely have to compromise on both.

Use the house hacking spreadsheet model to help analyze deals, but realize that the numbers are only 50% of the equation. The remaining 50% is your living situation, which is very hard to plug into a spreadsheet calculator!

Chapter 9: Property Management

"Hence it will not do for the Landlord to possess too fine a nature… He must have no idiosyncrasies, no particular bents or tendencies… but a general, uniform, and healthy development… offering himself equally on all sides to men."
-- Henry David Thoreau (1817–1862); Really, really smart philosopher

What is in this Chapter

We'll review the entire life cycle of property management and provide you with tips to run your properties like a pro. The information in this chapter will apply to a one bedroom condo as much as it will for a fifty unit building. The practices described below, at first read, sound like a LOT of work. It really isn't, especially for a smaller building. One of the authors had a nine unit building for a few years that was self-managed. After an initial few months of setup work, most months required no more than a few hours of work for all of these steps.

Executive Summary – Best Practices

- There are many cost effective methods to attract tenants. Try to match the methods you pick with the categories of tenants you wish to attract. Consider asking the existing tenants how they found out about the building. Don't forget to ask the tenants you like to refer their friends and family.
- If there are a lot of rentals in the immediate neighborhood of your property, consider making an effort to get to know some of the other owners. If you decide not to use a property manager, you might be able to work out an arrangement where an on-site owner could take some of the calls and do some of the showings for you for a nominal fee. Or you could take turns covering each other on vacations.
- Take the time to figure out when most units are shown and leased in your market, and make sure you have excellent coverage at those times. For example, in our market, weekends are much more popular than weekdays, and the last two weeks of the month are much busier than the first two weeks.
- The amount of time you spend on follow up will be governed by how comfortable you are working on the phone. If you practice, it quickly becomes easy and painless. You would be surprised how few landlords ever follow up. It can dramatically improve your conversion rate and reduce the amount of time that you have a unit vacant.
- Answer your phone!
- Take the time to screen your tenants carefully, just as you screened the professionals on your purchase team carefully. It will save you significant headaches.
- Do not limit yourself to signing just six or twelve month leases. You will probably find that some times of the year are more active months for leasing vacant properties than others, typically June and July. Try to time your

There are many cost effective methods to attract tenants. Try to match the methods you pick with the categories of tenants you wish to attract. Consider asking the existing tenants how they found out about the building. Don't forget to ask the tenants you like to refer their friends and family.

leases to expire when you know there will be more traffic. Try to stagger the leases so they don't all expire in the same month. This levels out your cash flow.

- Don't forget the lead based paint disclosure if your building was built before 1978 (consult your attorney).
- At move-in, take a few moments to explain anything the new tenant might need to know – what to do if the garbage disposal sticks (if it tends to do that), how to reset the electrical breakers (if they tend to go out), etc. This will reduce some of the simple maintenance calls. More sleep for you.

Tenant Management – Getting New Tenants

Once you have purchased the building, managing tenants becomes the primary focus of the property manager. The big steps in tenant management are getting new tenants, managing the existing tenants, and managing tenants leaving the building.

Typical Tasks for "Get New Tenants"
- Write and place ads
- Respond to calls
- Set up appointments
- Show property
- Take and evaluate applications (e.g., run credit report, background checks)
- Explain lease, get signatures and deposits, and pre-paid rents

Begin your process of finding tenants by understanding your market. Is the vacancy rate high, and is it easy for tenants to find a place to live? Are landlords "bending over backwards" with rent concessions and low security deposits? Or, is the rental market very tight, and is it hard for tenants to find a place to live, and does every landlord have a waiting list to get into their building? Determine who has the upper hand at the moment – the tenant or the landlord. This should guide your marketing efforts and how willing you are to make concessions to your prospective tenants. One of the authors swears the best way to gauge the state of the market is by how polite prospective tenants are when they call you on a For Rent sign.

BEST PRACTICES

If there are a lot of rentals in the immediate neighborhood of your property, consider making an effort to get to know some of the other owners. If you decide not to use a property manager, you might be able to work out an arrangement where an on-site owner could take some of the calls and do some of the showings for you for a nominal fee. Or you could take turns covering each other on vacations.

SAMPLE CHECKLIST

Methods to Attract Tenants

There are many potential methods for getting new tenants into your building:

Word of Mouth. If you have an apartment building, offer your tenants an incentive (say, $100 - $200) for a referral of a friend or coworker that signs a lease with you. Be sure to pay the incentive with the second month of rent received, and make it a rent credit versus an actual check. One of the authors with a couple of dozen tenants has innumerable "auntie," "uncle," and "grandma" referrals currently living in his units.

Yard Signs. This is an outstanding method if you are on a relatively busy street. Don't be cheap and get a three dollar sign at Home Depot that you hand-letter with a marker. Order a sign for $30 - $40 and have it professionally done with a LARGE phone number. Most prospective renters drive through the areas that interest them and write down numbers. They won't get out of their car to read your sign. You will need to be committed to answering the phone or being very diligent about returning the phone calls that you get.

Classified Ads. This is often the first thing that newer landlords consider using. These ads can work well, but they tend to be expensive. You will need to be committed to answering the phone, or being very diligent about returning the phone calls that you get. Try to add some text to your ad to make it stand out. If you read the ads in the paper before you run your ad, you will see that 99% all look identical. **Craigslist** is a fantastic alternative to the newspaper, and it's free.

Take the time to figure out when most units are shown and leased in your market, and make sure you have excellent coverage at those times. For example, in our market, weekends are much more popular than weekdays, and the last two weeks of the month are much busier than the first two weeks.

Fliers. Cutthroat, but in a market with too much capacity, we have had clients who were surprised to see fliers under the windshield wipers of their tenant's cars offering a free month to move into a building across the street. Not everyone will be comfortable with this technique, and it tends to attract the tenants that are going to have shorter than average stays.

Home Builders. Frequently a family will sell their current home before they are able to move in the home that is being built for them, and they will need to rent for several months.

Real estate agents. Some agents specialize in relocations and can be a good resource for finding short term renters.

Human Resources (HR) Departments. Sometimes employees will need to leave town for short term assignments (e.g., 2 to 4 months)… too long for a hotel but not long enough to buy something. Professional services firms are a good bet (e.g., engineers, attorneys, accountants, consultants).

The amount of time you spend on follow up will be governed by how comfortable you are working on the phone. If you practice, it quickly becomes easy and painless. You would be surprised how few landlords ever follow up. It can dramatically improve your conversion rate and reduce the amount of time that you have a unit vacant.

Getting the Prospect to Sign a Lease

Answer the Phone. This seems like common sense, but common sense is NOT common practice. When you were doing the due diligence before you purchased the building, you should have driven through the neighborhood to call for-rent signs. What percentage of the people answered the phone? 30%? Less? What percentage called you back in 5–10 minutes when you were still in the neighborhood and hadn't yet signed a lease with the competitor down the street? Usually, not many. How many even called back? This seems obvious, but close attention to detail here will pay enormous dividends. **Answer your phone!**

Set up Appointments. The property manager should be available to show units during normal hours (say, 10 AM to 6 PM Wednesday through Sunday). You could put a lock box, like the real estate agents use to sell homes on the vacant unit and give the combination to the tenant if you can't make it there quickly. You can purchase these lockboxes at Home Depot for about $30. This won't make sense in every neighborhood, but it does work well for most places.

Show Property. Think back to when you were doing your due diligence. For the disappointingly small number of landlords that were able to show you the property when it was convenient for you, how many of them did a good job of presenting their rental in the best possible light? Often times you will get an unenthusiastic person that mumbles a few things and doesn't explain the features at all. The more successful property managers will be enthusiastic, take some time to get to know the prospect, then explain the features of the property in a way that the prospect is most likely to respond favorably to.

The property and the unit really should be completely clean so that it shows well relative to the competition. Be sure to get the prospect's name and contact information so you can follow up with them.

Evaluate Applications. You should have a rental application for the prospect to fill out. A sample is included in the appendix, along with some of the criteria we think about when evaluating applications. Depending on your market conditions, you may also be able to charge an application fee. You can use this to offset the costs of running the credit check. You might want to consider signing up for a service like Safe Rent (www.saferent.com) to screen your applications in more detail. Your local Apartment Association will have other vendors for you to consider.

Take the time to screen your tenants carefully, just as you screened the professionals on your purchase team carefully. It will save you significant headaches and make the investment more fun.

Do not limit yourself to signing just six or twelve month leases. You will probably find that some times of the year are more active months for leasing vacant properties than others. For example, near a college, if you get a vacancy after a new term starts, you might have a vacant unit for a long time. In most markets, the holidays tend to be much less busy than the summer months. Try to time your leases to expire when you know there will be more traffic. Also, if you have more than one unit, try to stagger the leases so they don't all expire in the same month. This can do wonders to level out your cash flow.

Finalizing the Application

After you have approved the new tenant, you and the new tenant should complete a move-in check list. See the sample in the Appendix. At a minimum it will include these steps:

Don't forget the lead based paint disclosure if your building was built before 1978.

Signing the Lease. A sample lease is included in the appendix as a starting point. Be sure to have it reviewed to make sure it complies with your local and state regulatory requirements. The local Apartment Association will likely have standard leases that have been optimized for your city that will be landlord-friendly. Eviction attorneys also often have their own leases as well. Review it in detail with the tenant and take the time to answer their questions.

Lead based paint. If this is an older property built before 1978, have the tenant sign a lead based paint disclosure. This is a federal requirement. The odds of being audited are very small if you only have a few units, but the audit probability increases as you get more units. The penalties for non-compliance are significant. Don't take a risk when this simple one page form is so easy to complete.

Move-in Condition Checklist. Check the condition of everything in the unit with a checklist (sample in the appendix). Have them note the deficiencies and/or dirty items in the apartment, then both of you should sign and date the document. You will use this when they move out to note any maintenance items that are beyond "usual wear and tear," and you can withhold part of the security deposit to cover your maintenance costs. If you don't document this up front and the tenant decides to challenge you, it will become your word versus theirs in small claims court. This step only takes a few minutes and will help improve your margins. There is a sample in the appendix to get you started. You'll want to customize it to your specific situation.

Collect Security Deposit and First Month's Rent. If they don't have all of the money up front, draft a quick note – handwritten is fine – outlining when they will have the money and have them sign it. If you don't get another dime after they get the keys, you will have the paperwork needed to support the eviction process. If you are in a soft market where you have to offer rent concession (e.g., a month free for a year long lease), consider making the month free the last month of the lease, or if that won't work, month three. There are plenty of stories of landlords that offered "move in with no money" that never did collect anything – and had a lot more evictions as a result.

Take a few moments to explain anything the new tenant might need to know – what to do if the garbage disposal sticks (if it tends to do that), how to reset the electrical breakers (if they tend to go out), where to turn off the water in the case of an emergency, etc. This will reduce some of the simple maintenance calls that you will get, and will reduce the severity of some of the emergency calls.

Step-by-Step Guide to the Lease

We recommend that you get in touch with your local Apartment Association to get a lease that has been customized for your market. Alternatively, review this sample lease with your attorney to make sure that it is in compliance with the legal nuances in your market. A version of the lease without the comments is in the appendix. If you have a dispute with a tenant and you have to go to court to settle it, you want to be sure that you are in compliance with the law. The good news is that in our experience it is extremely rare to go all the way to court.

One of the authors successfully used this lease for several years. This section walks through the lease in detail. While it will be somewhat different in style and content from the local lease you use, the majority of the information will be the same. The explanations should get you up to speed on why certain clauses are included, and how to most easily explain them to your tenants. A good tenant will not be scared off by a strong lease; a bad tenant might… and this is a great time to identify the problem.

The lease should be a living document that you can update. As you gain experience with tenants you'll want to change some of the language or add additional clauses. An important balancing act is to have enough material to protect your interests without developing an intimidating document that frightens your tenants. Keep it reasonable.

REAL ESTATE LEASE

This Lease Agreement (this "Lease") is made effective as of *Month, Day, Year*, by and between

Holding Company, LLC
Address, Unit #
Denver, CO 80222 ("*Landlord*"), and

_____
_____
_____
_____ ("Tenant")

> *The first section of the lease simply establishes everyone's permanent mailing addresses. Try to get a name and phone number for the person at this permanent address. If you need to forward important mail (such as a security deposit) you will need it.*

The parties agree as follows:

JOINT RESPONSIBILITY. All parties understand this agreement is between the owner(s) and each tenant individually and severally. In the event of default by one tenant, each and every other tenant shall be responsible for timely payments of rent and all other provisions of this lease.

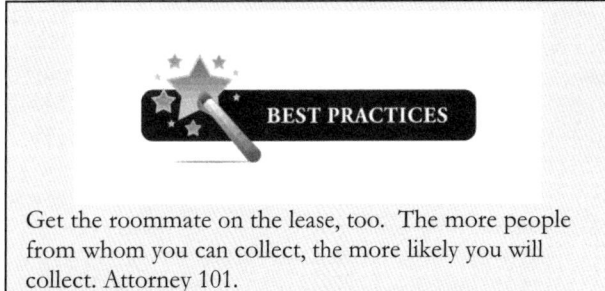

Get the roommate on the lease, too. The more people from whom you can collect, the more likely you will collect. Attorney 101.

> *This is an important clause to review if there is more than one tenant on the lease. Make sure they understand that if one person skips, the remaining people are still responsible for the lease payments. It is the tenant's problem to track down their wayward friend to collect the rent, not yours. If they object, it tells you something useful – if they don't trust their roommate, why should you? They certainly know him better than you do. Have each of them initial the clause.*

PREMISES. Landlord, in consideration of the lease payments provided in this Lease, leases to ___*(Tenant, Apartment #)*__ (the "Premises") located at_____*(Address)*_____, Denver, CO 80222.

TERM. The lease term will begin on ___*(Start Date)*_____ for a period of ___*(Duration)*___ months. The Tenant is required to give one month's notice, in writing, before vacating the unit.

> *Match the duration of the lease to when you would like for the unit to be vacant. Try not to have too many vacancies come up in the same month. Try to avoid holiday months or times that are slow in your market.*
>
> *When explaining the lease to the tenant, be sure to emphasize the importance of a month's notice in writing when they want to leave. Explain why it is important for you. Tell them if they get relocated or lose their job that you can start running ads immediately to re-rent the unit. If you work together, both parties can come out ahead. Consider having them initial this line.*

Don't let the unit become vacant because the lease ends at a time that is not convenient for you (e.g., you are on vacation or Christmas)

LEASE PAYMENTS. Tenant shall pay to Landlord $__*(rent)__*, for __*(starting month)*___ rent, due at move-in. Tenant shall pay to Landlord monthly payments of $__*(rent)*___ per month for each following month. Payment must be paid in check or money order. Rent is payable in advance on the first day of each month. Rent checks that arrive before the first of the month will not be cashed early. Lease payments shall be made to the Landlord at ___*(payment address)*___.

The first month's rent is often less than a typical month if they are moving in after the first of the month – you will need to prorate that month's rent. If you are in a market that requires rent concessions, it's OK to give a month free with a year lease if everyone else is (but if you have a nicer, cleaner product, you should not have to). However, don't give the free month at the beginning – do it at the end of the lease term. If you can't do that, try to make it the third month. We have had problems with tenants that moved in without any cash out of pocket.

Make sure to emphasize that you do not accept cash payments. This is particularly important if you leverage a property management company or an on-site assistant to help you collect rents. Also emphasize on what day the rent is due, and have them initial the clause.

The comment regarding not cashing the checks early is to encourage the tenants to get the checks in earlier. This enables you to recommend sending in the check a week early, since you can't cash it early. One of the authors once had a tenant that gave him twelve rent checks, post-dated to the appropriate months, when he moved in. He said he didn't want to have to remember to send them.

SECURITY DEPOSIT. Between the time of the signing of this Lease and ___*(date)*___ , Tenant shall pay to Landlord, in trust, a security deposit of $_*(Deposit $)*_ to be held and disbursed for Tenant damages to the Premises (if any) as provided by law. The security deposit cannot be used for the last month of rent. The security deposit will be returned to the Tenant within ___ business days of the end of the lease.

Security deposits should never be used for the last month of rent. If your unit has damage, it will be much harder to collect the money.

Ideally, you want the security deposit before they move into the building. For nicer properties that draw nicer tenants, this will certainly be the case. If you have a less desirable building in a rougher area, you are going to have some hard luck cases that don't have a dime at move in, and are relying on getting the security deposit back from their last apartment to give to you. Recognize there is a risk they won't get the deposit back, and you might be waiting a long time to collect the security deposit.

If you have a tenant that is short of cash, use the money they do have to fulfill the security deposit obligation first, and then use whatever is left for the rent. Fill out a separate sheet explaining the allocation. Both parties sign it. If they only have enough money for a half month of rent and you don't collect the second half of the rent on the 16th of the month, you can start eviction proceeding if you need to. If you had given them a full month's credit for rent and taken less as a security deposit, you would not have identified the cash shortfall problem until later. Also, in most areas, a security deposit shortfall will not be grounds for eviction.

Make sure to review with the tenants that the security deposit is not intended to be used for the last month's rent. You will need to collect the last month of rent and then return the security deposit to them after they have moved out and cleaned the unit. If they need the security deposit back rapidly to use the money for the security deposit on their next rental, try to be reasonable about your turnaround time. Perhaps they could set a time by which they will be moved out and have completed the cleaning, and you could do the inspection and give them a check on the spot. Alternatively, you could refund part of the deposit at the move-out inspection and the balance within the time specified by the lease, just in case you discover a problem a few days later (such as an unpaid water bill).

Each state will have a different guideline on when you must return the deposit. Find out what it is for your market and make sure you are in compliance. Make sure you get the deposit back to the tenant in the time that you promised when they move out. If they are not going to get a deposit back, use the form in the Appendix to explain why.

POSSESSION. Tenant shall be entitled to possession on the first day of the term of this Lease, and shall yield possession to Landlord on the last day of the term of this Lease, unless otherwise agreed by both parties in writing.

Usually your lease will expire on the last day of a month. Review this with the tenant, emphasize the importance that the unit is available for move-in on the first day of the month for the next tenant. This includes cleaning, as well. Have them initial this section.

USE OF PREMISES/ABSENCES. Tenant shall occupy and use the Premises as a dwelling unit. Tenant shall notify Landlord of any anticipated extended absence from the Premises not later than the first day of the extended absence.

SMOKING. Tenant agrees not to smoke within the Apartment, nor shall guests of the Tenant smoke in the Apartment.

The smoking ban is up to your discretion. If you have a nicer building, you might want to try to do this. Make sure this is legal in your market before you insert this clause.

PETS. The Landlord understands the tenant will have no pets in the Premises. Additional Pets shall not be allowed without the prior written consent of the Landlord.

In many markets you will be able to charge an additional security deposit and/or pet fee. Review this clause with the tenants and have them initial it. We have had extremely few problems with pets over the years, so consider accepting them.

PROPERTY INSURANCE. Tenant is not required to maintain casualty insurance on the Premises.

It would be helpful to tell the tenants to consider getting a renter insurance policy to cover their own possessions. It usually is very inexpensive.

KEYS. The Tenant will be given 1 (one) key to the Premises. The apartment does not have a mailbox key. If the key is not returned to the Landlord at the end of the Lease, the Tenant shall be charged $25.00.

Review this and have the tenant initial it. If they lose a key, you'll have fewer complaints about the fee.

MAINTENANCE. Landlord shall have the responsibility to maintain the Premises in good repair at all times and perform all repairs necessary to satisfy any implied warranty of habitation.

UTILITIES AND SERVICES. Landlord shall be responsible for the following utilities and services in connection with the Premises: Water and Sewer, Electric, Gas, Heating, Garbage and trash disposal. If the Tenant desires to add phone service or Cable TV, it will be at Tenant's expense. Tenant acknowledges that Landlord has fully explained to Tenant the utility rates, charges and services for which Tenant will be required to pay (if any), other than those to be paid directly to the utility company furnishing the service.

If the tenant is responsible for the utilities, consider making a quick reference sheet with the phone numbers for the different utility companies they will need to contact.

If the tenant pays the water bill, you might want to check with the water company periodically to make sure that it is actually being paid. In many areas, the electric and gas company won't be able to collect a tenant non-payment from the landlord, but the water company usually can.

BEST PRACTICES

Tenants that get behind on electric and gas (in most areas) create a collections problem for themselves. However, if they are supposed to pay the water, the local water utility can usually put a lien against the house, so you will pay if the tenant doesn't. Regularly check with the water company to make sure the tenant is paying if that is included in their lease.

TAXES. Taxes attributable to the Premises or the use of the Premises shall be allocated as follows: Landlord shall pay all real estate taxes and assessments for the Premises. Landlord shall pay all personal taxes and any other charges which may be levied against the Premises and which are attributable to Tenant's use of the Premises, along with all sales and/or use taxes (if any) that may be due in connection with lease payments.

This clause will need to be customized to your individual market.

TERMINATION UPON SALE OF PREMISES. Notwithstanding any other provision of this Lease, Landlord may terminate this lease upon 30 days written notice to Tenant that the Premises have been sold.

A very important clause if you are renting a single family home. Less important with a small to large apartment building, as the new owner will almost certainly want all of the tenants to remain in their units. Make sure such a clause is acceptable in your market.

DESTRUCTION OR CONDEMNATION OF PREMISES. If the Premises are partially destroyed in a manner that prevents the conducting of Tenant's use of the Premises in a normal manner, and if the damage is reasonably repairable within sixty days after the occurrence of the destruction, and if the cost of repair is less than $500.00, Landlord shall repair the Premises and lease payments shall abate during the period of the repair. However, if the damage is not repairable within sixty days, or if the cost of repair is $500.00 or more, or if Landlord is prevented from repairing the damage by forces beyond Landlord's control, or if the property is condemned, this Lease shall terminate upon twenty days' written notice of such event or condition by either party.

A clause that you hope you will never need. One of the authors had a tenant in a basement unit and a washing machine on the first floor malfunctioned and dumped ten gallons of water on the floor – and most of it ran into this tenant's basement unit. Fortunately not many of his personal effects were damaged (he didn't have renter's insurance), but the unit itself sustained significant plaster damage. We could have used this clause to terminate the lease. He was an exceptional tenant, so we helped him move into a different building where we had an empty unit while we repaired the damage.

HABITABILITY. Tenant has inspected the Premises and fixtures (or has had the Premises inspected on behalf of Tenant), and acknowledges that the Premises are in a reasonable and acceptable condition of habitability for their intended use, and the agreed lease payments are fair and reasonable. If the condition changes so that, in Tenant's opinion, the habitability and rental value of the Premises are adversely affected, Tenant shall promptly provide reasonable notice to Landlord.

EVICTION. Violation of any part of this agreement or non-payment of rent when due shall be cause for eviction. The tenant acknowledges that he or she has read this agreement and agrees to its terms, and has been given a copy.

DEFAULTS. Tenant shall be in default of this Lease if Tenant fails to fulfill any lease obligation or term by which Tenant is bound. Subject to any governing provisions of law to the contrary, if Tenant fails to cure any financial obligation within 30 days (or any other obligation within 30 days) after

Review the late payment policy with them. Have them initial the section so they will be more likely to remember it.

written notice of such default is provided by Landlord to Tenant, Landlord may take possession of the Premises without further notice (to the extent permitted by law), and without prejudicing Landlord's rights to damages. In the alternative, Landlord may elect to cure any default and the cost of such action shall be added to Tenant's financial obligations under this Lease. Tenant shall pay all costs, damages, and expenses (including reasonable attorney fees and expenses) suffered by Landlord by reason of Tenant's defaults. All sums of money or charges required to be paid by Tenant under this Lease shall be additional rent, whether or not such sums or charges are designated as "additional rent". The rights provided by this paragraph are cumulative in nature and are in addition to any other rights afforded by law.

Each market will have a slightly different method for managing late rent and its consequences. Often you'll need to explain more on the eviction process. Be sure to tune this section accordingly.

LATE PAYMENTS. Tenant shall pay a late fee equal to $__(Late Fee)__ for each payment that is not paid within seven business days after its due date.

Review this with the tenant and have them initial this clause. Amazingly, a percentage of tenants will be late every month and will just pay the late fee... giving you, in effect, a rent increase.

CUMULATIVE RIGHTS. The rights of the parties under this Lease are cumulative, and shall not be construed as exclusive unless otherwise required by law.

NON-SUFFICIENT FUNDS. Tenant shall be charged $__(Bounce Fee)__ for each check that is returned to Landlord for lack of sufficient funds.

Review this clause with the tenant and have them sign it.

REMODELING OR STRUCTURAL IMPROVEMENTS. Tenant shall have the obligation to conduct any construction or remodeling (at Tenant's expense) that may be required to use the Premises as specified above. Tenant may also construct such fixtures on the Premises (at Tenant's expense) that appropriately facilitate its use for such purposes. Such construction shall be undertaken and such fixtures may be erected only with the prior written consent of the Landlord, which shall not be unreasonably withheld. At the end of the lease term, Tenant shall be entitled to remove (or at the request of Landlord shall remove) such fixtures, and shall restore the Premises to substantially the same condition of the Premises at the commencement of this Lease.

Generally, you won't want your tenants to make modifications to the unit. Getting your written consent gives you a control point. Be sure to explain this to the tenant and have them initial this clause. Ask them if they had any construction needs in mind (the most common we have experienced is putting up a satellite dish). If they have something they want to do and feel strongly about it... and it isn't compatible with your goals for the building... perhaps neither of you should sign the lease.

ACCESS BY LANDLORD TO PREMISES. Subject to Tenant's consent (which shall not be unreasonably withheld), Landlord shall have the right to enter the Premises to make inspections, provide necessary services, or show the unit to prospective buyers, mortgagees, tenants or workers. As provided by law, in the case of an emergency, Landlord may enter the Premises without Tenant's consent.

Review this with the tenant. If you have not already, it would be a good time to discuss where the water shut-off valve(s), electrical box, and gas shut off valves are located.

DANGEROUS MATERIALS. Tenant shall not keep or have on the Premises any article or thing of a dangerous, flammable, or explosive character that might substantially increase the danger of fire on the Premises, or that might be considered hazardous by a responsible insurance company, unless the prior written consent of Landlord is obtained and proof of adequate insurance protection is provided by Tenant to Landlord.

This seems like common sense, but you'd be surprised how often the authors have found cans of paint or other combustibles next to furnaces and hot water heaters. Ideally, mechanical rooms should be off limits to tenants. Ask them what, if any, dangerous materials they might need to store. Most won't have any, but occasionally you will be surprised and you'll be glad that you asked.

SUBORDINATION OF LEASE. This Lease is subordinate to any mortgage that now exists, or may be given later by Landlord, with respect to the Premises.

This is a clause that many lenders require. You might need it if you decide to refinance the property.

ASSIGNABILITY/SUBLETTING. Tenant may not assign or sublease any interest in the Premises without the prior written consent of Landlord, which shall not be unreasonably withheld.

You will probably want to get a full application and to pull a credit report for any sub-let tenants. The reality is that the first tenant will often disappear and this new tenant is all that you will have for collection of rents.

NOTICE. Notices under this Lease shall not be deemed valid unless given or served in writing and forwarded by mail, postage prepaid, addressed as follows:

LANDLORD: *Name and address*

TENANT:

_____

_____

_____

Such addresses may be changed from time to time by either party by providing notice as set forth above.

GOVERNING LAW. This Lease shall be construed in accordance with the laws of the State of Colorado.

ENTIRE AGREEMENT/AMENDMENT. This Lease Agreement contains the entire agreement of the parties and there are no other promises or conditions in any other agreement whether oral or written. This Lease may be modified or amended in writing, if the writing is signed by the party obligated under the amendment.

SEVERABILITY. If any portion of this Lease shall be held to be invalid or unenforceable for any reason, the remaining provisions shall continue to be valid and enforceable. If a court finds that any provision of this Lease is invalid or unenforceable, but that by limiting such provision it would become valid and enforceable, then such provision shall be deemed to be written, construed, and enforced as so limited.

Does this seem like a lot of material? The Your Castle Real Estate team often offers classes (free!) on property management topics. Check the schedule at www.yourcastle.com and click on "Training."

SAMPLE CHECKLIST

Tenant Management – Monthly Process

"So cheat your landlord if you can and must…"
  -- William Burroughs (b. 1914), U.S. author

The hard work of screening the applicants to find great tenants pays off with an easier monthly process.

> Manage tenants in Building

 - Collect rent
 - Make deposits
 - Follow up with late tenants
 - Eviction process, if ever needed

Rent Collection. Make a policy of when and where the rent is due, and stick to it. Have a late fee and be firm about enforcing it. Almost all new landlords are too soft with tenants, falling for their hard luck stories. We've been softies. After being taking advantage of a number of times, you will become firmer.

Eviction. The methods for evicting a non-paying tenant vary widely by region and city. You will want to consult with your local Apartment Association for guidelines on the process and for recommendations of attorneys that can help you with the process. You can outsource the entire process for a reasonable fee in most areas, and entirely avoid this unpleasant task if you choose. We recommend you do so.

Tenant Management – Moving Out

All good things must come to an end. When your tenant gives notice that they plan to move out, begin planning immediately to locate a new tenant, and start lining up your contractors if you need to do work in the unit.

> Manage tenant leaving

 - Assess condition of apartment
 - Return damage deposit, as appropriate
 - Coordinate with planned maintenance
  team to do work between tenants

Assess Condition. Schedule a time to walk through the unit with the tenant. Bring the "move-in condition" sheet and note all of the work that will need to be done, if any, as a result of tenant misconduct or lack of cleaning. Have them sign off on the condition of the unit as they move out. If they disagree with you on the definition of "move-in condition," take lots of photos in case you need to back up your case. Get their forwarding address so you can mail their deposit back to them.

Return Deposit. Most states have a limit to the number of days that you have to return a security deposit. Sometimes your lease will have a limit, too. Be sure to get the money back in time. Most states have penalties for landlords that are late. If you are not sending back the entire deposit, include a letter explaining why. **There is a sample in the appendix.**

Maintenance Management

Maintenance and cleaning can be broken down into the things that you can predict and complete when you want to do them, and the periodic emergency.

Maintenance Management
Planned   Emergency

- Take off-hours calls
- Get bids
- Coordinate work
- Quickly respond
- Solve problem
- Ensure we get what we paid for

Planned work comprises all of the things you know you should be doing. Examples might be yard clean up and annual air condition maintenance. For a smaller building (four units or less), this should not be any more effort than you put into your own home.

The **Emergency work** happens during off hours. First time investors worry incessantly about these emergency problems, but the reality is that they don't occur that often. In case they do, know who to call.

General Management

The general management activities can be done off-site. Even if you hire a property manager, as the owner you will have to do some of these tasks. Most are simple.

Provide Oversight. Tenants and property managers (if any) will occasionally have questions or problems that they cannot (or, at least, they think they cannot) resolve on their own, so they get escalated to you, the owner. You'll spend some amount of time problem solving. It generally won't be a lot of time, but it is a point of differentiation between investing in a mutual fund and a building.

Internal Control. If you hire a property manager, you can delegate almost everything to him or her, so you just get a check each month and the occasional problem solving call. How do you know that you are getting what you are paying for and that the charges are reasonable? If you managed smaller buildings in the past yourself, you will have a good sense of what a plumber charges in your area to replace a sink or what a landscaping person might charge to mow a lawn. If you don't have this point of view, you might want to periodically look into how much the property manager is spending to make sure it is prudent.

Bookkeeping and Managing Cash. Many investors will have a property manager handle all of the on-site issues, but they like to retain control of the checkbook, pay their own bills, and maintain their own books. If you have the proper disposition for accounting, this isn't unpleasant and you'll have a much better understanding of how your building is performing – and *why* it is performing at that level. Try to maintain at least this level of control for yourself if you can.

Who is Going to Do all of this Work?

Now that you have a handle on what is really involved with property management, we can discuss three approaches to getting the work done – doing it yourself, hiring all of it out, or a hybrid approach.

Doing it Yourself. For a single family home or if you are getting a duplex where you live in one unit and rent the other, it might make the most sense for you to do most of the tasks yourself. The advantage is that you'll really understand what is going on with your property, and you will see first hand the sometimes great and occasionally awful known as your tenants. If you get bigger buildings in the future, you will be better equipped to ask the right questions of a prospective property manager, and you will have a better idea of what to check on to know if the property manager is doing a good job or not.

Hiring a Property Manager. When you get a bigger building or when you have a lot of smaller properties you might elect to hire out all of the tasks. Interviewing several managers and having some good internal control check points are important. When this works well, it is really nice.

Hybrid Approach. After their first investment, many investors buy slightly larger buildings and they will leverage a reliable and responsible tenant on-site to do some of the tasks for them, while they still perform the overall property management responsibilities. Examples of tasks to delegate are cleaning and yard maintenance and showing vacant units to prospective tenants. This is less expensive than turning over the whole process while eating up a lot less of the investor's time.

Chapter 10: How the Pros Sell Their Properties

"Next to the writer of real estate advertisements, the autobiographer is the most suspect of prose artists."
-- Donal Henahan, New York Times Literature Critic

What's in this Chapter. We'll open by determining if you should sell the property on your own or if you should hire a real estate agent to help you. Then we'll explore an oft-overlooked middle ground of sharing the work, which can often reduce the sales commission significantly while not placing too much of a burden on the investor. We'll review the importance of pricing the property and provide some tips on how to stage the property so that it shows its best. We'll share some contract and closing tips that apply specifically to sellers. We'll give you the inside track on how to negotiate a fair commission with your listing agent. And, we'll wrap up by looking at how agents fare in the actual sales process.

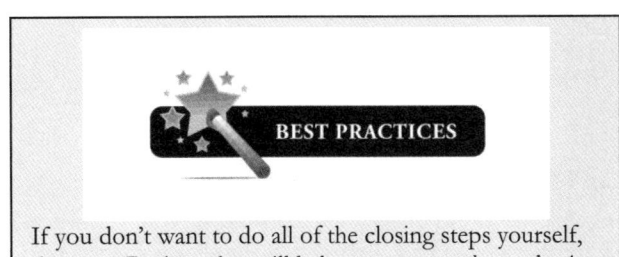

If you don't want to do all of the closing steps yourself, there are Brokers that will help you on an *a la carte* basis in most markets.

Executive Summary – Best Practices

- Hiring a Real Estate Agent does not have to be an either/or decision. You can usually do some of the work to reduce your costs while still getting the expertise you need.

- Getting your property into MLS is vital. Don't consider trying to sell it without the MLS unless you are in an amazingly hot market. Even in an overheated market, consider the "auction effect" you will generate if more Buyers are aware of your property.

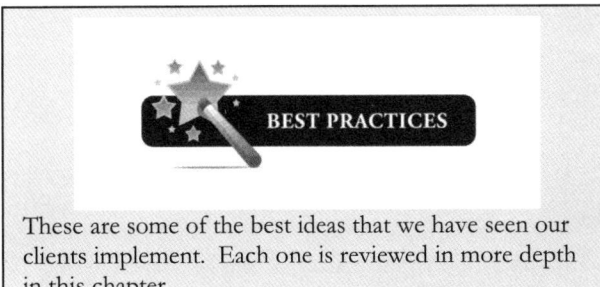

These are some of the best ideas that we have seen our clients implement. Each one is reviewed in more depth in this chapter.

- If you don't want to do all of the closing steps yourself, there are agents that will help you on an *a la carte* basis in most markets.

- Don't use the neighborhood "power agent." Most don't want to work with investors and will be less likely to give discounts.

- Whether a property is priced right and shows well matters much more in determining how fast the property will sell than the reputation or sales volume of the agent you pick.

- Visit your active competitors and drive by the sold comps to help you pinpoint your price.

- Price your property two to four percent above the price at which you expect to sell.

- Invest a little time and effort to stage the property to make it look its best. This matters almost as much for investment properties as it does for owner-occupant properties! It is NOT just about the numbers.

- Make the purchase contract deadlines as tight as you can. You don't want the buyer to tie up your property for any longer than necessary if the deal is going to bomb.

- Use your *Hold Open Policy* or a *Reissue Rate* to reduce your title insurance costs.

- If you are experiencing some Seller's remorse because you think you will be losing money – try to work through it as quickly as you can. Don't overprice the property, as you will just delay the closing and increase your holding costs.

- The real estate agent sets the commission. You may not have much flexibility with the buyer agent rate, but the listing agent's commission can be negotiated.

- The big national franchises are usually going to have to charge more money to cover their overheads, but they won't sell your property any faster or for any more money than the local boutique firms.

Can I Sell it Myself?

Yes, absolutely! Be willing to invest some time and effort, and you can save some money. You should evaluate the decision on whether or not to hire a real estate agent to help you sell the same way you evaluated whether you wanted to hire a Property Manager to run a rental, or a floor specialist to scrape, sand and refinish your wood floors. You can, with practice, figure out how to do everything – it's simply a question of what is the next best use of your time, would you enjoy it, and are you interested in learning how to do it as well as a full time specialist? The great thing about REALTORS®, versus all of the other contractors that help you, is that they only get paid when they deliver the results, whereas everyone else gets paid regardless.

Your Options. Break up the sales process into steps: marketing the property, then managing the closing once you have it under contract. *Consider that you really have five options*:

1) Do all of the marketing on your own. And, do your own closing. This is what most investors think of when they need to sell.
2) Do all of the marketing on your own. But, have an agent or attorney help you with the closing or do the closing for you.
3) Do some of the marketing, but get some selected marketing help from an agent. Do your own closing.
4) Do some of the marketing, but get some selected marketing help from an agent. Have the agent help you with the closing.
5) Traditional relationship: The agent does everything.

Hiring a real estate agent does not have to be an either/or decision. You can usually do some of the work to reduce your costs while still getting the expertise you need.

Many investors think of alternatives #1 and #5, but do not think there are options in between. Alternatives #3 or #4 will not cost much more than option #1, but will take a lot less effort from you and should make the process a lot more fun. The vast majority of *FSBOs* (for sale by owner properties) try approach #1, give up in less than six weeks, and then hire an agent as described in option #5. It's not all or nothing.

Importance of the MLS. Find a real estate agent (see the initial chapter on "Building a Team" and the Appendices on hiring a real estate agent) that is willing to help you on an *a la carte* basis. We'd suggest you do most of the marketing work on your own, but have the agent put your property into the MLS. The vast majority of the Buyer prospects are going to be found that way, and in most markets you will get a better price by being in the MLS. Investor-friendly agents are willing to do this for a nominal charge. They may tell you that entering the property into the MLS is a lot of work, takes hours of time, and/or costs them a lot of money. Maybe it is true in their market, but it is unlikely. In Denver, it takes an hour or so to prepare the input materials, a few minutes to take the photos, an hour or so to input the listing and the photos, and it costs us under $250 for listing fees. Ask around. Many national franchises will not permit their agents to do this. It's reasonable to pay a few hundred dollars to get it listed in most markets. If you just want MLS entry and not any assistance with anything else, be sure to explain it that way.

Other Marketing. Results will certainly vary by market. Our office has tinkered with a number of different marketing approaches for homes, and frankly none of them mattered much other than the big four:

- Is it priced right,
- Is it available to show,
- Does it show well,
- Is it in the MLS?

The real estate agent sets the Commission. You may not have much flexibility with the Buyer Agency, but the Listing Agent's commission can and should be negotiated.

Whether a property is priced right and shows well matters much more in determining how fast the property will sell than the reputation or sales volume of the agent you pick.

Listing agents will give you a great story about the many other things they will do to market your home so expect a big song and dance. The longer the list, the higher the commission will usually be. And, in your market there might be techniques that really do help properties sell faster. Ask the listing agent for some evidence to support that it really works (not just two or three personal stories). Verify it by asking a few other agents if they agree. In some cases an integrated internet marketing program can actually help sell a property faster, and it does cost some money and take some work to set up.

Perhaps the best idea is to price the home correctly and put it in MLS and give it a few weeks. This is a low cost way to sell the property. If you are not happy with the results, you can always switch to a more expensive listing agent with more marketing bells and whistles. Don't spend the money until you know you have to.

Assistance with Closing. Next, ask the agent if they would help you with the process from contract negotiation through to closing (or what it might cost to have them do all of it for you). The time requirements will vary by state; in Colorado it might take a skilled agent 10-15 hours to do all of the steps from contract negotiation through to close. This assumes that the first buyer actually closes. Many times it takes more than one buyer to get to a closing, if their financing falls through!

The agent might agree to do all of these steps for $3,000 to $5,000. Newer agents may certainly be willing to do it for a lot less. Be wary of green agents without experience – they won't be as good at negotiating or in watching for common pitfalls in the contract's fine print. Get someone who is experienced. Your initial reaction to the price might be that the agent is making as much as your Attorney. That's true, if the deal closes. Lots of

MLS – Multiple Listing Service. The MLS is a regional organization that collects, compiles and distributes information about properties listed for sale by its members, who are real estate agents.

deals don't close, and the agent only gets paid if it does. When your attorney helps you with an issue, they get paid regardless of the outcome.

Should You Seek a "Power Agent"? Probably not. Most are too busy to negotiate on an *a la carte* basis with investors. Many just don't work with investors. They have more prospective clients than hours in the day, so they are not going to waste their time with investors (many owner occupant agents don't like working with investors). As it turns out, you are not missing anything. We did a study of the market and looked at the agents that sell ten or more homes a year. We checked to see if their average DOM (Days on Market) was better than the market average? We found:

Here are the average discounts that sellers had to give to buyers (which includes price concessions, closing costs, etc) In 2014:

- Local / non-franchise: 3.1%
- Century 21: 3.0%
- Coldwell Banker: 2.9%
- Keller Williams: 2.8%
- Re/Max: 2.8%

Market average: 3.0%

- Power agents that sold 10+ homes sold 5 to 8% faster than average. If the average days on market in your area is 90 days, you would sell about a week faster.
- Above average agents that sell three to nine homes a year were 2 to 4% faster than average.
- Agents that sold two or fewer homes per year (the vast majority of the market) sold in a median 2 to 4% slower than average.

Conclusion: **Well known power brokers don't sell any faster** than Joe Average agent. The marketing time for your home is more a function of proper pricing and having it show well than whose name is on the sign. We think the experienced agents are more successful in getting the property listed at the right price right away – and this leads to a faster sale.

Understanding and Negotiating Commissions

Who Sets the Percentage? There is an amazing array of expectations about what it costs to sell a house. It's important to start by understanding that the commission is set by the negotiation between you and the real estate agent. The state regulators do not have authority to set commissions in most, if not all, states.

In most cases the real estate agent with whom you are working is employed by a Managing Broker (or Employing Broker, as they are sometimes called). The real estate agent may use the Managing Broker as the bad cop saying it is "Office Policy" that they "must" get 6% or 7% to sell your property. That is true in some cases, but in the majority of the cases the Office Policy would more likely say "*Try* to get 6 or 7%"… it likely is not mandatory. It's within your rights, in most states, to ask to see the Office Policy Manual. They will look at you strangely (the authors have never had a client or prospective client ask for this), but they should comply if you ask.

Where Does The 6% Go? In most larger areas (say, cities with more than 100,000 people), the odds of your agent selling the house to one of her own clients are very small (usually less than 1%). Don't let them tell you "I have a lot of Buyers in this neighborhood." Even if that is true, those Buyers are not likely to be the ones to purchase your property! The majority of the transactions will require the assistance of a Buyer's Agent that brings the Buyer to your property.

Getting your property into MLS is vital. Don't consider trying to sell it without the MLS unless you are in an amazingly hot market. Even then, consider the auction effect you will generate if more Buyers are aware of your property.

The Listing Agent (your real estate agent) usually agrees to split the commission with them. In this example, the Buyer's Agent would take 3% and the Listing Agent would take 3%. Both agents, unless they are Managing Brokers, would have to split some part of that commission with their Managing Broker to cover their office fees. How much will vary depending on the type of office. There are at least four types of offices:

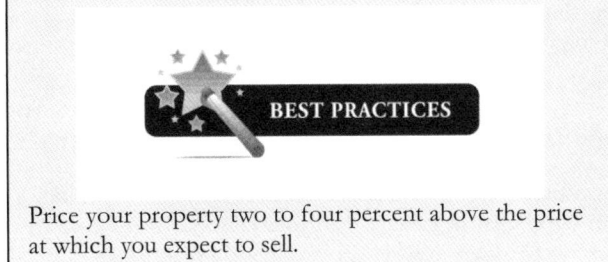

- If your agent works for an **Established National Franchises** like Century 21, Re/Max, or Coldwell Banker, they will often (but certainly not always) have a relatively large split they share with the office. Newer agents getting a lot of training and handholding with low production volumes could be on a 50/50 split. Agents with experience might be on an 80/20 or 70/30 split (70% to the agent). While it depends on the market, the franchises tend to do better with low to middle market homes. They certainly are trying to move upscale, however.
- **Growing Franchises** (e.g., Keller Williams) have a more attractive split than the established franchises, since they are still trying to capture agent market share. 70/30 with a commission cap (the amount that is paid to the company) in the $15,000 to $20,000 per year range might be typical.
- Most markets have some **local "prestigious" firms**. They often focus on luxury homes and have the extensive marketing programs expensive homes often require. Many do not accept inexperienced agents or agents that focus in the middle or lower price segments of the market. If they do take newer agents, they will almost certainly be on a 50/50 split. High production agents will be able to get better splits. Upscale homes will more often have these high-end local companies representing them.
- Most markets will have many **small, locally-owned offices.** These boutiques are all over the map in terms of pricing and capabilities. If they are specialists in a particular area or type of property, the office may charge their agents as much as the prestigious local offices. Others are just small offices with low cost structures and very attractive splits for their agents. Sometimes they just charge a monthly fee regardless of the agent's volume and the agent keeps all of the commission.
- Finally, some percentage of agents have a managing broker license and are **self-employed** as a one person shop. No splits, but their expenses are higher, since they pay their own liability insurance, rent, etc.

As with anything else, larger firms have more resources for marketing, technology, or market research.

Why guess? Just ask your agent in a conversational way how much they have to share with the office. Most of the time they will share it with you (along with the gripe of the week about their office). In summary, it doesn't matter which brand you pick. All of them sell in about the same amount of time.

You'll get essentially the same price no matter who you pick. For a $200,000 home, the difference in the discount from the best and worst performer on this list is about $600. Since the franchises have higher overheads, you will often have to pay more than $600 more for commissions for the big name firms.

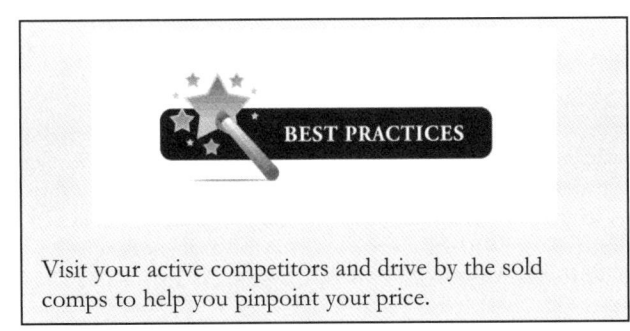

Getting Ready to Sell

SAMPLE CHECKLIST

Importance of Pricing. Everyone – investor or retail seller –thinks their property is special and worth more than it really is. The natural inclination is to price the property higher than it should be listed, and to think "I'm willing to negotiate." The reality is that buyers don't tend to write any offer at all on properties that are overpriced. Most retail buyers are afraid of "offending the seller" by writing a low priced offer. This is clearly a problem that investors don't face!

It is also worth mentioning here that despite all the hoopla about the big companies, it is the individual agent you are hiring. Buyers couldn't care less if the sign in front of the house has the right colors or decorations.

Foreclosure homes that take more time to sell, not surprisingly, sell for more of a discount. Be sure to ask your agent to look into this to see where the trends are in your market. Also, be aware that just because the average discount is, say, 2% for the entire market does not mean that every neighborhood averages a 2% discount. There will often be a lot of variation in marketing times and discounts from one neighborhood to the next. The more you can learn about this, the better you can negotiate!

If you are wrapping up a fix and flip project, you should have checked out your competition before you even purchased the property to get a sense for how properties are priced in your neighborhood. Now that you have finished the project, take a second look. It will also give you a chance to re-check the listings that were active when you did the research – did they sell? What did they sell for? Which ones did not sell? Is it a pricing problem?

Checking on the Competition.   Now is the time for the competitive assessment exercise. Spend an hour or two visiting the active homes on the market within a few block radius. Call your real estate agent and have them take you to all of them. Take lots of notes. Also have your agent print out the sales comps (all of them, not just the three that you are using to justify the price). Drive by them as well – are they really as nice as your property?

Pretend you are a retail buyer that has settled on this neighborhood. Given your active competitors and what has sold recently, what price would you have to be at to be the next house that would sell in this area? This is very hard to do but critical to get the price right. List the property within two to four percent of that price.

Making a Great First Impression with Staging.   Consider staging the house. Our objective with staging is not to have it look as polished as a new home construction model. Rather, many buyers and their real estate agents assume (often correctly) that Sellers are more motivated and will accept a lower price for a vacant property than one that is occupied. Often they are right. Also, having some items in the property helps buyers with poor imaginations (which is a larger segment than you might think) visualize how the property would look with *their* furniture in it.

Start with the **flooring**. If you have new, light colored carpets in a muddy climate (or during the winter), you might consider putting down plastic walkways in the heavy traffic areas to help keep the new carpets clean. Sure, you could have the listing service showing instructions indicate buyers should remove their shoes, but the directions don't always get conveyed (or obeyed). If you have wood floors, get some throw rugs to put down. In addition to warming up the look of the room, it does a lot to help reduce the echo in a vacant room.

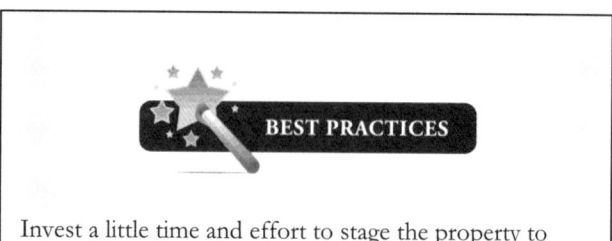

Invest a little time and effort to stage the property to make it look its best.

Kitchen and Bathrooms. Put in some modern towels and a few knick knacks. Candy is always a good idea for the kitchen. Have a new shower curtain and rings in the tubs. Everything, of course, should be exceptionally clean.

Furniture. Consider putting a table near the front as a location for the business cards that the Buyer's Agents drop off, and for your marketing material. Candles or potpourri are a good idea to lend a nice smell. You don't need anything in the bedrooms unless you don't have overhead lights. In that case, consider getting either floor lamps or small tables with table lamps to provide light so the buyers can really see the room. Consider getting some artificial plants to provide some color.

Wall Hangings. Don't go overboard, but a few framed prints will do a lot to break up the monotony of all of the bare walls. Mirrors in strategic locations can also help.

SAMPLE CHECKLIST

Tips for a Smooth Close

Contract Details. When you get a contract, you are generally going to look for the opposite of the things we discussed in the "How the Pro's Manage the Buying Process" chapter. You might need to modify some of these suggestions based on the customs of your market.

- The overall objective is to have the last of the buyer's "weasel" clauses (designed to get their earnest money back) expire as quickly as possible.
- Try to have the Inspection contingency completed in the first 10 days.
- The appraisal deadline should be about five business days after inspection resolution for any residential property.
- The financing commitment deadline should be just a few business days after the appraisal deadline. Call the mortgage broker that is managing the loan process for the buyer and ask them for an update on the status of the loan. Whatever they tell you, ask if there is any way to get to the loan commitment more quickly. They usually are helpful and come up with something. Use that for the date.
- Make sure you review all of the financing details closely. For example, make sure you are not committing to pay for an origination point on the loan.

Title Work. If you purchased the property in the last year or two and you had planned to sell it all along, you probably got a *Hold Open Policy* when you purchased the property. Be sure to use the same Title Company and remind them of this so you get the discount. If you did not get a Hold Open and it's been less than five years (this period varies by market) since you purchased the property, ask if you can get a *Reissue Rate* – sometimes that will cut the costs of your Title Insurance in half.

Facing a Loss and Moving On. Sometimes during the process you realize that you have made a mistake and either purchased a property that you should not have, or the property is OK but the price that you paid was too high. We have done this many times. The best time to address this is when you first list the property on the market.

Don't play games and use wishful thinking to price the property. It won't sell (and may not even attract any showings) and you will waste money increasing your holding costs. Price it right, take the hit, and move on. Most successful investors have had at least one project that they broke even on or even lost money. Babe Ruth had more strikeouts than anyone else in the league when he was playing. Taking risks means taking an occasional strike out to get the rewards. This is why you analyzed your risk tolerance in Chapter 1.

Final Thoughts

Real estate investing is a great way to expand your horizons and make money. We hope we have provided you with enough intelligent information for you to make intelligent decisions. Investing is a learning process, and we hope this book has helped that process to be less challenging and more fun. There is no silver bullet, and there will always be things that go wrong; such is the nature of the business.

This said, there are few better ways to make a decent living. Our experience has shown us that there has never been a better time to do what we do, and we enjoy *almost* all of it. However, the most rewarding thing for us is to help a great client secure a great property, and the more educated the client, the better they are to work with.

Appendix A – Sample Lender Letter

Here is a sample letter we have seen some lenders use. It will give you an idea of the major topics that a Seller would like to see addressed in a Lender Letter.

PRE-APPROVAL LETTER

RE: Roger Client

This letter is to certify that the above mentioned customer has received a conditional approval for a purchase amount of $100,000 with 0% down plus closing costs on a conventional primary residence loan. This is subject to:

- Satisfactory Appraisal
- Acceptable Title Commitment
- Survey (if required by Title)
- Satisfactory Purchase Agreement
- Final Verification of Income & Employment
- Final Verification of Assets
- Final Credit Approval

Please contact our office with any further questions.

Sincerely,

Bob Cash

_____

Loan Officer.

SAMPLE CHECKLIST

Appendix B – Hiring a Mortgage Broker

Suggested interview questions and what you should consider in their responses:

Are you a Full Time Mortgage Broker or do you do other things? If so, what else do you do?
You should really try to find a full time person that gives all of their thought and energy to writing loans. A less experienced person can do a fine job for a residential loan, which tends to be simpler, but you really deserve a strong player on your team for this important role.

How long have you been doing this in a full time capacity?
Experience helps, to a point. The mortgage industry changes so fast that a person with twenty years of full time experience is not likely to be any more proficient that someone with a few years of experience. At least one solid year of experience should be sufficient.

How many transactions did you complete in the last twelve months?
Different people define "full time" in different ways. Sometimes the first question tips your hand and the broker you are interviewing responds "full time" because they think that is what you want to hear. A good mortgage broker that really is full time should be doing, on average, four deals a month, and would likely close about fifty deals over the course of a year. If you hear "six deals" in the last twelve months, keep looking.

Tell me about your mix of clients – what types of clients did you work with and what sorts of loans did you write?
You will probably hear about a few refinancing jobs that they did, some residential purchases they completed, and hopefully a lot about the investors they worked with.

How many of your deals in last 12 months were for investors? Tell me about a few of the loans.
Ideally at least a third to a half of their loan volume was for investors, and they should have a few case studies of investors with a profile similar to yours purchasing properties at least somewhat similar to the property that you are considering.

What documents will you need from me?
The sooner you have a sense of what underwriting will require from you, the sooner you can get started with the wild goose chase to find all of the documents. Typically for a full-doc loan you will need:
- W2 or 1099 for the past two years (or full tax returns if self employed)
- Last two months worth of pay-stubs (if employed)
- Contact information for your insurance agent
- Complete 1003 loan application
- Signed loan documents, including 1003, GFE (good faith estimate) and Truth-in-Lending
- Bank statements to document six months of liquid reserves, down payment and closing costs

Do you do your underwriting in-house?

If so, this is great news – there should be fewer surprises and your chances of a delayed closing should be reduced. If not, it's not a deal breaker.

Since your underwriting is done by the Lender in a far-away headquarters, what steps do you take to make sure that our loan closes on time and we don't have a scramble six hours before the close to get some "the last thing underwriting needs"?
This is not really something that your mortgage broker can control – sometimes the folks at underwriting are backlogged and don't look at your file until the last minute. The value of working with a mortgage broker with experience and who understands investor loans is that they also understand what makes an underwriting file "clean" so that it has less chance of raising red flags at the last minute. They will have a perspective of which Lenders review files in advance and which procrastinate until the last minute – and they can set your expectations accordingly. One lender many of our clients have used is notorious for last minute delays, but their pricing is exceptional. If the mortgage broker doesn't set the expectation, we will – expect a great rate from this lender, but you should also expect a lousy closing experience. For some investors, it is worth it; for others it is not – but they all appreciate the advance warning.

Also listen for experiences where the mortgage broker had a closing delayed, any they discovered that X caused the problem, and now they double check that X is taken care of before they submit a file to that Lender. This is the experience that you want, and it's probably worth paying a little more for it, if you have to.

Do you work on a team? If you are sick or on vacation, who will be working on my file?
While it doesn't happen a lot, it has happened that our clients picked a one-person mortgage shop to do their loan, then the Loan Officer got the flu at a critical time in the process… and there was no one to back them up. Ideally, it would be nice if the Loan Officer had a partner that would look after their files in such an event.

What else should I know about your team and operation that makes you stand apart from your competition?
The mortgage business is very competitive and if the person you are interviewing has some unique advantages, this gives them an opportunity to point them out to you.

Describe the investment you are considering. What loan products would you suggest I consider? What types should I avoid? What have you seen other investors like me do?
A mortgage broker with experience with investors should have a well-developed point of view and some good war stories of investors in situations similar to yours. If you don't understand all of the terms or jargon, ask to have them explained. The world of mortgages is complex, and you should expect them to be able to patiently explain things at your level of knowledge. A good broker will be very willing to invest a bit of time in you to educate you – and you can make better decisions as a result. Consider "playing dumb" and asking questions that you know the answer to just to evaluate how they handle questions.

Could I get some references of three or four investors you have recently assisted?
Call up the investors and ask them …
- How comfortable they were working with the Loan Officer?
- How knowledgeable did seem about the different loan products that might apply?
- How responsive they were in answer questions and returning phone calls?
- Did they interact well with the real estate agent and the Title Company?
- Did the rates seem competitive?
- What is a smooth closing?

SAMPLE CHECKLIST

Appendix C – Hiring a Real Estate Agent – Investor Buyers Agent

Our overall objective is to find a full time agent with experience with investors. Bear in mind that the perfect agent with A+ answers on every question likely does not exist, and if they do, they will be so busy that they might not have time for more clients. Be willing to compromise. It's rare that you can find the perfect agent.

Suggested interview questions and what you should consider in their responses:

Are you a Full Time Real Estate Agent or do you do other things? If so, what else do you do?
You should really try to find a full time person that gives all of their thought and energy to real estate. A less experienced person can do a fine job for a residential home or condo, which tends to be simpler, but with your more sophisticated needs you want a strong player on your team.

Are you an investor yourself? Tell me about your investments.
It is nice to work with an agent that is fighting in the same trenches that you are. They will have better insight on most of the decisions points throughout the entire process.

How long have you been doing this in a full time capacity?
Experience helps a great deal. At least one solid year of experience of working with investors should be sufficient, but a few more years would be nice. The reality is that not many agents specialize in working with small investors, so you will have to be realistic in your expectations.

How many transactions did you complete in the last twelve months?
Different people define "full time" in different ways. Sometimes the first question tips your hand and the agent you are interviewing responds "full time" because they think that is what you want to hear. An agent that really is full time should be doing, on average, one or two deals a month, and would likely close at least a dozen deals over the course of a year. If you hear "three investor deals" in the last twelve months, keep looking.

Tell me about the mix of clients – what types of clients did you work with and what sorts of deals did you do?
You will probably hear about a few residential purchases they completed, and hopefully a lot about the investors they worked with.

How many of your deals in last 12 months were for investors? Tell me about a few of the transactions.
Ideally at least a half of their volume was for investors, and they should have a few case studies of investors with a profile similar to yours purchasing properties at least somewhat similar to the property that you are considering.

Can you recommend a lender that specializes in investor loans?
Real estate agents are usually a very good source of referrals for Mortgage Brokers that can reliably close loans.

Do you work on a team? If you are sick or on vacation, who will be helping me?
Ideally, it would be nice if the agent had a partner that would look after them in such an event.

What else should I know about your team and operation that makes you stand apart from your competition?
The real estate brokerage is quite competitive and if the person you are interviewing has some unique advantages, this gives them an opportunity to point them out to you.

Review your goals with the Agent.
Ask for feedback. Does this sound realistic?

What happens if I'm not satisfied? Can I get out of the contract? How long is the contract?
Be wary of agents that lock you into a lengthy contract. Will they give you a satisfaction guarantee?

Describe the investment you are considering. What properties do you suggest I consider? What have you seen other investors like me do? What specific returns did they achieve?
If the agent is really involved in the market segment you are interested in, they might have a few properties that immediately come to mind that they think would be a fit. This is a great sign that you have found a good person to work with. Ideally they will have had some experience with your specific type of project and walk you though some case studies of clients that have bought a similar project, how much they made, and what they learned.

How would we work together? What is your "Process"?
Look for a similar style to how you approach problems. Set expectations on who will be responsible for what.

Could I get some references of three or four investors you have recently assisted?
Call up the investors and ask them …
- How comfortable they were working with the agent?
- How knowledgeable did seem?
- How responsive they were in answering questions and returning phone calls?
- Did they interact well with the Mortgage Broker and the Title Company?
- What is a smooth closing?
- Did the investment turn out as they expected?

SAMPLE CHECKLIST

Appendix D – Hiring an Agent – Residential Listing Agent

Our objective is to find a seasoned, full time agent that can sell your property. If you are selling an investment property (e.g., an apartment building), please refer to the previous interview guide… it will have a more appropriate set of questions for your situation. If you are selling a home or condo and the intended market is a retail buyer (e.g., you bought a nasty house and just fixed it up), then you need an agent with good retail marketing skills – the investor skills will not be relevant.

The other item to keep in mind is that a good listing agent will have an impressive song and dance about how great they are and all of the super marketing ideas they have for your home. In all market conditions, the biggest driver of selling a home promptly is if the property is properly priced (don't be greedy) and does the property show well (or ideally better than competitors). No amount of marketing and fancy-schmancy bells and whistles will overcome a deficit in either area. Don't be suckered by a listing agent's dog and pony show. In some cases you are better off with a slightly less expensive real estate agent and lower the price of your property by the amount of money that you save.

Some questions to consider asking and how to evaluate the answers:

Are you a Full Time Real Estate Agent or do you do other things? If so, what else do you do?
You should really try to find a full time person that gives all of their thought and energy to real estate.

How long have you been doing this in a full time capacity?
Experience helps a great deal. At least two solid years of experience of working with retail sellers should be sufficient, but a few more years would be nice. Most agents focus on residential clients, so it should not be hard to find one.

How many transactions did you complete in the last twelve months?
The vast majority of agents only complete two or three deals a year (even those that are full time), and only one or two of those deals are likely to be listings. It is hard to gain proficiency without practice. A residential agent that really is full time should be doing a minimum of one or two deals a month, and would likely close at least a 12-18 deals over the course of a year. About half of those should be listings. If you hear "three deals" in the last twelve months, keep looking.

Tell me about your mix of clients. What types of clients did you work with and what sorts do transactions did you do?
You want to hear about the residential homes they sold and the great success they had.

What are your specific marketing plans for my home?
How much money does this agent spend on marketing versus the other agents that you are interviewing? If you are in a Seller's market, will they be conducting open houses (ineffective in a Buyer's market but useful for a Seller's market)? What media will they use for the ads? Does the agent have much insight as to which marketing channels are the most effective?

How would we work together? What is your "Process"?
Look for a similar style to how you approach problems. Get to a common understanding of who will be responsible for what.

What have you sold in my area?
There is some value in finding an agent with at least some basic level of familiarity with the neighborhood. If they work for a large office, many of the other agents in the office will have been active in the area you are interested in. That's nice, but completely irrelevant. What's critical is that your agent has specific knowledge of your area. However, if you find an agent with a good track record without specific knowledge of your neighborhood, they are likely to be the better bet than the agent that knows your area the best but doesn't understand marketing or have much deal volume.

Do you control your marketing budget or does the office Managing Broker?
If the agent does not control the ad budget, you will be competing not only with the other listings that this agent also has to promote, but the listing of every other agent in their office.

On average, how long did it take for your listings to sell in the last year?
Ask to see the sold sheets from the MLS – in most regions it will tell you the DOM (days on market). Ask the agent what the average is for the region (or you can look this up yourself on the local REALTOR® Board's web site). If the agent is selling his or her listings much faster than average, ask what drives this performance. They will usually have a good reason. If the homes are taking a lot longer to sell than average, ask about that. Unless you hear a compelling reason (there could be one), you might want to interview a few more agents.

On average, what percentage of the homes you listed actually sold?
Call the local REALTOR® board and ask what the metro average is. In a Seller's market, the figure will likely be more than 80%. In a Buyer's market, the figure might be only 55%. Compare this to the agent's performance.

On average, what discount did your listings sell for?
Visit the website or call the local REALTOR® board and ask what the metro average is. Compare this to the agent's performance. Did the agent sell their listing quickly because the caved in on the price?

Do you work on a team? If you are sick or on vacation, who will be helping me?
It would be nice if the agent had a partner that would look after them in such an event.

What else should I know about your team and operation that makes you stand apart from your competition?
Real Estate Brokerage is quite competitive and if the person you are interviewing has some unique advantages, this gives them an opportunity to point them out to you.

What happens if I'm not satisfied? Can I get out of the contract? How long is the contract?
Be wary of agents that lock you into a lengthy contract. If they just put a sign in the front yard and enter the listing into MLS then never return another phone call, you could be stuck for a long time. Will they give you a satisfaction guarantee?

Could I get some references of three or four recent clients you have recently assisted?
Call them up and ask them …
- How comfortable they were working with the agent?
- How knowledgeable did seem?
- How responsive they were in answering questions and returning phone calls?
- What is a smooth closing?
- Were they happy with the marketing time and the price?

Appendix E – Sample LOI (Letter of Intent)

This is a sample letter that we have used. It may or may not be legal and/or appropriate where you work so be sure to contact your attorney to have it reviewed before you use it.

TO: Listing Agent, Listing Office
FROM: Buyers Agent, Buyer's Office
DATE:

Please accept this Purchase Letter of Intent (LOI) for the Property at 5080 West Overpriced Lane, Your City, State Zip.

PRICE	$285,000.
TERMS	Cash offer, no lender or appraisal contingencies.
PROPERTY CONDITION	This offer is to purchase the home in "AS IS" condition. The Buyer will still conduct an inspection, but Buyer agrees not to ask for additional concessions. The Buyer reserves the right to cancel the contract if the home's condition is not satisfactory.
INSPECTION DEADLINE	Inspection to be completed within five business days of signed contract.
CLOSING:	Buyer prepared to close within fifteen business days of signed contract. This period can be extended if Seller requires more time.
CONTRACT	This LOI is not a binding contract, but a guide to how the contract will be written. If this LOI is acceptable, we will write up a standard purchase contract for your Seller immediately.
EXPLAINING THE OFFER	Our office has over 200 listings. Like you, we get a number of unsolicited "letters of intent" to purchase our homes each week. Our Sellers, like yours, usually have two concerns: (a) is this a real buyer and (b) why is the offer so low? Our Buyer purchased over twenty homes in 2008. Some of the homes are remodeled and sold. Other homes are held in their portfolio and rented. The offer is lower than the asking price because our Buyer has done a calculation of how much they can afford to pay and still meet their required investment parameters. The offer is not meant to be insulting to your Seller.
TITLE	It would be helpful to the Buyer if the closing and title work could be purchased from First Alliance Title, but this is not mandatory.
EARNEST MONEY	The earnest money, in the amount specified by the listing agent, shall be deposited with the Title Company within 24 hours of acceptance of the proposed contract.

Appendix F – Sample Lender Letter

Pre-Approval Notice

Date: 3/19/2021

Rick Wytt,

You have provided Castle & Cooke Mortgage, LLC with preliminary information regarding income sources and assets available to qualify for a residential mortgage loan. Based upon the information you provided, Castle & Cooke Mortgage has determined that you are available for such financing and are qualified to meet the financial requirements of the loan.

Please note that a pre-approval notice is not to be construed as a loan commitment. It is based solely upon the preliminary information you have provided. Prior to final approval, Castle & Cooke Mortgage will complete its credit review, property valuation and verification of assets and income.

Program and funds availability are not guaranteed and subject to change or termination, at any time without advance notice, as determined by investor guidelines, mortgage insurance availability and other factors in the market place.

Thank you for choosing Castle & Cooke Mortgage for your home purchase. I look forward to serving you through this buying experience.

The following terms were discussed with you:

Sales Price: $265,000

Base Loan Amount: $212,000

Loan Program: Conventional 30 Year Fixed

Loan Term: 360

Sincerely,

Joe Massey 3/19/2021
Joseph Thomas Massey
Senior Loan Officer
Castle & Cooke Mortgage, LLC, NMLS#1251
Originator: Joseph Massey, LIC# 100017422, NMLS# 7538
Direct: 303-809-7769
Email: jmassey@castlecookemortgage.com

GLOSSARY

1003 – The standardized loan application form for *Residential* mortgages. It consists of a list of your sources of income, your *Balance Sheet*, your *Credit Score* and other information needed by the Lender to determine which loan products for which you qualify.

1031, or *1031 Exchange* – a tax deferred method to sell one property and exchange it for another property of a similar type. If you follow all of the IRS rules carefully, you can postpone your payment of capital gains.

Acceleration – also called the *Due on Sale Clause.* If a property is sold, the entire amount of the loan is usually due immediately. Some other triggers for loan acceleration might include several late payments in a row. Acceleration can motivate a seller to want to move quickly, to avoid foreclosure.

Addendum – An extra document that is incorporated into a real estate contract. It might also modify the existing terms and conditions.

Adjustable Rate Mortgage – A mortgage that is fixed for a period of time, then the interest rate floats and is periodically adjusted based on the interest rate on which the loan is indexed.

Agency – a relationship where one person is authorized to act on the behalf of another. Your real estate agent will have an agency relationship with you, the investor, in many situations.

Amortize – the reduction of the principal of a mortgage with regular monthly payments. Residential loans are usually amortized over thirty years. Commercial loans are commonly amortized over fifteen to thirty years, but they might become due with a *Balloon Payment* in a shorter period of time.

Apartment – real estate property designed and built to be used for renting to tenants. Its highest and best use is usually renting to tenants. If the surrounding area has appreciated significantly in value, it occasionally becomes profitable to *Convert* the building from apartments to *condominiums.* Apartment buildings with four or less units are considered *Residential* property; five units or more are considered *Commercial* property.

Appraiser – Independent party that develops an assessment (the *Appraised Value*) of the value of a property. For residential real estate, they rely most heavily on recent history of similar properties (sales *Comps*) that have sold near your property. For *Commercial* properties, they will often use sales comps, an *Income Valuation*, and a *Cost Valuation.*

Appraised Value – The valuation the *Appraiser* calculates for your property, based on their analysis. This can be different from the *Market Value,* as it is only an estimate, and investors often influence the appraisal process.

Appreciation – an increase in the value of a parcel of property.

ARM – See *Adjustable Rate Mortgage*

ASF – Attached Single Family home; such as a duplex or a triplex. Usually less expensive, on $/ square foot basis, than a DSF (detached single family home), but usually a bit more expensive than a condo of a similar size in a given location.

Assets – What you own, such as your primary residence and your car. Part of the *Balance Sheet* on the *1003*, the standard mortgage application.

Assign or *Assignment* – usually "*Assign a Contract.*" An investor who is interested in Assignments gets a property under contract for an attractive price then assigns the contract to another buyer, usually another investor. The first investor will be paid a fee for the work.

Assumable Loan – A loan that can be transferred to another party, upon lender's approval. Common for commercial loans; much less common for residential.

Assumption – process of taking responsibility for a loan. You agree to take over the payments for the balance of the loan and the legal recourse for non-payment is transferred to you. A common feature of commercial loans, particularly the larger ones. Not commonly available on residential loans. More frequently, investors take over a property *Subject To* the existing mortgage.

At Par – The loan rate that you qualify for with a given type of property, LTV and credit score (among other variables). You can *Buy Down* the interest rate (get a lower interest rate) by paying more point(s) at the closing. Alternatively, you can get a point credited to you at closing to offset some closing costs by accepting a higher interest rate.

AVM – Automated Valuation Model; e.g., an automated appraisal.

Balance Sheet – A list of your *Assets* (what you own, such as your house and your car) less your *Liabilities* (what you owe, such as your mortgage and your car loan). The difference between the two is hopefully a positive number and represents your *Net Worth*. The Balance sheet is part of the *1003* mortgage application for *Full Doc* loans. The higher your *Net Worth* (also expressed in slang as "the stronger your Balance Sheet"), the better the terms the Lender can give you on your mortgage.

Balloon or *Balloon Loan* – a mortgage that does not fully amortize; in other words it has a shorter life and a lump sum payment is due at the end of its life. Common for commercial loans.

Balloon Payment – The amount of principal that is due at the end of a *Balloon Loan.*

Bankruptcy – A provision of Federal Law that a debtor can give assets to the court, and have many types of debts eliminated.

Basis – The investor's purchase price of the property, plus any purchase costs, plus any improvements (e.g., replacement of a boiler or roof) less accumulated depreciation.

Basis Points – 0.01%. Also referred to as *Bips*. One mortgage broker might whine to another that "rates on the five year fixed are up thirty bips today, and I lost a deal as a result."

BATNA – See *Best Alternative to Negotiated Agreement*

Best Alternative to Negotiated Agreement – also known as *BATNA*. In any negotiation setting, this is what your next best option is if you and the other party cannot come to terms.

Bips – See *Basis Points*.

Buyers Agent – A real estate agent that is representing a Buyer and has the financial responsibility to get the best possible deal for their client. A Buyer could also be represented by a real estate agent in the capacity of a *Transaction Broker*. In this case, the agent would be trying to get the transaction completed in a way that is fair and ethical to all parties, without looking out for the interests of any one party to the transaction.

Capital Gain – The sales price of the property, less selling costs, les the purchase price, less purchase costs, less any capital improvements. If the gain has been realized in less than a year, it is often taxed as *Ordinary Income*, which is usually a higher tax rate. If it has been held for more than a year, it is often taxed as the *Capital Gains* tax rate, which is usually lower.

Capital Gain Tax Rate – taxation applied to capital gains, usually of assets held for more than a year. Usually a lower rate than *Ordinary Income*.

Capitalization Rate (Cap Rate) – Used by investors to evaluate income properties, the NOI divided by the Cap Rate gives an estimate of the buildings value. Similar to return on investment for other types of investments, this is the return that you would get from investing in a building if you paid all cash. Cap Rates are roughly tied to interest rates – as rates go up, Cap Rates usually go up as well. As Cap Rates increase, the value of the building (assuming no change in NOI) declines.

Cash – When purchasing a property, most state-regulated real estate contracts allow you to put provisions into the contract that state if you cannot get the loan you want on the terms you want, you can back out of the deal. Investors usually purchase properties using "Cash." Most of them don't actually have the purchase price sitting in their checking account; they have made arrangements to get the money from some source, such as a *Hard Money Lender*. However, from the Seller's point of view, it looks like cash. Sellers find this to be highly desirable and will occasionally accept less money for the certainty and speed of a cash closing.

Cash on cash return – The ratio of before tax cash flow to the total amount of cash invested.

Certified Public Accountant (CPA) – An accountant who has passed the Uniform Certified Public Accountant Examination and other state regulations. He is licensed to be able to give advice and opinions on financial matters.

Closing – Ceremony where Title is passed from Seller to Buyer. Usually a large number of supporting documents are also signed.

Closing Agent or *Closer* – the person at the Title Company that conducts the closing and manages the blizzard of paperwork and checks.

Closing Costs – the expenses paid by the buyer and the seller when the deal closes, which include: commissions, mortgage fees, escrow or attorney's settlement charges, transfer taxes, recording fees, and title insurance.

Cloud or *Cloud on Title* – a doubt or uncertainty about who is authorized to sell a property, or who has value liens/claims against it. Clouds must be resolved before Title can pass from Seller to Buyer and the deal can close.

CMA – Competitive Market Analysis. See *Comps*

COFI – See Cost of Funds Index

Collateral – property (real or personal) that is pledged to secure a loan.

Commercial property – the opposite of *Residential* property. Commercial properties, for the purpose of this book, are apartment buildings with more than four units. Financing for these buildings is more difficult to arrange than for residential properties. Lower *LTV's* are typically available.

Comps – Slang for "sales comparables." If you purchasing a three bedroom, two bathroom home with a two car garage and 2,000 square feet, the homes that generally meet those same parameters and sold in the last six to twelve months in a half mile to mile radius would be the "comps" for your property. Generally, all of them should sell for about the same price. There will be a bit of a range, as some homes will have been sold in better condition than others, or will have had more upgrades than others. An investor will often as their real estate agent to "pull comps" for them for a property in which they are interested.

Condominium – A building with multiple units that share some common elements. For example, an apartment building that has been *Converted* into a condo will often have a common roof, boiler, and hallways. The condo will have a *Home Owners Association* that pays the common expenses and collects a periodic assessment from the building's owners.

Conduit Loan – A commercial loan that meets exacting criteria that is re-sold to Wall Street. Usually has a million dollar minimum, and offers lower interest rates and potentially slightly higher LTV than the portfolio alternatives. Often is non-recourse. However, they are harder to qualify for and are very difficult to pre-pay.

Conforming Loan – most residential loans adhere to strict underwriting guidelines. This enables the bank to package up large bundles of loans and sell them on Wall Street. If your property is within the tolerances of a conforming loan, you will get better terms. A loan that is not part of FHA or VA.

Construction Loan – A shorter term loan, often for 24 months or less, used to purchase an *Apartment* that an investor wishes to *Convert* to *Condominiums*. Often the lender will loan 75-80% of *LTV* or *LTC*, whichever is lower.

Contingency -- a provision of a contract that keeps it from being fully legally binding until a certain condition is met. For example, the Buyer's usually has a contractual right to get a professional home inspection before purchasing the home.

Contract – a legal document that binds two parties to perform some action. Often in real estate it refers to the *Purchase Contract*, though it could also refer to the many other documents involved in a purchase or sale of property.
Contractors – the trade people (e.g., plumbers, electricians, carpenters) that assist you with a renovation project.

Conversion – transforming an *Apartment* building into a *Condominium*. Involves a number of steps and can generate significant profits.

Conventional Mortgage – see *Conforming Loan*

Cost of Funds Index (COFI) – an index used for variable rate commercial loans. It adjusts rather slowly to changes in the interest rate. Often contrasted to LIBOR, which is another common choice for a commercial loan index, which tends to adjust to rate changes much more quickly. Often a better choice than LIBOR when rates are low and you expect for them to rise in the near future.

Cost Valuation (or Replacement Cost Valuation) – an analysis by the *Appraiser* for a *Commercial* property of how much it would cost to rebuild the property in the event of a major mishap.

Counter – see *Counteroffer*.

Counteroffer – A rejection of the initial offer proposed by the Buyer. The seller outlines different terms that would be acceptable.

Coverage Ratio – For apartment buildings, the Coverage Ratio = *Net Operating Income* divided by the *Debt Service*. Typically the debt service will be amortized over twenty five years. The minimum coverage ratio varies by lender, but will often be at least 120%.

Credit Report – the file that is independently maintained by three reporting agencies of what credit products you have applied for, received, and if you are making payments as agreed. The information in the credit report is used to calculate a credit score.

Credit Score – An independent, third party assessment of how well you have managed your credit in the past. Three national companies track your credit scores; a lender will usually request all three and take the middle value (the *Mid Score*) for determining the terms of your loan. As slang, you will often hear the *Loan Officer* say that they need to "pull your credit," which is to get the three credit reports to discover your mid score.

Debt Service – for commercial loans, the principal and interest payment for the loan. Often, commercial loans are amortized on a basis less than thirty years (25 is common). The under writer will want to make sure that the *Coverage Ratio* of the *NOI* divided by the *Debt Service* achieves a target ratio, often 120%.

Deed of Trust – See *Mortgage*

Defeasance – When a borrow must pre-pay a *Conduit* loan, they are often required to purchase a set of securities that will generate the same amount of interest as the loan payments they contractually committed to make. These securities are held by a trust which makes the payments for the life of the loan. This process is expensive to set up.

Depreciation – An accounting concept that lets the investor write-off a portion of the value of the property each year. For many types of real estate investments, you will calculate the value of the land (perhaps using a tax assessment as a guide), and then the value of the improvements can be depreciated over 27.5 years. This doesn't impact the actual cash flow of the asset, but it does reduce your current-year tax liability. When you sell the asset, the IRS *Recaptures* the depreciation.

DSF -- Detached Single Family Home.

DOM – Days on Market; number of days from the time that the property was listing the MLS to the time it was placed under contract.

Due on Sale Clause – a provision of most lender contracts. If you take over the payments of the mortgage without going through the formal *Assumption* process (if any), then the lender has the right to *Call the Loan* and make it payable immediately. This happens extremely rarely in practice.

Earnest Money – A good faith deposit, usually included with a purchase contract.

Equity – The difference between net market value after closing costs and the mortgage amount. The amount of money the Seller clears after the closing.

Escrow – Delivery of deed by the seller, which is contingent on some other event (such as the Buyer's loan being funded).

Escrow Agent – see *Closing Agent*

Escrow Payment – funds collected by the lender, usually monthly, in addition to the principal and interest payment. May include property taxes and hazard insurance.

Exit Strategy – The investor's plan for what they will do with the property when they have finished adding their value to it. Often the exit strategy is to sell to a retail buyer at top dollar, or to rent the property to a tenant. The better your understanding of your exit strategy, the more effective you will be as an investor.

Fannie or *Fannie Mae* -- a government agency that facilitates the mortgage market.

FHA – The Federal Housing Administration. They facilitate loans at high *LTV*. Often, but not exclusively, used by first time buyers.

Fix and Flip (F&F) – Purchase of a property with the intention to do something to it to add value, and then quickly resell at a profit. Renovation work is the most common value added by investors.

For Sale By Owner – a property that is being marketing by the owner of the property without the assistance of a real estate agent.

Foreclosure – a legal set of events that eliminates the legal rights of the property owner to use or sell the property.

Freddie or *Freddie Mac* – a government agency that facilitates the mortgage market.

FSBO – See *For Sale By Owner*

Full Documentation ("Full Doc") Loan – a mortgage where you document everything about your income and assets. Usually results in a lower interest rates and the potential for a higher *LTV*. Compare to *Stated Loan*. Usually used by investors with steady employment and/ or a strong *Balance Sheet*.

Good Faith Estimate – (GFE) – an estimate of your mortgage's closing costs; provided by your Loan Officer.

Grant – A monetary gift, usually from a third party, such as a city or county government, or a non-profit agency. In most cases, the investor will actually pay for the so-called grant by rolling the cost into the mortgage for the property. Neighborhood Gold is a typical example.

Grantee – the person receiving an interest in a property.

Grantor – the person giving up an interest in a property.

Gross Rent – the scheduled rent multiplied by the number of units. The theoretical maximum income that a building could produce if all of the units were occupied all of the time. In reality, some units are vacant some times, so the *Net Rents* after vacancy are lower.

Gross Square Feet – the measurement approach often used for single family homes and for apartment buildings. The appraiser measures the *outside* of the building. The square footage includes hallways, boiler rooms and the thickness of the exterior walls.

Hard Money Lender – Lend you money based on the value of the property you are purchasing. If the property is worth $200,000 and you are able to purchase it for $150,000, a Hard Money

Lender will probably give you a loan regardless of your down payment or credit score. However, the fees and the interest rate will be much less desirable than more conventional forms of financing. Hard Money Lenders can usually close very quickly, and from the Sellers' point of view, you are purchasing with *Cash*.

HOA – see *Home Owners Association*

Home Owners Association (HOA) – Group that pays the common expenses and collects a periodic assessment from *Condominium*'s owners

Hold Open Policy – A title policy that costs about 20% more at the time of purchase (the difference is paid by the buyer). If the investor sells in two years or less (the time varies by Title Company), the investor doesn't have to purchase a new title policy – they only pay the difference in the value of the purchase price and the sales price. Usually this is a nominal amount and it saves the investor about $1000.

HUD – A home owned by HUD, a government agency. Frequently a foreclosure on an FHA loan.

HUD or *HUD Statement* – see *Settlement Statement*.

Income Valuation – For commercial real estate, the appraiser will estimate the property's value using the income approach, as well as the cost approach and sales comps. This consists of estimating the income the building can generate (usually from rents), then deducting the expenses to operate the building (e.g., property taxes, utilities, maintenance) to arrive at *Net Operating Income* (NOI). The NOI is divided by a *Capitalization Rate* ("Cap Rate") to determine the buildings value from the income approach.

Inspector – Independent party that you may hire to inspect a property you are considering purchasing. In many states, inspectors are not regulated, so anyone can call themselves an inspector without any minimum level of training or certification.

Insurance Broker – Independent party that works with multiple insurance companies to find the best insurance product to manage your liabilities.

Interest Rate – the percentage amount of money that is due for the privilege of using money via a loan for a period of time.

Joint and Several Liability – the Lender can collect the full amount of the debt from anyone who signed the note.

Lease – A rental contract for a set period of time with a predetermined payment, usually monthly, for exclusive use of a property.

Lease Option (L/O) – Acquiring control of a property (though not necessarily ownership), then leasing the property to a tenant. The lease is bundled with an option, so the tenant can (but does not have to) purchase the property for a given price within a given time frame.

Lease Option – Investor Carry – A L/O where the investor purchases the property.

Lease Option – Owner Carry – A L/O where the investor does not purchase the property, the seller continues to be accountable for the mortgage.

Lender Letter – A letter from your lender that states you have made an application for a mortgage and gives a general outline of the financial terms and maximum loan amount for which you qualify. The listing agent for the property you purchase will likely call the Loan Officer to confirm the arrangements and that you have the financial capacity to complete the transaction.

Letter of Intent – also known as *LOI*. A letter that a prospective buyer can send to a prospective seller – whether the property is listed or not. Rather than using the formal state-regulated offer contract, this one page letter briefly outlines the important terms of a purchase contract in a non-binding manner. If the prospective seller has interest, the Buyer can then take the time to draft a complete contract.

Liabilities – what you owe. Examples would be the mortgage for your primary residence, or the loan balance for your car. Combined with your *Assets*, this forms a *Balance Sheet* that a lender can use to assess which loans for which you qualify. The liability statement is a part of the *1003*, the standard loan application.

LIBOR – The London Inter Bank Offer Rate. An interest rate index for commercial and residential loans. For some commercial loans the borrower can pick between the LIBOR or COFI indexes. COFI adjusts slowly to interest rate changes; LIBOR adjusts quickly. LIBOR tends to be a better choice when rates are high and you expect for them to decline.

Lien – an encumbrance against a property that must be paid or resolved before it can be sold.

Listing -- an agreement between a real estate agent and the entity selling the property that allows the agent to market and arrange for the sale of the property. "Listing" also refers to the property for sale.

Listing Agent -- A real estate agent that is representing a Seller and has the financial responsibility to get the best possible terms for their client. A Seller could also be represented by a real estate agent in the capacity of a *Transaction Broker*. In this case, the agent would be trying to get the transaction completed in a way that is fair and ethical to all parties, without looking out for the interests of any one party to the transaction.

Loan Officer (LO) – the person who gathers your financial information in a standardized format (the *1003*), gathers rate and term quotes from lenders, helps you select the best loan for your situation, then helps coordinate the closing of the loan.

Loan to Cost – The amount of money a Lender may be willing to provide for a construction loan. The cost might be the purchase price of the building ($100,000) plus the costs renovation costs needed ($50,000), or $150,000. If the lender is willing to loan 80%, the loan amount would be $120,000.

Loan to Value – The amount of money that the Lender is willing to provide for the purchase of a given property. For example, if you are purchasing a home for $100,000 and you want to borrow $80,000, the LTV is 80%. Higher LTVs are generally available for *Residential* properties than for *Commercial* properties.

LOI – See *Letter of Intent*

LTC – Loan to Cost. A term used for assessment of loans for *Commercial* property and *Construction* loans.

LTV – Loan to Value. A term used for the assessment of loans for *Commercial* and *Residential* property. Also used for *Construction* loans.

Market Value – what a property will sell for in a reasonable period of time with normal marketing efforts. Often less than the *Appraised Value*.

Mechanics Lien – an encumbrance on a property placed by a contractor.

Mid Score – The middle *Credit Score* from the three national companies that track your credit history. This value is the one most commonly used by your lender.

MLS – Multiple Listing Service. The MLS is a regional organization that collects, compiles and distributes information about properties listed for sale by its members, who are real estate agents.

Mortgage – A debt used to purchase a real estate investment. The property serves as collateral for the debt. Mortgages are usually the least expensive source of funds for a purchase.

Mortgage Broker – Independent party that works with multiple lenders to find the best loan for your specific needs. In most states they are licensed and regulated.

Mortgage Insurance (MI) – insurance for loans whose LTV exceeds 80%. Alternatively, the borrower can get a first mortgage at 80% LTV and a second mortgage for the balance of the required amount to avoid MI.

Multiple Listing Service – see *MLS*

Net Operating Income (NOI) – The amount of money an income property generates for the owner after all expenses for running the building, but before financing costs are paid.

Net Rent – The theoretical maximum income that a building could produce (the *Gross Rent*) less an allowance for vacant units.

Net Square Feet – the measurement approach often used for condos. The appraiser measures the *inside* of the building. This square footage measurement does not include hallways, boiler rooms or the thickness of the exterior walls.

Net Worth – On the *Balance Sheet,* Net Worth is your *Assets* less your *Liabilities.*

Non-Conforming Loan – A loan that does not adhere to strict, national underwriting guidelines. Since this loan cannot be packaged up into a large bundles and resold on Wall Street, the lender (often called a *Portfolio Lender*) often holds on to the loan themselves. The rates and terms will be less favorable than for a *Conforming* loan.

Offer – A proposal to purchase a property.

Option – A real estate contract that gives a prospective buyer the right to purchase a given property for a set price for a set period of time. Usually the prospective buyer pays an *Option Fee* for this privilege. The fee is usually non-refundable.

Option Fee – consideration given by a prospective buyer to have the exclusive right but not the obligation (option) to purchase a property for a set period of time at a predetermined price.

Ordinary Income Tax Rate – taxation applied to earned income and capital gains of assets held for less than a year. Usually a higher rate than the *Capital Gains Tax Rate.*

Origination Fee – A fee charged by a Mortgage Broker to recoup the costs of setting up the loan. Often about 1% of the loan balance.

Owner Occupied (sometimes abbreviated as O/O) – real estate when there owner lives on-site the majority of the time. Lenders perceive an O/O loan to be less risky than a non-O/O loan for a real estate investment. As a result, O/O loans have lower interest rates and can usually offer higher *LTV.*

Non-Owner Occupied (sometimes abbreviated non-O/O) -- real estate where the owner does not live, e.g., an investment. Lenders perceive non-O/O to be riskier than O/O loans, so the interest rates are typically higher and the maximum *LTV* offered is typically lower.

Non-Recourse. A loan where the borrower is not liable to the lender if the loan goes into default. Typically only an option with larger (at least $1 million) commercial loans, particularly *Conduit* loans.

P&I – part of the total mortgage payment. Principal payment and interest, but not taxes and insurance.

P&L – abbreviation for *Profit and Loss* statement.

Partial Recourse – If the borrower defaults on a loan, the borrower is only partially liable for the debt with their other personal assets. For larger commercial loans, the Lender may ask the Borrower to pledge assets to secure 50% of the loan balance, for example. This would be common on loan sites well over 1 million.

Partial Release of Lien – A feature of a construction loan to convert an apartment building into condos. As each unit in the project is sold off, the bank takes some of the sales proceeds to pay down the debt of the project in exchange for releasing some of the lien that is help against the property. This is a feature most standard commercial loans do not offer.

Payoff – amount of money to fully satisfy a mortgage; the Title Company will order a *Payoff* statement from the lender as part of the closing process.

PITI – The "total" mortgage payment: Principal, Interest, Property Taxes and Insurance.

Plat – a map showing how a parcel of land is divided.

Point – 1% of something, typically a loan amount or a purchase price. Often expressed with mortgages as "a point in front." This would be a 1% fee charged by the lender to originate the loan.

Portfolio Lender – Lender that holds on to the loan over the course of its life. This is in contrast to most residential lenders that re-sell their loans. Portfolio lenders charge more and often have less favorable terms, but offer more flexibility in the properties for which they can lend you money.

Power of Attorney (POA) – a written document that authorizes one person to act on the behalf of another and sign documents. If done for a real estate closing, the Title Company usually has to prepare and notarize the POA.

Prepayment Penalty – Fee imposed by a lender for paying off a loan before a specified time. Very common for commercial loans for borrowers of all credit scores; for residential loans most often seen for credit-challenged applicants or for certain non-owner occupied loans.

Profit and Loss – also called the *P&L.* For a rental building, the income generated (e.g., rents, laundry income) less the operating expenses (e.g., insurance, property taxes) to get to *Net Operating Income.* Usually the financing costs (e.g., the mortgage payment) are deducted, which leaves the profit for the owner after financing.

Pro-Forma – An estimate, often of a *Profit and Loss* Statement.

Property Manager -- A third party that takes on some of your responsibilities in the ongoing operations of your rental property. Some of the tasks include cleaning and maintenance, collecting rents, showing units to prospective tenants, answering questions, and managing tenants as they move out of the building. Some Property Managers will also run the operating account for you and pay the building's bills.

Prorate – to divide into proportional amounts. For example, the property taxes are prorated between the buyer and seller at closing.

Purchase Contract – the agreement between the buyer and seller regarding the sale of a property. Usually is completed on a contract form approved by the state government body that regulates real estate.

Real Estate – the land and anything permanently attached to the land.

Real Estate Agent – A person who has passed your state's regulatory board requirements and has some minimal level of training to offer real estate services to the general public. In most states it is illegal to buy and sell real estate for third parties unless you are licensed. Note that having a license doesn't mean that you are experienced in servicing all different types of property. A real estate agent that has joined the National Association of REALTORS® is allowed to use the trade name of REALTOR®. About half of the people with a license are also REALTORS®. In most transactions there will be a real estate agent representing the Buyer (often, but not always, a *Buyer's Agent*), and an agent representing the Seller (often, but not always, a *Sellers Agent*). Those two roles could also be filled by agents in a *Transaction Broker* capacity.

REALTOR® – A person with a license to practice real estate in your state who has also joined the National Association of REALTORS®. REALTORS® usually have some additional training in ethics and agree to abide by a strict code of ethical behavior when working with clients.

Record – the act of publicly filing a document, usually with the County government. Deeds and mortgages are filed to give constructive notice to the world that the Owner must repay a loan before they can sell the property.

Recourse – If the borrower defaults on a loan, the borrower pledges all of their other assets to repay the loan.

Refinance – replacement of one loan with another, usually at a higher LTV or better terms.

Reissue Rate – If you sell a property within seven years of purchasing it, many title companies can give you a discount (as much as 50%) for your title policy. Check out www.FirstAllianceTitle.com

REIT – Real Estate Investment Trust. An institutional investor that purchases real estate, such as very large apartment complexes.

Release – a document that terminates a lien or mortgage from a property. See also *Partial Release*.

REO – Real Estate Owned. The foreclosure properties in a Lender's portfolio.

Replacement Cost Valuation – see *Cost Valuation*.

Residential property – single family homes, town homes, condominiums and small apartment building with fewer than five units. Financing for these buildings is typically easier to arrange than for commercial buildings. High *LTVs* are typically available.

Retail Buyer – the typical owner occupant, who wants to move into a perfect property that needs no work of any kind. Retail buyers are willing to pay more for better condition and style.

Return on Investment – Often abbreviated as *ROI*. ROI is the profit made from an investment divided by how much money you had to invest to earn that return. For example, if you make a $5,000 profit on a $10,000 investment, your ROI is 50%. The ROI is often expressed in annual terms. If you have a 50% ROI in six months, you annualized ROI is 50% * (12 months / 6 months) = 100%. Conversely, if you have a 50% ROI in two years, your annualized ROI is 50% * (12 months / 24 months) = 25%.

ROI – See *Return on Investment*

Sales Comps – See *Comps*

Seller's Agent – See *Listing Agent*

Selling Agent – See *Buyers Agent*. Yes, this is confusing.

Settlement Statement – the document prepared by the closing agent that shows the buyer's and seller's charges and costs to accomplish a real estate closing. Also called a *HUD Statement*.

Short Sale – A property that has not yet been foreclosed on, but the clock is running. Sometimes it is possible to negotiate with bank(s) that hold the mortgage(s) to arrange a payment amount that is less than the amount owed to fully satisfy the debt. This is called a short sale.

Special Assessment – an ad-hoc tax from the government, usually to fund a one-time project (such as a new school). Alternatively, an ad-hoc charge from a HOA to pay for a one time large project (such as a new boiler).

Subject To – Transferring title from the seller to the buyer without paying off the mortgage. The new buyer continues to make the payments but the loan is not formally transferred or *Assumed*. The loan remains on the seller's credit report.

Stated Loan – As opposed to a *Full Doc* loan, you will not be required to fully document your income or your assets – you "state" what you have and the lender takes you at your word. Since there is more risk, the loan will usually have a higher interest rate and won't offer as high of a *LTV* as a Full Doc loan. This is the loan that many self-employed investors use. The Stated Loan still will examine your *Credit Score*.

Title – Evidence of ownership.

Title Company – a firm that sells *Title Insurance* and manages the *Closing Agent*.

Title Insurance – An insurance policy, purchased by the Seller in most states, that warrants that the Seller has the authority to sell a given property and that the property is being transferred to the Buyer free of all liens and encumbrances. The Buyer usually pays for the part of the Title insurance that protects the Lender.

Title Search – a review of the public records to determine who owns a parcel of property and what liens, if any, encumber it.

Transaction Broker —A real estate agent attempting to get the transaction completed in a way that is fair and ethical to all parties, without looking out for the interests of any one party to the transaction. If the real estate agent is working for both Buyer and Seller, they will need to be a transaction broker role. If they represent just one party, they can wear the transaction broker hat, but will usually either be a *Buyers Agent* or a *Listing Agent*.

Tri-Merge Credit Report – The combination of the information from all three credit reporting agencies and their credit score analyses. Usually the middle score is used for loan qualification analysis.

Underwriters – Group at the Lender that examines all of the Borrower's documents to be sure they are credit worthy and examine the appraisal to ensure the property is worth what the Buyer claims it is worth. They check all of facets of the loan to make sure they are within the lending guidelines of the program. When they are satisfied that all conditions are met, they approve the release of funds from the Lender so you can complete your purchase.

Vacancy – An empty rental unit that is not currently generating income.

Vacancy Allowance – In a *Pro-Forma Profit and Loss*, an estimate of how frequently a rental will not be occupied and not generating rental income.

Vacancy Rate – the average level of vacancy for a type of building in a given neighborhood. Most cities have an Apartment Association that collects this information on a periodic basis.

Walk-Away Price – As a Buyer, the most you can pay for a project to still have a viable project. You should determine this value before you start negotiations and stick to it, unless you uncover material facts that change your assumptions.

Wholesale – an investor that finds an assignment property that does not want to fix it and up and clean it so that it can be sold to a *Retail* buyer will usually *Assign* the contract to an investor interested in this type of work. This is called *Wholesaling a Deal*.

Yield Spread Premium – (abbreviated YSP). Points that are not obvious to the borrower (in most cases). Comprises additional compensation for the Loan Officer and / or their office.

YSP – See *Yield Spread Premium*.

Notes

Notes